RHETORIC AND POLITICAL CULTURE IN NINETEENTH-CENTURY AMERICA

RHETORIC AND PUBLIC AFFAIRS SERIES

RHETORIC AND POLITICAL CULTURE IN NINETEENTH-CENTURY AMERICA

EDITED BY THOMAS W. BENSON

Michigan State University Press
East Lansing

Copyright © 1997 Michigan State University Press

All Michigan State University Press books are produced on paper which meets the requirements of American National Standards of Information Sciences—Permanence of paper for printed materials ANSI Z23.48-1984.

Printed in the United States of America

Michigan State University Press
East Lansing, Michigan 48823-5202

04 03 02 01 00 99 98 97 1 2 3 4 5 6 7 8 9 10

Library of Congress Cataloging-in-Publication Data

Rhetoric and political culture in nineteenth-century America / edited by Thomas W. Benson.
    p. cm. — (Rhetoric and public affairs series)
    Includes bibliographical references.
    ISBN 0-87013-468-X
    1. Political oratory—United States—History—19th century—Congresses.
2. Rhetoric—political aspects—United States—History—19th century—Congresses.
3. English Language—19th century—Rhetoric—Congresses. 4. United States—Politics and government—19th century—Congresses. I. Benson, Thomas W. II. Series.
PN4055.R48   1997
808.5'1'08835—dc20   96-38913
                            CIP

to Robert G. Gunderson

CONTENTS

FOREWORD:
CONTEXTUALIZING AMERICAN RHETORIC

James R. Andrews

Each of the past two Public Address Conferences paid tribute to our intellectual heritage by extending special recognition to the work of a pioneering scholar; the third conference honored Robert G. Gunderson. Beginning with an essay, "The Calamity Howlers," which appeared in the *Quarterly Journal of Speech* in October of 1940, and continuing for over half a century, Professor Gunderson's work has left an indelible impression on rhetorical scholarship. The critical study of public address has, of course, changed in the twentieth century and will continue to change in the twenty-first. As the studies in this volume demonstrate, methodological pluralism is the standard of contemporary work, and active rhetorical critics today are more consciously aware of the theoretical implications and extensions of their work than were their critical forebears. What links the past with the present, however, and what will continue to engage us in the future, is the search for meaning in human rhetorical action.

Robert Gunderson and most of his contemporaries tended to eschew the grand generalization seeking, rather, to understand the meaning of events and the rhetoric that surrounded, connected, and made sense of those events in identifiable contexts. William B. Hesseltine, the distinguished historian who was Gunderson's mentor at the University of Wisconsin, once wrote that what separated historians from antiquarians was that antiquarians liked to collect facts as ends in themselves whereas historians sought meaning in events. Hesseltine attacked those who contended that "the human past is so complex, so inexplicable, so inflicted with innumerable factors, that its reconstruction is impossible. These people deny the possibility of determining causation or assessing consequences. They are content to establish facts . . . and arrange them to illustrate some particular concept." Hesseltine viewed such activity as anti-intellectual because "fundamentally they are denying the capacity of the human intellect to penetrate the mysteries of human experience."[1]

In the formative years of public address scholarship, Robert Gunderson, in his own critical search for meaning, attempted to penetrate the mysteries of human experience by uncovering, describing, and explaining relationships between rhetoric and events in a given situation and telling the story of those relationships vividly and clearly without regard to how that story supported any broad theoretical conception of human communicative behavior. What the best early studies of public address taught us was that recreating the tone and texture of a time is prerequisite to answering some of the questions (certainly not all of the questions that could be asked) that have engaged students of public address. Critics trying to understand the problems of rhetors and the predispositions of audiences, and to discern precisely how context constrained discourse, sought out the salient antecedents to discourse, delving into archives in an effort to understand the details of life in another time—details that connect, clash, sometimes mystify but ultimately help to clarify actions and reactions. Robert Gunderson always took a dim view of those who observed and documented their observations second or third hand, condemning what he called "academic podiatry": living off the footnotes of others. For him, critical analysis not buttressed by and connected to concrete examples of the milieu out of which the discourse arose was "custard pie" history; "Throw it against the wall and nothing sticks," he would say.

George Bernard Shaw once observed that "he who has nothing to assert has no style and can have none." Gunderson had much to assert and his assertions are reflected in his style. Indeed, a number of the early critics—skillful, imaginative, and steeped in the context out of which the rhetoric emerged—exhibited a style both muscular and clear; relevant facts, interwoven with the public expression of ideas, were cast in compelling narratives whose arguments were propelled by the style in which they were cast and which served the critical function of demonstrating how rhetoric works in a given situation.

Consider, for example, Gunderson's essay on Daniel Webster's speaking tour in 1840 on behalf of the Whig candidate, William Henry Harrison. "Putting aside his satin-lined coat, white vest, diamond knee buckles, and shirt with lace-point ruffles (which he had worn for his audience with young Queen Victoria)," Gunderson wrote, "the Godlike Daniel donned a linsey-woolsey coat, a wide-brimmed hat, knee-high boots, and a flowing necktie, and set out on a stump speaking expedition which took him from the crest of Mount Stratton in Vermont to the steps of the State Capitol in Richmond, Virginia. To identify himself with the new coonskin Whiggery, Webster camped with Green Mountain boys in a pine wood before an open fire, ate meals from shingles, paid tribute to log cabins, and challenged at fisticuffs anyone who dared called him an aristocrat."[2]

Gunderson's discussion of Webster within the context of the 1840 campaign displays, in its vivid particulars, the great ideological shift from the elite republicanism of the founders to rough egalitarian democracy of the frontiersman which surfaced in the Jacksonian era and that was in full and evident flood when Harrison sought the presidency. The story he tells of Webster in linsey-woolsey, skillfully weaving into his narrative the account of Webster's modifications in style, delivery, popular appeals, and choice of topics, is a story of a society whose political culture was in flux, changing and being changed by the political rhetoric that both drove and reflected it.

While it is true that many of the early critics were especially adept at lively description, one who reads such works as *The Log Cabin Campaign* or *The Old Gentlemen's Convention* is convinced that the vivid reconstruction of events was not achieved at the expense of argument and analysis.[3] Much of the past scholarship in our field, of which Robert Gunderson's is a gleaming example, has been the progeny of imagination married to evidence, of analysis wedded to style, and of insight sharpened by wit. In "The Oxymoron Strain in American Rhetoric," for example, Gunderson's pungent style and trenchant example reinforces his argument that American rhetoric is characterized by a struggle between transcendental and pragmatic values in which, as Gunderson sees it, greed has an edge over ideals—but not so much so that our rhetoric can allow us to admit it. He sardonically observes:

> Pity politicians in America, always having to justify their selfish impulses to demanding voters. To please a majority in a badly divided society they resort to a rhetoric of negative opposites. This *oxymoron* strain is evident in the paradox of fighting Quakers like A. Mitchell Palmer and Richard Nixon, conforming individualists like Herbert Hoover, transcendental opportunists like Thaddeus Stevens, honest grafters like George Washington Plunkett, and repressive champions of liberty like Woodrow Wilson. A Janus-faced duplicity may thus account for the courageous conformity of Grover Cleveland, the energetic absence of trust busting by Teddy Roosevelt, the "balder and dash" of Warren Harding, and the silent profundity of Calvin Coolidge. Perhaps it might even explain the lustful moralism of Jimmy Carter.[4]

It is said that Thomas Jefferson, when he arrived in Paris to take up his ambassadorial post, replied to a welcome that characterized him as Benjamin Franklin's *replacement*, that no one could replace Dr. Franklin; Jefferson was merely his *successor*. Well, we are the successors of previous generations of scholars. We cannot replace them, and they and we would not want us to try to duplicate them. We must confront our own struggles and create our own triumphs; the essays in this volume are clearly efforts to do just that. Nevertheless, we must also be humble enough, and sagacious enough, to learn from men and women who took the careful, critical study of public discourse to be a serious and worthy scholarly discipline. As we look at the history of public address criticism, and as we sift out the inevitable chaff, we remember the likes of Robert Gunderson, Loren Reid, Waldo Braden, Ernest Wrage, Marie Nichols, Jeffery Auer, Donald Bryant, Robert T. Oliver, Carroll C. Arnold, and we save and savor the golden wheat left by scholars such as these.

NOTES

1. William B. Hesseltine, "The Challenge of the Artifact," *Wisconsin Magazine of History* 66 (winter 1982-83): 126.
2. Robert G. Gunderson, "Webster in Linsey-Woolsey," *The Quarterly Journal of Speech* 37 (February 1951): 23-30.
3. *The Log Cabin Campaign* (Lexington: University of Kentucky Press, 1957); *The Old Gentlemen's Convention* (Madison: University of Wisconsin Press, 1961).
4. Robert G. Gunderson, "The Oxymoron Strain in American Rhetoric," *Central States Speech Journal* 28 (summer 1977): 95.

PREFACE

Thomas W. Benson

The authors of this book explore the claim that public discourse—spoken and written but in either case governed by oratorical models—importantly constituted and continues to illuminate nineteenth-century American political culture. The book is a series of close textual readings of significant texts in American rhetoric, inquiring into the text, the context, the influence of pervasive rhetorical forms and genres, the intentions of the speaker, the response of the audience, and the role of the critic.

This book is based on the proceedings of the third biennial conference on Public Address that convened at the campus of the University of Minnesota in Minneapolis in September 1992. Earlier conferences in this series were held at the University of Wisconsin in Madison, Wisconsin, in 1988 and at Northwestern University, Evanston, Illinois, in 1990. The idea for this series of conferences, and the primary organizational work for the first two meetings, were contributed by Professor Michael Leff, currently of Northwestern University. The 1988 conference was the basis for *Texts in Context: Critical Dialogues on Significant Episodes in American Political Rhetoric*, edited by Michael C. Leff and Fred J. Kauffeld (Davis, Calif.: Hermagoras Press, 1989).

Based on the advice of series editor Martin Medhurst and his editorial board at the Michigan State University Press series in rhetoric and public affairs, we have chosen those conference papers that focused on nineteenth-century American public address.

A unifying aim of the work is to enact some of the central issues of current rhetorical criticism in actual critical practice, and to make that practice contestable. These spirited essays are concrete, committed, dialogic explorations of significant moments in American public discourse. That they do not reduce to a single voice or theory will be taken, it is hoped, as part of their virtue. A spirit of eager contestation and respect for intellectual diversity was a marked feature of the conference and one that may at least partly show through in the following pages.

Each of the chapters treats in some detail issues relating to the theme of "time" in rhetorical practice and rhetorical studies. Time appears as an issue here especially in considerations of the persistence of themes and forms; in recurrent attempts to transcend and re-shape public memory; in the choice of speakers and critics to celebrate, appropriate, revise, re-frame, or reject earlier texts; and of course in the use of public oratory to influence the future.

Our book begins with Edwin Black's "The Aesthetics of Rhetoric, American Style," based on his keynote address to the Minneapolis conference. Black argues that American public discourse continues to be shaped by two "aesthetic modalities"—"a dispositional or structural aesthetic that is associated with a rhetoric of power, and a stylistic or textural aesthetic that is associated with a rhetoric of character."

There then follow four major critical essays on significant texts in American public discourse of the nineteenth century; each of these essays is the subject of a response chapter. This pattern of critique and response is one that helps to give the present book much of its sense of intellectual challenge and critical zest, and helps to capture many of the themes that dominate discussions of rhetorical criticism today.

The paired critical chapters include James Farrell and Stephen Browne on Webster's Eulogy to Adams and Jefferson; John Lucaites and James Jasinski on Frederick Douglass's "What to the Slave Is the Fourth of July?"; Martha Solomon Watson and David Henry on the "Declaration of Sentiments" of the 1833 American Anti-Slavery Society and the 1848 Seneca Falls Women's Rights Convention; Michael Leff and Maurice Charland on the appropriation of Lincoln by Grady, Douglass, and Addams. In each of the texts central to these chapters, earlier American texts are interrogated, appropriated, and transformed by later speakers for new purposes. Together these critics describe a culture in which speeches and public declarations were read, remembered, and regarded as instruments of power. Robert Hariman writes in an afterword that oratory has suffered a "precipitous decline," and he undertakes to articulate the critical agenda in studies of American public address for an age in which public address has been transformed. Together these essays address central issues in contemporary criticism of public address and treat in detail crucial American moments in the definition of nation, self, race, and gender.

The editor and authors convey their special thanks to the faculty and students of the Department of Speech-Communication at the University of Minnesota, and especially to Robert L. Scott, who hosted the conference and handled local arrangements; and to the program committee for the conference—Robert L. Ivie, chair (in 1992 of Texas A&M University and now at Indiana University), Robert Hariman (Drake University), and Karlyn Kohrs Campbell (University of Minnesota).

A striking feature of the conference design, in contrast to the fragmentation and brevity of annual convention formats of the major academic associations, is that at each conference there is only one session at a time, devoted to a lengthy opening paper, a full-scale response written well in advance, and ample time for general discussion among those attending. By design, the conference is kept small enough to allow for considerable interaction. Among those attending the conference whose names do not appear in the table of contents or elsewhere in this preface were Fred Antczak (University of Iowa); Moya Ball (Trinity University); Sandra Berkowitz (University of Minnesota); Ernest Bormann (University of Minnesota); Jeff Bineham (St. Cloud State University); John Angus Campbell (University of Washington); Ann Chisholm (University of Minnesota); Adrienne Christiansen (Macalester College); Suzanne Daughton (Southern Illinois University); Nathan Dick (University of Minnesota); Bonnie J. Dow (North Dakota State University); Thomas Goodnight (Northwestern University); Robert Gunderson (Indiana University); James Hayes (Augsburg College); Laurie Hayes (University of Minnesota); J. Michael Hogan (Indiana University); Phyllis Japp (University of Nebraska); Vernon Jensen (University of Minnesota); Fred Kauffeld (Edgewood College); Alan Kennedy (Carnegie Mellon University); Ronald Lee (University of Nebraska); William Lewis (Drake University); Stephen E. Lucas (University of Wisconsin); John Murphy (North Dakota State University); Karen Musolf (University of Minnesota); Paul Oehlke (University of Minnesota); Gregory Olson (Marquette University); Kathryn Olson (University of Wisconsin, Milwaukee); Sian Owen-Cruise (University of Minnesota); Tarla Rai Peterson (Texas A&M University); Malcolm O. Sillars (University of Utah); Herbert Simons (Temple University); John Sloop (Drake University); Peter Solie (University of Minnesota); Shane Stafford (University of Minnesota); Douglas Thomas (Gustavus Adolphus College); Kathleen Turner (Tulane University); Kristin Vonnegut (St. John's University); Arthur Walzer (University of Minnesota); Michelle Zurakowski (University of Minnesota).

State College, Pennsylvania
4 December 1995

THE AESTHETICS OF RHETORIC, AMERICAN STYLE

Edwin Black

Since the decline and discrediting of the elocutionary movement, rhetorical critics have been exceedingly reluctant to apply aesthetic values to public discourse. Those old elocutionary textbooks, with their illustrations of gesture and posture and their voice exercises, are so intellectually sterile and so historically aberrant that we refuse any association even with their implications.

Perhaps our rejection of elocutionary values has been too undiscriminating. At least one element of the elocutionary movement merits our consideration, and it is the fundamental conviction of the movement that aesthetic experience is a component of rhetorical activity, that—in its simplest formulation—an attraction to beauty and a repulsion by ugliness influence the composition and reception of discourse.

A major part of our problem with the elocutionary movement, of course, is with the particular aesthetic values that it championed. The extravagant posturing and chronic superficiality that the movement sponsored seem to us now prescriptions for ridicule; but to at least some of our forebears, elocutionary histrionics were the marks of eloquence. In now contemplating the historical disparity between them and us, we are brought to reflect on how radically one generation's conception of aesthetic excellence can differ from another's.

Repeatedly, as we muse among aesthetic objects of the past, we experience the shock of estrangement at representations of obsolete taste. When we see, for example, a preservation of a late nineteenth century parlor, or we read a melodrama or hear a popular song of the era, we may be charmed by the experience, but we are still conscious of our temporal disengagement. We are reminded of the mutability of aesthetic values, at least as they are manifested in popular taste.

This inconstancy affects not only such purely aesthetic exercises as decoration, but also such more pragmatic efforts as rhetorical activity. Some of us are old enough to remember the oleaginous locutions of Senator Everett Dirksen, and

1

probably all of us have watched flickering films of Huey Long or of Billy Sunday. Those examples, which could be endlessly multiplied, present us with procedures of advocacy that were once serious and powerful, and that now represent such obsolete rhetorical taste that their imitation is indistinguishable from their parody. Such taste, and especially its associated regulatory apparatus, may reward our attention.

We do not commonly talk of "rhetorical taste," but the concept of such a sensibility is indispensable to criticism. Aesthetic preferences for one mode of rhetorical activity over another are manifested all the time. Rhetors yield to such preferences when speaking to different groups on different occasions in different ways, even when they intend their messages to be constant. And audiences—even sophisticated ones—routinely refuse to distinguish between attraction and conviction, and allow their credulity to be affected by their interest in, or indifference to, or repulsion by the discourses that they encounter.

The discipline of rhetoric is concerned with the ways that minds are changed, and with the circumstances—especially the discursive ones—that generate such changes. And it follows that if variations in rhetorical tastes over time reflect concomitant variations in the ways that people are persuaded, then that historical instability is immensely important to rhetorical studies. Perhaps the best way of exploring such possibilities is to focus on a time and a set of rhetorical fashions different from the present. The nineteenth century presents just such antipodal possibilities.

Jeremy Bernstein's observations concerning Henry Stanley, the Victorian journalist and explorer, testify to a characteristic attitude of the age:

> after Florence Nightingale read "How I Found Livingstone"—which by then was a best-seller both here and in Britain—she commented that it was "the very worst book on the very best subject I ever saw in my life."
>
> Miss Nightingale's objection to Stanley's book may have been similar to objections that many Victorians had. The books were just too graphic. Stanley made no attempt to conceal . . . brutalities. . . . He does not prettify anything. The Victorians probably objected less to what he had done than to his having made no attempt to cover it up.[1]

The operative terms in the quotation are "conceal," "prettify," and "cover up." The Victorians—British and American alike—exercised censorship. It was too habitual a censorship to be wholly visible to most of its contemporaries, but we can see it clearly from the perspective of our time, not because we are more liberated than our ancestors, but because some of our inhibitions are different from theirs, and so too are some of our disguises.

Victorian censorship took two principal forms: one, overt; the other, reflexive. There were restrictions on the material that could be communicated, and there were restrictions on the material that one allowed oneself to perceive. We need briefly to consider each of those forms of censorship and their implications for rhetorical activity.

Our forebears' most overt strictures about aesthetic propriety took the form of official legislation, and were buttressed by the sanctions of criminal law. Fastidious as the nineteenth century legal code was, however, a much more extensive administration of aesthetic propriety operated through custom and convention: looser and more taciturn forms of regulation than the law, but scarcely less punitive. Custom and convention alone could not imprison offenders of taste, but renegades could be excluded from respectability and made exiles within their own societies.

Two walls, then, were erected to serve as barriers against aesthetic impropriety. One was the literal wall surrounding a prison, which assured that offenders against the legal code would be confined. The other was the figurative wall bounding respectability, which assured that transgressors against the code of taste would dine alone.

This overt proscription of unacceptable material was facilitated by the radical disjunction between public and private life that the age sponsored. To Chaucer, writing in the fourteenth century, "homely" meant, in the words of the *Oxford English Dictionary*, "of or belonging to the home or household." Over time the word gained in disapprobative implication until, in our own day, it has come to mean "unattractive." For six hundred years the English language has been working to consign unattractiveness to the private realm, outside the public's view. This process of censorship through social allocation reached its modern apogee in the last century.

The other principal form of censorship was reflexive: a regulation of the apparatus of perception itself. Gentility, which was a widely desired condition, involved the cultivation of a sensibility that deflected incipient perceptions, that refused admission into the human sensorium of offensive impressions. The genteel sensibility had to be selectively blind and discriminatingly deaf; it had to screen out infractions of propriety. This reflexive censorship insulated the minds of its adherents and, in collaboration with the more overt censorships that were being enforced, it made a nullity of whatever was deemed unfitting.[2]

Here, then, were two general tendencies in the aesthetic regulation of sensory material. One proceeded outwardly, and worked to banish unacceptable material from the public sphere either through explicit legal prohibition or, more subtly, through the operation of social pressures. The other proceeded inwardly, and worked to focus perception itself so selectively that unacceptable material was simply excluded from consciousness.

My thesis is that each of these tendencies in turn generated its own aesthetic modality and, further, that each of those modalities has been distinctively realized in public discourse. They have left us historically with a dispositional or structural aesthetic that is associated with a rhetoric of power, and a stylistic or textural aesthetic that is associated with a rhetoric of character.

The aestheticism of structure is best illustrated, at least in its rhetorical manifestations, in the ways in which news is transmitted or public events represented, especially on television. No matter what random chaos may occur in the world, our media take account of it only in terms of dramatic events—organized units of experience that an audience can assimilate within a moral order.

This dispositional mode of comprehension works to satisfy our Kantian appetites; it nourishes our moral hunger for understanding and control. We require that events have form, that they be so ordered and arranged that familiar categories of plot and role, suspense and adversarial tension be operative in our communication of them. This requirement also encourages the creation of artifacts that provide corresponding satisfactions until, in the end, we are left in the hackneyed, but no less poignant, philosophical condition of being unable to disentangle the world from our schemata for apprehending it.[3]

The categories that I mentioned—plot and role, suspense and adversarial tension—are illustrative rather than exhaustive, but clearly they are categories of structure, not of detail. Indeed—as the local news programs on television daily remind us—the categories are perfectly compatible with a style that is maladroit, even sometimes repugnant.

The practitioner of a structural aesthetic may look unflinchingly on obnoxious displays—may even feel an obligation especially to confront such displays—but would require that they be subsumed under an aprioristic organizational principle. The anti-abortionist who displays pictures of a destroyed fetus, or the revivalist who depicts the torments that sinners suffer in hell, or the reformer who portrays the careworn vagrants who haunt our cities' streets: each focuses the auditor on a disagreeable object of perception in what the rhetor, at least, takes to be the service of a higher good. The rhetor transmits an image from which the auditor is disposed to turn away in aversion, but the ugliness is requited in becoming illustrative and monitory. The image, repellent in itself, subserves a larger mosaic of truth. Horrific appearance becomes redemptive reality.

The pleasures provided by a structural aesthetic are, generically, intellectual pleasures. They are the pleasures of a conception that has a place for everything: a universe of discourse that accounts for and appropriately consigns even those subjects whose existence is regrettable. They are the pleasures of comprehension and mastery. They are architectonic satisfactions.

Among recent rhetors, Lyndon Johnson and Richard Nixon were exceptionally successful practitioners of a structural aesthetic, an aesthetic concerned with large patterns of order. Both Johnson and Nixon were capable of being clear and forceful—and Johnson, indeed, of being exceptionally colorful—but neither exhibited much talent, at least in their public speeches, for stylistic distinction. The irreducible atomic unit of their discourses was typically not the phrase or the sentence; it was the argument. Their stylistic nuances, which occurred rarely, were much more often demonstrations of tact than refinements of expressivity: linguistic symptoms that marked them not as notably articulate, but rather as notably political. Their speeches were, for the most part, slabs of prose: efficient, commonplace, and pedestrian.

On rare occasions, in a strained effort to be eloquent or poetic, each would include in a public discourse a passage that struggled for stylistic distinction, a passage that drudged and grubbed to be visionary. In the context of a structural aesthetic, the patch of purple prose is the deviation that individuates, the exception that personalizes, the conventional anomaly, the orthodox idiosyncrasy. Even in the monotonously prosaic public discourses of both Johnson and Nixon, we can sometimes find the rare essay at preciosity. It appears as a laborious toiling after stylistic distinction in those portions of their speeches when they are trying to project a telos.

I have commented elsewhere on the passage in Lyndon Johnson's Voting Rights speech of 15 March 1965 in which he envisions his presidential ambitions:

> I want to be the President who educated young children to the wonders of their world. I want to be the President who helped to feed the hungry and to prepare them to be taxpayers instead of taxeaters.
>
> I want to be the President who helped the poor to find their own way and who protected the right of every citizen to vote in every election.
>
> I want to be the President who helped to end hatred among his fellow men and who promoted love among the people of all races and all regions and all parties.
>
> I want to be the President who helped to end war among the brothers of this earth.

Amidst a national crisis and before the whole republic as his audience, Lyndon Johnson proclaims his bloated vanity. One cannot contemplate this self-indulgent passage without experiencing an emotion that has, as far as I know, no name. It is a fusion of awe, astonishment, and disgust.

In Nixon's speech of 8 August 1968 accepting the Republican nomination for the presidency, a crude attempt at eloquence occurs in the passage when he recollects his childhood dreams and then projects them onto all American children. Richard Nixon was a willfully public man, sedulous—and often ineffectual—in his efforts to conceal his resentments and fears behind a prosaic mask, but the writers of his 1968 acceptance speech developed an unnaturally poeticized passage near the end. The speech culminates in Nixon's seeing visions—of the glorious future that he will institute, and of his own rise from obscurity to eminence.

> Tonight, I see the face of a child. He lives in a great city, he's black, or he's white, he's Mexican, Italian, Polish, none of that matters. What matters is he's an American child. . . .
>
> I see another child tonight. He hears a train go by at night and he dreams of far away places where he'd like to go. It seems like an impossible dream.
>
> But he is helped on his journey through life. A father who had to go to work before he finished the sixth grade, sacrificed everything he had so that his sons could go to college.
>
> A gentle Quaker mother, with a passionate concern for peace, quietly wept when he went to war but she understood why he had to go.
>
> A great teacher, a remarkable football coach, an inspirational minister encouraged him on his way. A courageous wife and loyal children stood by him in victory and also in defeat.
>
> And in his chosen profession of politics, first there were scores, then hundreds, then thousands, and finally millions who worked for his success.
>
> And tonight he stands before you, nominated for President of the United States of America.
>
> You can see why I believe so deeply in the American dream.

The passage is ostensibly concerned with Nixon's past. Like the correspondingly narcissistic passage in Johnson, it is, as the personal usurpation of a communal occasion, the unbandaged festering of a swollen ego. However, in its implicit invitation to its audience that they fulfill "the American dream" by electing him president, this Nixonian flourish, like its Johnsonian equivalent, describes an uncompleted trajectory. Both passages, therefore—despite their coarse egoism—may have generated a certain momentum of credulity among those faithful whose disbelief had been suspended.

It is not critical perversity alone that has brought me to quote atypical passages from Johnson's and Nixon's speeches. The passages are remarkable because they roil with aesthetic pretensions. Their gaudery stands in instructive contrast to the stylistic mediocrity, the homeliness of texture, that otherwise pervaded the public discourses of Johnson and Nixon.

Insofar as the structural aesthetic can be associated with a characteristic style, that style is echoic, mimetic: a style that enables auditors to hear a purified version of themselves. The rhetor working in a structural mode employs a wholly public idiom, but an idiom purged of dross. If there is any stylistic accomplishment characteristic of the structural aesthetic, it is in making an articulate instrument of the conventional mumble—in saying what is said in the language of the ordinary—in expounding power in an everyday tongue. The structural rhetor is a simulacrum of the public, and structural aesthetics is an exhibition of conformity with the scruples of the public domain.

In the long campaign leading to the presidential election of 1992, neither Paul Tsongas nor Ross Perot was a notably scintillating rhetor. However effective or impressive, neither flirted with sublimity; neither could be accused of eloquence. Both were clearly practitioners of a structural aesthetic, and both were intensely appealing to some audiences. The stylistic simplicity of each suggested sincerity: they were acclaimed for not behaving like "politicians." They appeared to their followers to be direct and plain spoken, to abjure the aesthetics of texture, which can too easily seem artful, insincere—a fabrication, sometimes even in the odious sense.

The purple patches from Johnson and Nixon are ornamentations of their discourses: supererogatory embellishments, having the same relation to communication as cosmetics do to hygiene. We sense in such visionary excursuses as Johnson's and Nixon's that a gratuitous adornment has been engrafted onto a speech, that it has no essential or organic connection with its context, that it expresses a fundamentally frivolous ambition to be eloquent just to be eloquent. Such grandiloquence is not a projection of the rhetor's essential perspective. It is less a symptom of passionate conviction than the flush of fevered ambition.

By contrast, although the discourses of a Martin Luther King, Jr. have passages that are every bit as florid as the labored concoctions of Johnson and Nixon, those passages in King reflect the orientation of the rhetor's mind. However maudlin the sentences, they connect; however exaggerated the figures, they are products of a metaphorical imagination. Indeed, one cannot find the public King talking in any way other than in tropes of heat and cold, vision and dream, height and depth, distance and duration, illumination and darkness: all, the imperfect articulations of his moralistic comprehension of the world, his millenarian comprehension of its history, and his prophetic comprehension of his role in it.

Typically the structural discourse achieves its maximum of expressive vividness in the projection of an ideal, a cynosure, a telos, a fulfillment. Because the future can be envisaged only in the imagination, it is a subject on which even rhetors who are verbally sedentary must try to exercise a style. Through futuristic projections a predominately structural aesthetic is adapted to the temporality of action.

The association of futurity with stylistic ambition is intimate and indissoluble in our culture. Its origin may be in the chiliastic vision that has incited our culture from the beginning of the Christian era, a vision in which the future, of both the individual and the human race, culminates in cosmic resolutions that are beyond simple utterance.

In contrast to the structural rhetor, who may strain occasionally to reach beyond the mundane style, the textural rhetor practices a discriminating reticence. The stylistic aesthetic is notable for its filtering of experience: its tendency to exclude material that cannot be vividly rendered. Strictly speaking, such an exclusion is a prejudice. That is, it renders a verdict about an object prior to any judgmental procedure. The process of self-censorship requires that any object laying claim on one's attention must first qualify as to appearance, that an image must meet certain minimum standards before its underlying essence can be engaged. That requirement, in turn, is predicated on the belief that there is a direct link between appearances and essences; that appearances are true symptoms: not infallible necessarily, but at least true enough to provide reliable warrants for the expenditure of moral energy.

It stands to reason that a general attitude that closely regulated the admission of data into the human sensorium on the basis of those data's aesthetic qualities would place a great value on appearances. Aesthetic qualities are, after all, wholly matters of perception and appearance.

Another assumption that seems to undergird this attitude is of the priority of privacy. To lay claim on one's moral attention, an object must somehow have deserved that attention. Prima facie, we do not acknowledge subjects that have not, by virtue of their appearance, earned our acknowledgment. Given the temporal limitations and unavoidable selectivity of our perceptions, we do not accept accident and chance as the factors that determine what fills our minds. Rather, we construct a moral apparatus to discriminate among the claims on our attention. Thus, there is control being exercised in this attitude too, but it is a reflexive and inhibitory control rather than a managerial one.

Because the expression of a textural aesthetic is individuated, it invites attention to the persona of the rhetor. In structural aesthetics, on the other hand, the persona of the rhetor is less obtrusive, unless, of course, the rhetor is the subject of the discourse. In the practice of textural aesthetics, the rhetor's voice is distinctive, and thus the rhetor's persona emerges as a unique and individual character. To be sure, an exponent of structural aesthetics may become celebrated too, but it is likely to be because the rhetor is somehow a mirror of the audience, and is to be explained in those terms. The structural celebrity is an archetype; the textural celebrity is an original.

The association of stylistic aesthetics with a rhetoric of character is appropriate because discourse in that mode signals a self-conscious transfiguration of communication itself. What, after all, makes a style noticeable? It is its singularity. To speak the conventional attitudes in the conventional ways is to be unremarkable, to pass from agent to scenery. And, by contrast, to say something uniquely is to assert a personality.

We have to understand stylistic distinctiveness as an act of will and of effort. One does not spontaneously assimilate an individual style. It is an earned condition—sometimes, strenuously earned—and it invariably makes its inventing persona more salient than does discourse in the common idiom.

Generalizing about broad classes of discourse can, of course, be precarious; it is so easy to slip into stereotyping. Nevertheless, I want to propose the hypothesis that much of the public discourse of African Americans has been, in the aggregate, strikingly stylistic in its aesthetic character. No doubt the strong influence of sermonic form plays a role here, together with the high proportion of preachers among African American leaders, and the central role of the church in African American communities.[4] Furthermore, the principal motif of African American discourse has necessarily been the subject of appearance—sheer physical appearance—and its fateful effects on public life.

If there is, in fact, a markedly stylistic aesthetic informing much African American discourse, it has likely been nurtured by a colocation of historical experiences. There is, importantly, a call-response tradition in which the texture of public discourse is fashioned to accommodate spontaneous interjections from the audience, a tradition that assumes a prominence but not a monopoly by the rhetor. Reflected in that discursive egalitarianism, and germane to our present concern, may be a diffidence, a less covetous attitude toward power than is displayed in more structural discourse, along with a greater tendency to reconstruct the internal world rather than the external one.

A group of people who become convinced that their power is severely attenuated—that it is extremely difficult and potentially dangerous to exercise authority—would be moved toward a stylistic aesthetic, toward a mode of persuasion that focused on attitude more than on action. And from this perspective, it would be a virtual redundancy to observe that those African Americans who do display a predominantly structural aesthetic are those who, having acquired a sense of social control, exhibit a mastery of the idiom of social control. When black executives, black jurists, or black legislators speak deliberatively, they speak the common language of authority. There is, in sum, a correlation between employing the rhetoric of power and believing that one has actually acquired some power.

It is important to understand that the association I am arguing does not involve the possession of power so much as the sense of its possession. I do not mean to suggest any sort of objective calculus by which the deprivation of power would, in time, produce a stylistic aesthetic. Rather, I mean to suggest that even a Hercules may, at a given moment, feel overwhelmed and impotent, and his proclamation of his despair will be as poetic as he is capable. Indeed, it may be that certain sorts of especially powerful people—people of exceptional moral imagination or of exceptional intellectual penetration—sense more keenly than the rest of us how straitened their mastery is. Their eloquence, if it appears, can be taken as compensatory. It flouts their demons. Their speeches struggle to give form to the chaotic, fluency to the mute. The eloquence of a Lincoln or a King may seem to us the very articulation of power, but perhaps we hear it more truly if we hear it as the cry of their limits, the defiance of their human insufficiency.

In 1838, the twenty-nine-year-old Abraham Lincoln delivered an address to the Young Men's Lyceum of Springfield, Illinois. It was entitled "The Perpetuation of Our Political Institutions." In it, the young Mr. Lincoln said:

> Many great and good men sufficiently qualified for any task they should undertake, may ever be found, whose ambition would aspire to nothing beyond a seat in Congress, a gubernatorial or a presidential chair; *but such belong not to the family of the lion, or the tribe of the eagle.* What! think you these places would satisfy an Alexander, a Caesar, or a Napoleon?—Never! Towering genius disdains a beaten path. It seeks regions hitherto unexplored.—It sees *no distinction* in adding story to story, upon the monuments of fame, erected to the memory of others. It *denies* that it is glory enough to serve under any chief. It *scorns* to tread in the footsteps of *any* predecessor, however illustrious. It thirsts and burns for distinction; and, if possible, it will have it, whether at the expense of emancipating slaves, or enslaving freemen. Is it unreasonable then to expect, that some man possessed of the loftiest genius, coupled with ambition sufficient to push it to its utmost stretch, will at some time, spring up among us?

Edmund Wilson wrote of that passage, ". . . it is evident that Lincoln has projected himself into the role against which he is warning them."[5] If Wilson was right, if Lincoln did see himself as a "man possessed of the loftiest genius, coupled with ambition sufficient to push it to its utmost stretch"—an ambition that not even "a presidential chair" would appease—then who can imagine a Lincoln who was, even for a moment, satiated by his dominion or insensitive to his limits?

Textural aesthetics is situated at the boundary between the public and private spheres. That is its situation because it works to affect the individual's internal organization while, at the same time, it addresses groups as groups on public matters. Structural aesthetics is wholly in the public sphere. It engages its audience in their civic capacities, but it does not encumber their inner selves. The difference between textural and structural aesthetics is therefore one of degree. They are not incompatible with one another; indeed, they are, in some instances, amalgamated; but they are located differently in relation to the distinction between public and private, which is itself always fluid and often contested.

Because, as the failed experiments of Lenin and Mao have taught us, individuals remain individuals, irrespective of social arrangements, the taste for stylistic refinement seems inextinguishable. People admire eloquence, even when they are not persuaded by it. However, because the adhesiveness of social networks can vary over time, especially in our dispersed and fluctuant society, the attractiveness of structural aesthetics is inconstant. Its popularity will depend on the inclination of people to concern themselves with public matters.

The aesthetic nature of rhetoric is most conspicuous in an artificial polity—that is, a polity which is the arbitrary creation of a small group who do their work in a limited period of time. The French revolutionary regime, the Soviet Union, the Third Reich were not organic creations that accumulated their identities in the course of history. It is true that in all of these cases, virtuosi of power expropriated elements of history to graft onto their creations, and they did it with a skill sufficient to establish for their audiences an emotional continuity from the old order to the new, a transition to novel forms of community that they yet could recognize as communal. But each of these social orders was a rapid creation, consciously designed to occupy the empty place left by a desolated older system. Each was a fulfillment, but not of the daily habits and variegated interchanges of a multitude. Rather, each was the realization of a few political artists' febrile dreams, artists who sculpted a state from the mire of disorder and modulated a clamor into a fanfare.

The American republic too was the creation of a limited number of political craftsmen who composed a design for a commonwealth. That creation was remarkable for its modesty—for the fact that the framers of the Constitution invented only the machinery of governance, but then deferred to indeterminacy the elaboration of its symbols. Unlike the Jacobins, who sought to create "a new breed of citizen," or the Soviet Communists and the Nazis, who aspired to cultural totality, the American founders did not try to suffuse the lives of their subjects with their political ethos; they did no more than adumbrate the machinery of a republic.[6] Venturing less, they risked less, and that constraint may have made their design less vulnerable to the vagaries of history.

It remained for the country's greatest civic poet, Lincoln, to articulate a vision of the union that had the capacity of subsuming virtually all of its cultural expressions. Lincoln's eloquence, his personal legend, and his martyrdom coalesced finally in a drama of mythic proportion, a drama that has constituted the supreme aesthetic model so far of our national experience. That model has had its occasional rival—most recently, the Hollywood western, and the Camelot fantasy associated with Kennedy—but yet the Lincolnian model abides. We sustain it through generations because it defines us, and because it inspires us, and because it extends succor where we are riven.

This essay began with a focus on the elocutionary movement, and it should end there as well. Among Americans who taught or studied rhetoric, the *coup de grâce* administered the elocutionary movement was the publication of James Albert Winans's immensely popular textbook on public speaking, whose first edition appeared in 1915.[7] In that textbook, Winans advocated, with an elegance that is unmatched by any other public speaking textbook of this century, a conversational mode of delivery and a style that was simply the candid projection of the rhetor's internal condition: a style that was, in a word, "sincere." Winans conceived of what we would call style entirely as a means of controlling the attention of auditors, and he was unyielding in subordinating his discussion of stylistic matters to psychological rather than ornamental considerations. Significantly, the word "style" does not appear in the table of contents or the index of Winans's book, or, apparently, anywhere in the book itself. Yet, because Winans insisted on the centrality of audience attention to rhetorical transactions, his view of persuasion retained an orientation that could still be characterized as aesthetic.[8] That orientation, however, was utilitarian and functional rather than normative and formalistic.

Winans was pivotal in turning practical instruction in public speaking from the stylistic aesthetic of the elocutionists to a structural aesthetic. His book was the vehicle for assimilating to rhetorical studies in this country the great cultural transvaluation that followed the Enlightenment: the fading of virtue as the *summum bonum* of the West, and the installation in its place of power as the greatest good. In performing that assimilation, Winans was not following any moral or ideological program so much as he was responding to the spirit of the age—an outward facing age, impatient with the niceties of self-protection, lustful for control, proud of its ability to "face facts" without flinching, seeking always power and the instruments of power: an age that Winans's near contemporary, Henry

Adams, was rendering with nostalgic disenchantment through his images of the Virgin and the dynamo.[9]

Our moral attitudes and our aesthetic tastes are, after all, of a piece. They partake of one another. What we admire in discourse is intermixed with what we value. We exalt what we think beautiful, and think beautiful what we exalt. Those are blunt axioms, and perhaps too close to commonplaces to reward much reflection, but we dare not ignore them if we hope to understand the discipline of rhetoric's history and, beyond that, the objects of its study.

NOTES

1. Jeremy Bernstein, "A Critic at Large. The Dark Continent of Henry Stanley," *The New Yorker*, 31 December 1990, 95.

2. Genteel women of the nineteenth century were reputedly disposed to fainting. They are often portrayed in popular literature of the time as having a relatively low threshold for shock, and of reacting to it by losing consciousness, to be revived by fanning and smelling salts. That genteel women in the nineteenth century suffered from conversion hysteria more often than do their great-granddaughters may seem remote from our consideration of the aesthetics of rhetoric, but the historical datum can, in fact, be read as another bit of illuminating evidence. It comports with the hypothesis that self-censorship is a historically variable instrument that may have reached a maximum use around a hundred and fifty years ago.

3. I have tried to amplify some of these themes in *Rhetorical Questions: Studies of Public Discourse* (Chicago: University of Chicago Press, 1992), esp. 147-70.

4. "American blacks are, by some measures, the most religious people in the world. In 1981, for example, Gallup International organizations conducted surveys on religious beliefs in twenty-three nations. One question asked respondents to rank the importance of God in their lives, with 10 the top score. The highest score recorded was by American blacks— 9.04." George Gallup, Jr. and Jim Castelli, *The People's Religion: American Faith in the 90's* (New York: Macmillan, 1989), 122. Gallup and Castelli cite additional polling data showing that, by virtually every measure, African Americans attach more importance to religion than does the general American population (123-24).

5. Edmund Wilson, *Patriotic Gore* (New York: Oxford University Press, 1966), 108.

6. James A. Leith, *Media and Revolution: Moulding a New Citizenry in France during the Terror* (Toronto: Canadian Broadcasting Corporation, 1968), 7. The old identities, however, stubbornly persisted. See: Georges Lefebvre, *La Révolution Francaise* (Paris: Presses Universitaires de France, 1957), esp. 540-58.

7. James Albert Winans, *Public Speaking* (New York: The Century Co., 1915). The book was reproduced in various subsequent editions.

8. "Persuasion is the process of inducing others to give fair, favorable, or undivided attention to propositions." James Albert Winans, *Public Speaking*, rev. ed. (New York: The Century Co., 1919), 194.

9. See: Henry Adams, *The Education of Henry Adams: An Autobiography* (Boston and New York: Houghton Mifflin Company, 1918), esp. 379-90. Adams's book was first published in 1905 under private auspices. Its reputation grew over the subsequent decade until it was more widely disseminated by a commercial publisher.

THE SPEECH WITHIN: TROPE AND PERFORMANCE IN DANIEL WEBSTER'S EULOGY TO ADAMS AND JEFFERSON

James M. Farrell

On July 8th, 1826, President John Quincy Adams received a letter from his niece, dated July 3rd, informing him that his "father's end was approaching," and that "he would probably not survive two days."[1] What the President could not know was that his venerable father, at the age of 90, had in fact passed away on the afternoon of the fourth of July. Reportedly, the last words of John Adams were "Thomas Jefferson still survives." What John Adams could not know was that earlier that day, Jefferson himself had given up the ghost. The death of these two Founding Fathers, on the anniversary of Independence, exactly fifty years after both had played an instrumental role in the birth of the nation, was a coincidence of providential proportions.

The City of Boston, desiring to mark the passing of these great statesmen, invited Daniel Webster to pronounce a commemorative oration at Faneuil Hall on August 2nd. The orator of Plymouth and Bunker Hill would have another opportunity to display his rhetorical craft and add to the lustre of his own growing reputation. "It has, perhaps, never been the fortune of an orator to treat a subject in all respects so extraordinary as that which called forth the eulogy on Adams and Jefferson," wrote Edward Everett, who himself delivered an address to mark the occasion. It was an opportunity in which "the characters commemorated, the field of action, the magnitude of the events, and the peculiar personal relations, were so important and unusual."[2]

Webster's effort in commemorating the two fallen founders of the republic received wide praise. Josiah Quincy told Webster "Your perfect success yesterday ought to be as satisfactory to you as it is to your friends. I think nothing ever exceeded or perhaps equalled it."[3] Joseph Hopkinson offered his "unqualified applause," while Tobias Watkins thought the address "the best production of its kind I have ever read."[4] One Boston newspaper wrote that "to say of this production that it was eloquent, would be too common an expression to apply to such a performance. It was profound—it was sublime—it was godlike."[5]

Twenty years after his famous eulogy, Webster was still receiving inquiries about the oration. Despite his repeated efforts to clarify the historical record, admirers of his eloquence still wondered about the authenticity of the speech by John Adams that Webster had included as the centerpiece of the eulogy. "Even among our 'liberally' educated men there is nearly an equal division of opinion," wrote Peter J. Becker, in 1846, "many of the 'great' lawyers contending most strenuously that the said speech is the veritable address, word for word, delivered by Mr. Adams when deliberating upon the Declaration. Not only our lawyers, but merchants of the first standing, as well as intelligent mechanics entertain these views, while others contend that it is all your composition."[6] Webster graciously replied to as many such letters as possible. "Your inquiry is easily answered," he wrote to Becker, "So far as I know, there is not existing in print or manuscript, the speech, or any part or fragment of the speech, delivered by Mr. Adams on the question of the Declaration of Independence. We only know from the testimony of his auditors, that he spoke with remarkable ability and characteristic earnestness." Adams's letters and *Autobiography* may have provided Webster with a few ideas, but "For the rest," he said, "I must be answerable. The speech was written by me, in my house in Boston, the day before the delivery of the Discourse in Faneuil Hall."[7]

The Adams speech, which so concerned Becker and the other patriotic citizens of Auburn, New York, was immediately heralded by Webster's contemporaries as an example of his unparalleled rhetorical abilities. "The speech ascribed to John Adams in the Continental Congress," wrote Edward Everett, "is not excelled by anything of the kind in our language. It thrills and delights alike the student of history, who recognizes it at once as the creation of the orator, and the common reader, who takes it to be the composition, not of Mr. Webster, but of Mr. Adams."[8] Tobias Watkins pronounced the Adams speech "worth all the eulogies that ever were conceived,"[9] while Richard Rush told Webster that the imaginary speech, "made my hair rise." "It wears the character of a startling, historical discovery," Rush wrote, "that bursts upon us at this extraordinary moment after sleeping half a century. Curiosity, admiration, the very blood, all are set on fire by it. Nothing of Livy's ever moved me so much."[10]

For later critics and biographers, the Adams speech remained one of the most eloquent and interesting sections of the famous eulogy, and indeed in all of Webster's works. The passage, said Henry Cabot Lodge, is "absolutely startling in its life-like force," and is "perhaps the best example we have of Mr. Webster's historical imagination."[11] The Adams speech, said Claude Fuess, "formed the climax of Webster's eloquence and thrilled the audience at Faneuil Hall."[12] This display of rhetorical craft, Wilbur S. Howell and Hoyt H. Hudson believed, demonstrated "the orator's highest virtuosity."[13]

The supposed speech by John Adams, so widely and for so long anointed as the triumph of Webster's eulogy, invites our critical attention. How does this work of "historical imagination," contribute to the status of the eulogy as a masterwork of American eloquence? In part, the answer lies in the capacity of the Adams speech to serve as the primary field of rhetorical action in the text. The fictional address is the space where Webster's artistic and historical strategies come into sharp focus. That critical focus is achieved here by examining the unmistakable figurative dimension of the imaginary speech. Taking the fictional address as an instance of one or more of what Kenneth Burke called the four master tropes, we gain critical insight into many of the key structural, generic, historical, performatory, and ideological aspects of Webster's eulogy.

When viewed as a master trope, what appears as a simple exercise in creative writing provides a critical code to the complex dimensions of Webster's oration. Each element of the compound trope—metaphor, metonymy, synecdoche, and irony—becomes a critical screen with which we may sift through the sediment of meaning in the famous eulogy.

FOUR MASTER TROPES

In his essay "Four Master Tropes," Kenneth Burke reminds us that metaphor, metonymy, synecdoche, and irony share principles of figurative construction, and consequently "shade into one another." "Give a man but one of them," he writes, "tell him to exploit its possibilities, and if he is thorough in doing so, he will come upon the other three." As with Burke, my concern is not with the strictly ornamental character of the trope in question, but rather with its "role in the discovery and description of 'the truth.'"[14] That discovery and description is facilitated by Burke's theory of the tropes. For each purely figurative trope, Burke "substitutes" an underlying "realistic" principle—perspective, reduction, representation, dialectic—affording the critic a wider latitude for exploration of "figurative" elements in discourse. And although critics ordinarily deal with tropes as figurative constructions at the level of the word or sentence, the understanding of larger passages of discourse is also facilitated by consideration of their capacity to shift perspective, reduce, represent, and synthesize through dialectic.

REPRESENTATION AND STRUCTURE

The imaginary Adams speech has multiple functions within the larger eulogy. The first of these is to establish a formal connection within the eulogy between the present occasion and the historical past. Within the structure of the eulogy, the fictional Adams address acts as the keystone. It appears in the center of the eulogy, at a pause in the life stories of Adams and Jefferson, in the place where past and present merge through the coincidence of time.

The fictional oration briefly arrests the biographical narratives at the point in time when both Adams and Jefferson made their most significant contributions to the nation. That historical moment, echoed in their simultaneous departure from life on the fiftieth Independence Day, becomes the focus of Webster's concentration. "On our fiftieth anniversary," Webster observes, "the great day of national jubilee, in the very hour of public rejoicing, in the midst of echoing and reechoing voices of thanksgiving, while their own names were on all tongues, they took their flight together to the world of spirits."[15] Webster's recollection of Adams's eloquence in the debate over independence allows him to exploit more fully this potent coincidence and permits him to illuminate the historic occasion which most firmly connects the nation's past to the present moment in Faneuil Hall. The fictional address is encouraged by a sense of temporal and occasional propriety, while at the same time it contributes to the structural coherence of the eulogy at large.

The inclusion of the Adams speech is also demanded by a sense of structural balance. Following the introduction, the narrative of the eulogy progresses toward 1776 and slows as it approaches the eventful date by focusing more specifically on the details of the service of its two principal subjects. The timing of the narrative is accompanied by a spatial merging of Adams and Jefferson as they move from opposite ends of the American colonies to a fateful convention in Philadelphia. Thus the life lines merge, the paths cross, at the birthplace of the nation, in its creation moment, a moment which is now invested with added significance as the date when "these aged patriots, these illustrious fellow-laborers, have left our world together."[16]

Webster begins with the narrative of Adams's early life in Massachusetts. Here, the narrative moves rapidly, and years are covered in a matter of a few lines. The narrative slows as Webster moves to his review of Adams's Revolutionary service. Beginning with Adams's attendance at the Writs of Assistance case in 1761, Webster follows the development of Adams's political career as he becomes increasingly active in the Revolutionary movement. In the course of the political biography, the orator brings his subject to the Continental Congress, where he interrupts the story and begins his discourse on Jefferson.

After a brief account of Jefferson's early career and patriotic service Webster joins the heroes at Philadelphia in 1776. As the narrative slows, he emphasizes their connection spatially by joining them on the committee to draft the Declaration, and even segregating them from the committee of five "to act as a sub-committee to prepare the draft."[17] In this sub-committee, then, Adams and Jefferson are intimately united in patriotic action as they would be linked, exactly fifty years later, in a death rich with patriotic symbolism.

Lingering at this moment of cooperation, Webster selects the Declaration of Independence as the paradigm of Jefferson's service to the nation. He remarks on the nation's "title deed" at some length, giving Jefferson full credit for the merit of the paper. But, having offered a compelling, concrete example of Jefferson's eloquence, Webster, if he is to maintain the balance that has marked the narrative thus far, must discover some comparable text, situated in the same intense historical moment, which he may display as the trophy of Adams's patriotism and service.[18]

The imaginary speech, therefore, serves as the counterweight to Jefferson's Declaration and helps preserve the balanced structure of the eulogy. Moreover, the fictional address reminds us that both writing and speech were necessary to justify independence and define the Revolution. In Webster's view, the contributions of Jefferson the writer are equaled and perhaps surpassed by those of Adams the orator. The insertion of the supposed address by Adams, then, allows Webster to recall the oral tradition of American eloquence in an age when academic rhetoric was turning to written composition. The oral tradition of eloquence, a tradition with which Webster himself closely identifies, is thus rediscovered in the fictional recomposition of a discourse lost to history.

The principle of balance within the structure of the eulogy is retained by Webster through the remainder of the oration as he proceeds through the later careers of both statesmen. As the Revolution passes into memory, Adams and Jefferson again move apart, geographically and ideologically, and the pace of the narrative quickens. The effect of Webster's timing, and of his decision to compose an oration for Adams, serve to focus our attention on Independence Day as the original moment in American history. The fictional speech allows Webster to pause at that vital juncture while at the same time capturing and articulating its meaning for the audience of 1826.

The meaning that Webster communicates is the message that defined his own career: "Liberty and Union, now and for ever." The perpetuity of the republic of 1776 stands as one of the principal themes of the commemorative discourse. It is also a theme Webster announces clearly in the composition he invents for Adams.

Webster begins his eulogy with a prayer for the republic. "The honors that are paid, when the founders of the republic die, give hope that the republic itself may be immortal."[19] Within the fictional address, he has Adams confidently assent to that prayer. "This Declaration will stand," Adams is supposed to have said. "When we are in our graves, our children will honor it. They will celebrate it with thanksgiving, with festivity, with bonfires, and illuminations. On its annual return they will shed tears, copious gushing tears, not of subjection and slavery, not of agony and distress, but of exultation, of gratitude, and of joy."[20] Webster, in a dramatic apostrophe to the dead hero, assures him "And so that day shall be honored, illustrious prophet and patriot! so that day shall be honored, and as often as it returns, thy renown shall come along with it, and the glory of thy life, like the day of thy death, shall not fail from the remembrance of men."[21]

The conclusion of the fictional address further declares the theme, and strengthens the structural connections with the larger text. Webster has Adams tell his fellow delegates "It is my living sentiment, and by the blessing of God it shall be my dying sentiment, Independence, *now*, and INDEPENDENCE FOR EVER."[22] At the end of Webster's narrative of Adams's life, the phrase appears again, here offered as the dying words of John Adams. "Thus honored in life, thus happy at death, he saw the JUBILEE, and he died; and with the last prayers which trembled on his lips was the fervent supplication for his country, 'Independence for ever!'"[23]

Webster uses the phrase "Independence For Ever" not only to give a sense of melodramatic closure to Adams's speech and life, but also to tie the fictional address more firmly to the eulogistic occasion, and to secure an additional structural connection with the eulogy as a whole. That structural connection, moreover, invites an identification between the orator and his subject, who share the vision of an eternal republic. The phrase leads Webster comfortably into his closing paragraphs, where the sentiment is repeated in a call unifying the generations. "Let us, then, acknowledge the blessing, let us feel it deeply and powerfully, let us cherish a strong affection for it, and resolve to maintain and perpetuate it," he implores the audience. "The blood of our fathers, let it not have been shed in vain; the great hope of posterity, let it not be blasted."[24]

The fictional Adams speech, therefore, acts as both the structural centerpiece and the thematic essence of Webster's commemorative discourse. Here the action of the whole text is concentrated. The imaginary address, therefore, acts as a synecdoche—a "representation" of the whole. As Kenneth Burke observed, "the well-formed work of art is internally synecdochic, as the beginning of a drama contains its close or the close sums up the beginning, the parts all thus being consubstantially related."[25] Present in the fictional Adams speech are strong reminders of the introduction of the eulogy, and an anticipation of its conclusion. The Adams address, in structure and essential nationalist message, is the "microcosm," of the whole oration. In a larger sense, the Adams speech also represents the most essential elements of the Revolution itself. Within the eulogy, the fictional composition articulates Daniel Webster's own "revolutionary" sentiment and his understanding of the events of 1776.

The success of the Adams address as synecdoche is borne out in the fact that the fictional speech was so widely anthologized on its own. It is its capacity to "contain" the whole message which enables the Adams speech to "represent" the eulogy and the eloquence of the Revolution, as it reappears and is rehearsed in schoolbooks, classrooms, and patriotic assemblies across the nation.[26]

REDUCTION AND REMEMBRANCE

The wide distribution of the Adams address in school readers and anthologies confirmed Webster's success in meeting one of the principal goals of any eulogy—that of assisting the remembrance of the deceased. Kathleen Jamieson has outlined the generic character of eulogies: "Eulogistic rhetoric has traditionally affirmed the reality of death, eased confrontation with one's own mortality, psychologically transformed the relationship between the bereaved and the deceased, and refashioned relationships of members of the community in the absence of the deceased."[27] In the eulogy to Adams and Jefferson, Webster participates in this generic tradition. Indeed, the eulogistic psychology described by Jamieson would seem to form the emotional foundation for Webster's oration.

"Adams and Jefferson are no more," Webster repeats in the first section of the eulogy, "they are no more. They are dead."[28] He demands recognition of the fact, but in a way which inspires awe rather than grief or terror. "If it be true that no one can safely be pronounced happy while he live, if that event which terminates life can alone crown its honors and its glory, what felicity is here! The great epic of their lives, how happily concluded! Poetry itself has hardly terminated illustrious lives, and finished the career of early renown, by such consummation." Inventing fully from the remarkable circumstances of the deaths of Adams and Jefferson, Webster assures his audience that although "our patriots have fallen," they have done so at "such age, with such coincidence, on such a day, that we cannot rationally lament that the end has come, which we knew could not be long deferred."[29]

Webster eases this confrontation with mortality by assuring that Adams and Jefferson "yet live, and live for ever. They live in all that perpetuates the remembrance of men on earth." Their service to the republic, their intellectual production, their legacy of wise leadership, will all be remembered, Webster promises.

But especially, "they live, emphatically, and will live, in the influence which their lives and efforts, their principles and opinions, now exercise, and will continue to exercise, on the affairs of men, not only in their own country, but throughout the civilized world."[30]

The orator next helps the transformation of the relationship between the living and the dead. The essential move is one "from physical encounter to encounter in memory," which is usually accomplished, says Jamieson, "by rehearsing the virtues of the deceased in the past tense."[31] Webster's narratives begin this task by assembling the important moments in the lives of Adams and Jefferson, and structuring them in a memorable discourse. Webster's attempt to secure a place for Adams and Jefferson in the collective memory constitutes by far the largest portion of his eulogy.

Finally Webster assists the community in restructuring their own relationships by insisting that the duties of citizenship have fallen fully upon them. After completing the biographical narratives of his subjects, telling his audience "their name liveth ever more,"[32] Webster speaks no more of the dead. Instead, he turns to Charles Carroll, the only surviving signer of the Declaration, as the remaining link between the present generation and that of the Revolution. Carroll is the "aged oak standing alone on the plain, which time has spared a little longer after all its contemporaries have been levelled with the dust." He invites his audience to "gather round its trunk, while yet it stands, and to dwell beneath its shadow."

Carroll personifies the startling wonder Webster wishes to communicate as he once again knits together American generations and recalls the principal theme of the eulogy. "If he dwell on the past, how touching its recollections; if he survey the present, how happy, how joyous how full of the fruition of that hope, which his ardent patriotism indulged; if he glance at the future, how does the prospect of his country's advancement almost bewilder his weakened conception!"[33]

Webster places the yoke of office firmly upon his audience as the new generation of leadership. "Let us not retire from this occasion," he implores, "without a deep and solemn conviction of the duties which have devolved upon us." The weight of public service, the responsibility for preservation of the union, now falls upon them. "Generations past and generations to come hold us responsible for this sacred trust. Our fathers, from behind, admonish us, with their anxious paternal voices; posterity calls out to us, from the bosom of the future; the world turns hither its solicitous eyes; all conjure us to act wisely, and faithfully, in the relation which we sustain."[34]

Within this psychological scheme falls the centerpiece of the oration—the fictional Adams speech. The imaginary address permits Webster to offer a concrete, visible, example of the service of John Adams, in effect inviting a memorable encounter with Adams in the past tense. We should not underestimate the importance of this eulogistic task. Raised on the classics, as were both Adams and Jefferson, Webster appreciated how historical fame acted as a compelling motive to public service. The early republic was crowded with public men who sought their greatest rewards, not in immediate popularity, nor riches, but in "Immortality in the Memories of all the Worthy, to the End of Time."[35]

Ironically, the responsibility for such fame rested with historians and eulogists, and it was a responsibility Webster took seriously. Indeed, the need to secure a measure of fame for Adams explains Webster's decision to compose a memorable oration for him. Webster especially understood the desire to achieve fame through oratory, which no doubt motivated much of his own public conduct. And in composing a great oration for Adams, Webster was defining Adams as a man of eloquence and obtaining for him the brand of fame Adams himself most desired. Adams had lamented that his contribution to the Revolution, and especially his service as an orator, would be forgotten. "Mausoleums, statues, monuments will never be erected to me," Adams wrote in 1809. "Panegyrical romances will never be written, nor flattering orations spoken, to transmit me to posterity in brilliant colors."[36] Yet as Webster said in the eulogy, "The eloquence of Mr. Adams resembled his general character, and formed, indeed, a part of it." His speech in the Continental Congress won him fame, and "no age will come in which it shall cease to be seen and felt, on either continent, that a mighty step, a great advance, not only in American affairs, but in human affairs, was made on the 4th of July, 1776. And no age will come, we trust, so ignorant or so unjust as not to see and acknowledge the efficient agency of those we now honor in producing that momentous event."[37]

We can better appreciate Webster's historical burden if we here view the imaginary Adams address as metonymy. The speech acts as a "reduction" of the abstract virtue of eloquence to the concrete action of speech. Webster makes the connection clearly by prefacing the fictional debate on Independence with the now famous dissertation on true eloquence. "True eloquence, indeed, does not consist in speech," he advises. "It must exist in the man, in the subject, and in the occasion." Webster's vision of eloquence rejects "the graces taught in schools, the costly ornaments and studied contrivances of speech," in favor of situated action "noble sublime, godlike action!"[38]

The Adams oration, therefore, becomes the manifestation of this virtue and the means by which Adams will be remembered. The need to demonstrate the practical manifestation of his ideal of eloquence also affords Webster another opportunity to advance the cause of spoken eloquence over written discourse. Webster's bias is evident as we compare the treatment he gives Adams's speech with that afforded the written Declaration of Jefferson. The Declaration is praised as Jefferson's accomplishment, as a "production of his mind," a "composition," his "work." True, it was a paper of "high dignity" and "merit," but it remains, in Webster's hands, merely "the paper to be drawn" to "set forth those causes, and justify the authors of the measure, in any event of fortune, to the country and to posterity."[39]

In contrast, the eloquence of Adams is part of his character, and is "godlike." We see it "speaking on the tongue, beaming from the eye, informing every feature, and urging the whole man onward, right onward to his object." Adams's eloquence was "bold, manly, and energetic," and connected with his "high intellectual and moral endowments." It consists of a "spontaneous, original, native force."[40]

Webster was not satisfied, however, to give an abstract description of eloquence. He had to present that eloquence to the audience. The imaginary speech acts as metonymy insofar as it embodies that principle of eloquence. The basic figurative architecture here is not complex, and operates any time a theoretical construct is made manifest by a practical paradigm. But consider briefly the type of paradigm chosen by Webster. There was no attempt by Webster to conjure up Adams's legal defense of the British soldiers in the Boston Massacre trial. Nor does he rehearse lines from Adams's Inaugural oration. And while it is true that Webster is constrained by structure to focus on 1776, and constrained by history to recreate a political speech, it may have been the case that the motivation to undertake the composition existed in the challenge to produce a memorable deliberative text. The subtle message is that not oratory in general, but primarily deliberative speech is the scene of the truest eloquence. It is political speech that is most demanding and calls on "education and discipline . . . natural talent and natural temperament" to achieve success.[41]

The Adams speech acts as metonymy in a different way as well. The fictional address captures and articulates Webster's own sense of appreciation for the eloquence of his hero. Inspired by Adams's excellence, Webster issues what Lawrence W. Rosenfield would call an invitation to "join with our community in giving thought to what we witness." In epideictic discourse, Rosenfield explains, such appreciation is communicated and such witness invited by "setting an example before the community." The commemorative speaker "seizes on and embellishes particular incidents in his subject's career in order to set free on the audience the radiance incorporated in the events." The audience recognizes the excellence as the speaker "recreates for his listeners the splendor residing in the temporal and contingent," and thereby makes that moment "more permanent in the collective memory."[42]

The imaginary speech captures the excellence of Adams and reduces it to memorable discourse. The discourse operates as metonymy because it contains the "reduction" of Webster's original inspiration. As Burke explains, a work of art, "reduces a state of consciousness to a 'corresponding' sensory body," a text for example. "But the aim of such *embodiment*," says Burke, "is to produce in the observer a corresponding state of *consciousness*."[43]

Webster disclosed the intensity of his own inspiration, his state of consciousness, in a letter to Millard Fillmore. The president, like other admirers of Webster's oration, once asked about the authenticity of the Adams address. "I will tell you what is not generally known," Webster wrote in return. "I wrote that speech one morning before breakfast, in my library, and when it was finished my paper was wet with my tears."[44] Webster's inspiration was successfully communicated through the metonymy of the fictional speech. Tobias Watkins, after receiving a copy of the eulogy by mail, wrote and told Webster that he could not contain "the spontaneous, irrepressible outpouring of my feelings," when he read the speech. He credited Webster with "a consciousness of superior powers" which inspired and enabled the author to compose "the reply of Mr. Adams."[45]

Others made similar observations. "In joy and in grief," wrote Samuel Knapp, in 1831, "there often is a feeling so intense that the mind cannot find repose until the heart has discharged itself in words." Webster provided such words, according to Henry Cabot Lodge. The Adams address was another instance when Webster "gave form and expression, at once noble and moving, to the national sentiment of his people. In what he said men saw clearly what they themselves thought, but which they could not express."[46] The Adams address, therefore, works as the trope of expression—the discourse which communicates the vision of history which so moved the orator himself.

PERSPECTIVE AND HISTORY

In his concern to secure the fame of Adams and ensure that his services would pass safely into the collective memory of the early republic, Webster no doubt had a consciousness of his own role as historian. In 1826, professional history was still in its infancy. Before Bancroft and Fiske it was often the orators who assembled the remarkable events of the past and composed them into a discourse worthy to be remembered.[47] Webster took this responsibility seriously, not only in his eulogy to Adams and Jefferson, but in his speech at Plymouth, and in his Bunker Hill oration. These orations, and others by Webster, form a body of discourse that served the young nation as "an education in history and statescraft," and "an outline framework of the American Character and the American History."[48]

In the Eulogy to Adams and Jefferson, "it was Webster's distinction to be among the first in New England to summarize the dramatic careers of these two founders of our nation."[49] Not surprisingly, then, there is a strong narrative element in the oration. "The occasion, fellow-citizens, requires some account of the lives and services of John Adams and Thomas Jefferson," he tells his audience. "This duty must necessarily be performed with great brevity, and in the discharge of it I shall be obliged to confine myself, principally to those parts of their history and character which belonged to them as public men."[50]

The history that Webster understood, however, was not the empirical discovery of past fact, nor the unbiased disclosure of cause and consequence. It was rather a confident political history, a history for use. Webster would no doubt have been delighted to know that his fictional Adams address was "read aloud and memorized by generations of schoolchildren."[51] As Caleb Cushing wrote, the recitation of the Adams speech, along with other passages from Webster's oratory, served to "mould the boy to the destinies of the future patriot and statesman."[52] It was Webster's goal, then, at least in part, to assist in the cultivation of a growing American nationalism by composing orations that popularized important historical events. He wished to fix among the stars "the American constellation," which might inspire a respect for "our position and our character among the nations of the earth."[53]

It was of little concern to Webster that no records existed of the debates in the Continental Congress. Whether perfectly genuine or not, the speech composed by Webster had the appearance of authenticity. Adams "made no Preparation beforehand, and never committed any minutes . . . to writing," but the fictional Adams speech was a convincing substitute. It had "such an air of truth and reality about it," thought George Curtis. Indeed it was, said Charles Richardson "true as truth."[54]

Webster, of course, was familiar with both the classical and contemporary examples of historians who composed orations for their subjects. Whether in Thucydides or Sallust, Shakespeare, Botta, or William Wirt, the fictional oration was a mainstay of the historical literature familiar to Webster.[55] Nevertheless, the composition of such an oration as a means of enhancing historical narrative cannot claim historical authority and will necessarily involve creation of new meaning. The new meaning results from what is essentially a metaphorical shift in perspective. In the case of the fictional—or figurative—Adams speech, the shift occurs on two levels.

First, in its figurative recomposition by Webster, the original Adams speech becomes something it never aspired to. It takes on a permanence it could not have gained on its own. Adams's original address was a discourse of the moment, an extemporaneous deliberative argument situated firmly within the environs of

Revolutionary Philadelphia. Webster's substitution, while filling the historical vacuum, cannot recapture the living moment. As a consequence, the revolutionary character of the speech is diminished. Its daring, its radicalism, is tempered by its new surroundings and by its performance as a "privileged cultural text."[56] The speech, which in its own day had been considered seditious, in Webster's hands becomes calcified as part of increasingly well rehearsed national myth. Webster tries to preserve the original anxiety of the moment by reminding the audience that Adams "stood in the hour of utmost peril," and "met the frown of power," but the relative stability and comfort of his own situation prevents him from resurrecting the radicalism of Adams's discourse. Instead, the fictional oration takes on a decidedly conservative ideological force as it assumes its place in the national literature.

The composition by Webster further alters our perspective on the original Adams speech by demanding a consciousness of the text as artistic performance. However aware Adams may have been of the aesthetic element of his argument in Philadelphia, Webster's substitution brings to the forefront, not the revolutionary doctrine, nor the force of the speech as philosophical or legal argument, but its character as embodied eloquence. "This, this is eloquence" says Webster as he introduces the Adams address.

Webster encourages this alternative perspective by prefacing his creation with the discourse on true eloquence. The prefatory dissertation directs our admiration not to Adams's courage or wisdom, but to his eloquence. This shift in perspective is quite significant when we consider that it is the same virtue of eloquence which must sustain Webster's own public standing and which he hopes will remain a prominent force in the conduct of the public's business.

These subtle shifts in perspective were accompanied by some considerable risk for the orator, risks recognized by contemporaries and critics alike. "Certainly your attempt to pass the doors of that most august sanctuary, the congress of 76, and become a listener and reporter of its immortal debates, was extremely bold, extremely hazardous," wrote Richard Rush. "Nothing but success could have justified it, and you have succeeded." It was, said Allan Benson, "A daring thing."[57]

By prefacing the Adams text with his remarks on eloquence, Webster would inevitably invite his audience to turn the light of that discourse on the orator himself. Webster's skill comes in his ability to remain present but transparent in the performance. In other words, the Adams text attains a degree of verisimilitude without calling attention to itself as a performance by Webster.

Webster removes himself from the scene—invites the audience to suspend its awareness of his presence—by crafting a new scene for the "godlike action" of John Adams. By this scenic construction, Adams is placed within the context of a historical drama, and removed temporarily from the context of Webster's eulogy. Webster bid his audience "Let us, then, bring before us the assembly, which was about to decide a question thus big with the fate of empire. Let us open their doors and look in upon their deliberation. Let us survey the anxious and care-worn countenances, let us hear the firm-toned voices, of this band of patriots."[58]

The fiction is made more plausible by Webster's ability to compose the Adams speech in a distinctively argumentative oral style, in contrast to the steady narrative prose of the biographical accounts. For authenticity, Webster adds material borrowed from Adams's *Autobiography* and letters. "There was no attempt to deceive," wrote Benson, "but the art with which Webster did the thing *did* deceive. It was both great oratory and great acting."[59] For many who later read the oration, said Irving Bartlett, "Webster's John Adams and the John Adams of history had fused as one."[60]

Verisimilitude in the metaphoric substitution is also vital to discourage critical attention to the basic paradox of Webster's eulogy. In his remarks on eloquence Webster achieves status for Adams's oratory by contrasting it with the studied rhetoric of the schools. "Rhetoric is in vain," he says, "words and phrases may be marshalled in every way," but they cannot achieve eloquence. Nor can eloquence be reached by "affected passion, intense expression, the pomp of declamation," nor by "labor and learning."[61] Yet the imaginary oration is itself a piece of carefully crafted rhetoric. If the paradox is noticed, the dissertation on eloquence would arrest any authority claimed by the fictional oration. Because of Webster's craft, however, the Adams argument can be both eloquent and not eloquent at the same time.

DIALECTIC AND IDEOLOGY

What I have here called paradox might by some critics be labeled irony. But I wish to reserve that term to refer to the contributory dialectic within discourse described by Kenneth Burke, the dialectic which results when "ideas are in action" and when discourse produces a development which subsumes all its parts.[62]

The effectiveness of the Adams speech as a historical document results in large measure from Webster's ability to create the proper dramatic context for the Adams text. Perhaps the most vital element of that context is the fictional opponent gotten up by Webster to challenge the move toward independence. That opponent is essential to create the drama of a heroic triumph for John Adams. At the Continental Congress, John Dickinson had commanded the floor as the most eloquent opponent of the Declaration of Independence. Within Webster's speech, the "Pennsylvania Farmer" is not named, but is represented as "one of those not yet prepared to pronounce for absolute independence."[63]

The speech by this anonymous opponent is rehearsed by Webster. "Let us pause," says the imaginary colonial moderate. "This step, once taken, cannot be retraced. This resolution, once passed, will cut off all hope of reconciliation." Webster goes on to compose a series of compelling reasons to hesitate in the vote for separation from England. "While we stand on our old ground, and insist on redress of grievances, we know we are right, and are not answerable for consequences. . . . But if we now change our object, carry our pretensions farther, and set up for absolute independence, we shall lose the sympathy of mankind." As Webster tells his audience, "it was for Mr. Adams to reply to arguments like these."[64]

Webster, therefore, aims to create the sense of dramatic deliberation which no doubt characterized the original moment in the Congress at Philadelphia. And although the speech composed by Webster for the less radical delegate is shorter than that invented for Adams, it nevertheless advances a powerful case against independence. In fact, several of Webster's contemporaries remarked upon the substantive and formal superiority of the argument made by Adams's opposite. "Mr. Walsh and myself, without any previous communication, were both struck with the circumstance that the *argument* given against the Declaration of Independence is much stronger than that in support of it," wrote Joseph Hopkinson to Webster. It was apparent, he continued, that "the strength of all human reasoning was with those who opposed the measure, although every elevated and noble feeling was in favour of it."[65]

By allowing the Adams speech to rest primarily on emotional appeal, Howell and Hudson believe, Webster was "showing that the Declaration was an act of faith, that the signers could rest not on certainties but only on their own strength of resolution."[66] Beyond this explanation, however, it seems important to consider the larger effect of the dramatic clash between the imaginary Adams and his rival.

The political disagreement between Dickinson and Adams mirrors the long ideological dispute between Adams and Jefferson. Webster's ability to negotiate and resolve the Adams-Dickinson argument, therefore, prefigures his handling of the Adams-Jefferson struggle. Although both subjects of the eulogy were together for Independence, their later careers were marked by often bitter political rivalry. Nevertheless, Webster and the country honor both Adams and Jefferson. The extraordinary occasion transcends partisan politics. Both contributed to the birth of the nation, and the American experiment has become larger than the political doctrine espoused by either man. The Webster eulogy thus restates the point Jefferson himself made in his famous inaugural: "We have called by different names brethren of the same principle. We are all republicans—we are all federalists."

Webster directs our attention away from the division between Adams and Jefferson by focusing on their unity—in Philadelphia, in diplomatic service, in high office, in scholarship, and in death. They were rivals, he acknowledges, "but this is not the time, nor this the occasion, for entering into the grounds of that difference." Instead, Webster says, we should "imitate the great men themselves in the forbearance and moderation which they have cherished, and in the mutual respect and kindness they have been so much inclined to feel and to reciprocate."[67]

The capacity of Webster's own eulogy to praise two men of such different political creeds encourages a view of history, and of future politics, which is equally generous. The clarion note of "E Pluribus Unum," rehearsed throughout the eulogy, also gives Webster grounds to reconsider the historical events in Philadelphia in an ironic fashion.

In casting his historical drama, Webster has deliberately chosen to include the moderate or more conservative message within the meaning of the events at Philadelphia. He has given that message considerable force by resting it upon compelling arguments. Webster was quite comfortable articulating a conservative doctrine. He was, after all, in his early career, "the foremost spokesman of New England conservatism."[68] In this case, the orator suggests that the conservative voice, too, was present at the creation and was indeed what Burke would call "neither true nor false, but contributory."[69]

As Webster moves to reclaim elements of the conservative past, we can begin to construct a view of the Adams oration, not in isolation, but in dialectic. It is no longer purely "Revolutionary," but ironic. The irony exists in the fact that the fictional Adams address provides the occasion and becomes the instrument by which Webster recovers an important appearance of American conservatism. In Burke's terms, Webster uses the Adams speech, in dialogue with the Dickinson character, to create "the interaction of terms upon one another, to produce a development which uses all the terms."[70]

Webster's history is therefore decidedly revisionist in that it intentionally recalls the conservative voice to its role in the deliberative mythology of American politics. To be sure, Webster is not subverting the revolutionary accomplishment of the Founding Fathers. He knows he can depend on the hermeneutic impulse of his audience to fit the conservative message within the meaningful context of the full eulogistic text. He relies on what Robert Ferguson calls the "animated obedience" of nineteenth century listeners to ensure that his inclusion of the conservative position is not mistaken as a debunking of the national mythology he himself helped invent.[71] Dickinson was defeated in 1776, and that does not change here. Adams remains the orator-hero of the day. But Webster has accomplished something by announcing the presence (and perhaps re-emergence) of the conservative message in American politics.

The key point in this ironic development is that both Adams and Dickinson become necessary to comprehend the politics of 1826, as they were both necessary to accomplish the drama of 1776. As Burke explains, "history in this sense would be a dialectic of character," in which we "should note elements of all such positions (or 'voices') existing always, but attaining greater clarity of expression or imperiousness of proportion of one period than another."[72]

The timing of Webster's recovery of the conservative voice is also important, for in a matter of a few years, when he himself would take center stage to be the eloquent defender of the republic, his own discourse would recall the topics, not from the fictional Adams speech, but rather those from the discourse composed for the opponent of the Declaration. Substitute "Nullification" or "Secession" for "Independence" and the words of the Dickinson character might easily find room in the Second Reply to Hayne, or Webster's debates with Calhoun. "It will be on us," warned that conservative voice, "if, relinquishing the ground on which we have stood so long, and stood safely, we now proclaim independence, and carry on the war for that object, while these cities burn, these pleasant fields whiten and bleach with the bones of their owners, and these streams run blood."[73]

The strong presence of the conservative voice has led some critics and historians to wonder how Webster himself would have voted had he been at Philadelphia in 1776. But the question, in fact, is misdirected. We need to look instead to how Webster fashioned a history of 1776 for use in 1826. Burke explains that in irony, "although all the characters in a dramatic or dialectic development are necessary qualifiers of the definition, there is usually some one character that enjoys the role of *primus inter pares*."[74] Unquestionably, the first character of the eulogy is John Adams. But as Burke suggests further, the principal character has a dual role. He is "'adjectival' as embodying one of the qualifications necessary to the total definition, but is 'substantial' as embodying the conclusions of the development as a whole."[75]

As "adjective" Adams clearly represents the Revolutionary sentiment of 1776. His counterpart is the conservative "adjective." What is the conclusion? At one level it is a nationalist political ideology which glories in the success of the Revolution as the chief event and unifying moment of its history. But at another level, the conclusion is more immediately useful to the orator himself. The conclusion is eloquence. Adams is "substantial" insofar as he embodies eloquence. "The eloquence of Mr. Adams," says Webster, "resembled his general character, and formed, indeed, a part of it."[76] The clash between Dickinson and Adams is necessary to produce "noble, sublime, godlike action." In this sense, Adams is "indebted" to Dickinson in true ironic fashion. His greatest deliberative effort is impossible without the challenge of a capable rival (as Webster's later success would be impossible without the challenge of Hayne or Calhoun). Thus, both Adams and Dickinson—radical and conservative—combine to produce the man, the subject, and the occasion for eloquence. Webster is therefore motivated to produce not a set-piece oration by Adams alone, but the full drama of deliberative debate.

What might ordinarily be seen as merely the necessary staging for a dramatic performance, therefore, when considered through the lens of Burkean irony, becomes a powerful instrument for the promotion of a conservative ideology. Moreover, consideration of the fictional Adams address as irony once again reveals Webster's ability to promote eloquence and to advance principles that are consistent with his image and public conduct.

CONCLUSION

By examining the imaginary Adams address as a master trope in the Eulogy to Adams and Jefferson, we can recognize its status as a field of primary rhetorical action in the text. The trope not only assists Webster in meeting the structural, generic, and historical demands of his commemorative discourse, but also empowers him to cast the revolutionary eloquence of John Adams in a fashion that serves the ideological needs of Webster's day. Webster's invention of a speech for Adams not only supplies the text for one of the nation's most significant rhetorical acts, it also makes eloquence itself a historical force. And, as eloquence is advanced as the glorious paradigm of public service, the value of Webster's own stock in patriotic oratory appreciates dramatically. He has reinforced those tenets of the national mythology upon which later eulogists would found their commemoration of Daniel Webster's godlike action.

NOTES

1. *Memoirs of John Quincy Adams comprising portions of his Diary from 1795-1848*, ed. Charles Francis Adams (Philadelphia: J. B. Lippincott, 1875), 7:124.
2. Edward Everett, "Biographical Memoir of the Public Life of Daniel Webster," in *The Works of Daniel Webster*, 4th ed. (Boston: Little Brown, 1853), 1:lxviii.
3. Josiah Quincy to Daniel Webster, 3 August 1826, in *The Writings and Speeches of Daniel Webster*, National Edition (Boston: Little Brown, 1903), 17:408.
4. Joseph Hopkinson to Daniel Webster, 30 August 1826, in George Ticknor Curtis, *Life of Daniel Webster*, 4th ed., 2 vols. (New York: D. Appleton, 1872), 1:279. Tobias Watkins to

Daniel Webster, 1 September 1826, Manuscript in the Baker Special Collections of the Dartmouth College Library, MS. 826501.

5. Merrill D. Peterson, *The Great Triumvirate: Webster, Clay, and Calhoun* (New York: Oxford, 1987), 111.

6. Peter J. Becker to Daniel Webster, 16 January 1846, in Curtis, *Life of Webster*, 1:294.

7. Daniel Webster to Peter Becker, 22 January 1846, in Curtis, *Life of Webster*, 2:295. In a letter to George Ticknor, Webster laments that "I cannot answer all these, one after another." The question about the Adams speech, he said, "has been a great many times asked me." Webster asks Ticknor to answer future inquiries and to publish his response to Becker to help clarify the historical record. (Daniel Webster to George Ticknor, 24 January 1826, in Curtis, *Life of Webster* 2:296) Webster's letter to Becker was published in several editions of his collected speeches. See for example, *The Great Speeches and Orations of Daniel Webster* (Boston: Little Brown, 1879), 177-78.

8. Everett, "Biographical Memoir," lxviii.

9. Tobias Watkins to Daniel Webster, 1 September 1826, Dartmouth manuscript.

10. Richard Rush to Daniel Webster, 30 August 1826, in *The Papers of Daniel Webster: Correspondence, 1825-1829*, ed. Charles M. Wiltse (Hanover, N.H.: University Press of New England, 1976), 2:129.

11. Henry Cabot Lodge, *Daniel Webster* (Boston: Houghton Mifflin, 1885), 125-26.

12. Claude Moore Fuess, *Daniel Webster* (Boston: Little Brown, 1930), 1:303.

13. Wilbur Samuel Howell and Hoyt Hopewell Hudson, "Daniel Webster," in *A History and Criticism of American Public Address*, ed. William Norwood Brigance (1943; reprint New York: Russell & Russell, 1960), 2:684.

14. Kenneth Burke, "Four Master Tropes," in *A Grammar of Motives* (Berkeley: University of California Press, 1969), 503.

15. Daniel Webster, "Adams and Jefferson," 2 August 1826, in *The Papers of Daniel Webster: Speeches and Formal Writings, 1800-1833*, ed. Charles M. Wiltse (Hanover, N.H.: University Press of New England, 1986), 1:239. All quotes from the eulogy will be from this edition.

16. Webster, "Adams and Jefferson," 243.

17. Ibid., 250.

18. On the balance in the structure of the Eulogy see Craig R. Smith, *Defender of the Union: The Oratory of Daniel Webster* (New York: Greenwood, 1989), 36.

19. Webster, "Adams and Jefferson," 238-39.

20. Ibid., 259. Webster based this passage on a letter John Adams wrote to his wife following the vote for independence. See John Adams to Abigail Adams, 3 July 1776, in *Adams Family Correspondence*, ed. L. H. Butterfield (Cambridge: Harvard University Press, 1963), 2:29-31.

21. Webster, "Adams and Jefferson," 259-60.

22. Ibid., 259. This peroration written for Adams, of course, anticipates the dramatic close of Webster's greatest deliberative address, his Reply to Hayne in 1830. There Webster ended with "Liberty and Union, now and for ever, one and inseparable!"

23. Ibid., 263.

24. Ibid., 270.

25. Burke, "Four Master Tropes," 508.

26. The supposed oration by Adams was reprinted alone in many school readers. "The two speeches attributed to Mr. Adams and his opponent attracted great attention from the first," wrote George T. Curtis. "Soon they were put into school-books, as specimens of English and of eloquence. In time, men began to believe they were genuine speeches," (Curtis, *Life of Webster* 1:275). "Thousands of Americans never realized that this was Webster's language," wrote Irving Barlett ("Daniel Webster the Orator and Writer," in Kenneth Shewmaker, ed., *Daniel Webster the Completest Man* [Hanover, N.H.: University Press of New England, 1990], 84). Numerous school readers contain the "Adams" oration. See for example, John D. Philbrick, *The American Union Speaker* (Boston: Thompson, Bigelow & Brown, 1871); George S. Hillard, *The Franklin Sixth Reader and Speaker* (Boston: Brewer & Tileston, 1875); Asa Fitz, *Fitz's American School Speaker, and School Reader* (Boston: N. L. Dayton, 1856); Charles Dudley Warner, *The Book of Eloquence* (Concord, N.H.: Edson and Eastman, 1877).

27. Kathleen M. Jamieson, *Critical Anthology of Public Speeches* (Chicago: SRA, 1978), 40.

28. Webster, "Adams and Jefferson," 239-40.

29. Ibid., 239.

30. Ibid., 240.

31. Jamieson, *Critical Anthology*, 40.

32. Webster, "Adams and Jefferson," 269.

33. Ibid. The image of the aging Carroll peering into the past and imagining the future, calls to mind the compelling image of Lord Bathurst, introduced by Edmund Burke in his Speech on Conciliation with America. Webster admired Burke's oratory.

34. Webster, "Adams and Jefferson," 269.

35. John Adams to Jonathan Sewell, February 1760, *Papers of John Adams*, ed. Robert J. Taylor, Mary-Jo Kline, and Gregg L. Lint (Cambridge: Harvard University Press, 1977), 1:41-42. On the importance of historical fame to John Adams, see James M. Farrell, "John Adams's Autobiography: The Ciceronian Paradigm and the Quest for Fame," *New England Quarterly* 62 (1989): 505-28.

36. John Adams to Benjamin Rush, 23 March 1809, *The Spur of Fame: Dialogues of John Adams and Benjamin Rush, 1805-1813*, eds. John A Schutz and Douglass Adair (San Marino, Calif.: Huntington Library, 1966), 139.

37. Webster, "Adams and Jefferson," 255, 241.

38 Ibid., 255.

39. Ibid., 251-53.

40. Ibid., 255.

41. Ibid. Here I am following an argument made by Michael Leff in his analysis of Antonius's discourse in Cicero's *De Oratore*. See Michael C. Leff, "Genre and Paradigm in the Second Book of *De Oratore*," *Southern Speech Communication Journal* 51 (1986): 308-25.

42. Lawrence W. Rosenfield, "The Practical Celebration of Epideictic," in *Rhetoric in Transition*, ed. Eugene E. White (University Park: Penn State University Press, 1980), 131-

55, esp. 133-41. Rosenfield's essay is also helpful in understanding the contrast Webster has formulated between Jefferson's "accomplishment" and Adams's "character."

43. Burke, "Four Master Tropes," 509.

44. Allan L. Benson, *Daniel Webster* (New York: Cosmopolitan, 1929), 167-68.

45. Tobias Watkins to Daniel Webster, 1 September 1826, Dartmouth Manuscript.

46. Samuel L. Knapp, *A Memoir of the Life of Daniel Webster* (Boston: Stimpson and Clapp, 1831), 76; Henry Cabot Lodge, "Daniel Webster—His Oratory and His Influence," in *A Fighting Frigate and other Essays and Addresses* (New York: Charles Scribner's Sons, 1902), 131.

47. On the importance of oratory as historical discourse see Daniel Boorstin, *The Americans: The National Experience* (New York: Random House, 1966), 307-69.

48. Charles F. Richardson, "Webster, the American Orator," in *Daniel Webster for Young Americans* (Boston: Little Brown, 1903), xxxiii; Robert A. Ferguson, *Law and Letters in American Culture* (Cambridge: Harvard University Press, 1984), 213.

49. Fuess, *Daniel Webster,* 1:303.

50. Webster, "Adams and Jefferson," 243.

51. Boorstin, *The Americans: The National Experience,* 310.

52. Peterson, *The Great Triumvirate: Webster, Clay, and Calhoun,* 112.

53. Webster, "Adams and Jefferson," 270-71. Four days before the Webster oration, John Quincy Adams recorded in his diary that "The evening was uncommonly clear, starlight, and I passed from one to two hours with George and T. B. Adams, Jr., in the road fronting the house, showing them the constellations." (*Memoirs of John Quincy Adams,* 7:137).

54. John Adams, *Diary and Autobiography,* ed. L. H. Butterfield, (Cambridge: Harvard University Press, 1961), 3:396; Curtis, *Life of Daniel Webster,* 1:275; Charles F. Richardson, "Webster, the American Orator," in *Daniel Webster for Young Americans,* xxxiii.

55. Webster was probably motivated, in part, by the challenge to outdo William Wirt and his very successful *Sketches of the Life and Character of Patrick Henry* (Philadelphia, 1817), which contained the remarkable "Liberty or Death" speech reconstructed by the biographer. Webster may have sought to strike a blow for Massachusetts in the rivalry between local orator-heroes of the Revolution. On this point see Boorstin, *The Americans: The National Experience,* 307-10, and 357-60; O. M. Dickerson, "Writs of Assistance as a Cause of the Revolution," in *The Era of the American Revolution: Studies Inscribed to Evarts Boutell Greene,* ed. R. B. Morris (New York, 1939), 40-75; Farrell, "John Adams's Autobiography: The Ciceronian Paradigm and the Quest for Fame." During his visit to see Jefferson, in 1824, Webster discovered that Jefferson thought Wirt's *Life of Henry* was "a poor book, written in bad taste, and gives an imperfect idea of Patrick Henry." Jefferson believed, however, that "John Adams was our Colossus on the floor. He was not graceful nor elegant, nor remarkably fluent, but he came out occasionally with a power of thought and expression, that moved us from our seats." See Curtis, *Life of Daniel Webster,* 2:585-89. See also Webster, "Adams and Jefferson," 254. Tobias Watkins, knowing that William Wirt would also deliver a eulogy to Adams and Jefferson, wrote "I pity my poor friend Wirt, that he has to come before the publick after such a display . . . if he gives the chance to the critic of

comparison in the closet, I would not suffer the sentence which must be passed upon him for all his present reputation." Watkins to Webster, 1 September 1826, Dartmouth Manuscript.

56. I am borrowing the term from Dilip Parameshwar Gaonkar. See "The Oratorical Text: The Enigma of Arrival," in *Texts in Context: Critical Dialogues on Significant Episodes in American Political Rhetoric,* ed. Michael C. Leff and Fred J. Kauffeld (Davis, Calif.: Hermagoras, 1989), 271.

57. Richard Rush to Daniel Webster, 30 August 1826, in *Papers of Daniel Webster: Correspondence, 1825-1829,* 2:129; Benson, *Daniel Webster,* 162.

58. Webster, "Adams and Jefferson," 256.

59. Benson, *Daniel Webster,* 162.

60. Bartlett, "Daniel Webster the Orator and Writer," 84.

61. Webster, "Adams and Jefferson," 255. I am here borrowing the idea of "status" for eloquence from Robert Hariman, "Status, Marginality, and Rhetorical Theory," *Quarterly Journal of Speech* 72 (1986): 38-54.

62. Burke, "Four Master Tropes," 512.

63. Webster, "Adams and Jefferson," 256.

64. Ibid., 256-57.

65. Joseph Hopkinson to Daniel Webster, 30 August 1826, in Curtis, *Life of Daniel Webster,* 1:279.

66. Howell and Hudson, "Daniel Webster," 684.

67. Webster, "Adams and Jefferson," 267-68.

68. Thomas Brown, *Politics and Statesmanship: Essays on the American Whig Party* (New York: Columbia University Press, 1985), 58.

69. Burke, "Four Master Tropes," 513.

70. Ibid., 512.

71. Ferguson, *Law and Letters in American Culture,* 220.

72. Burke, "Four Master Tropes," 513.

73. Webster, "Adams and Jefferson," 257. The parallel between this fictional speech and Webster's "Reply to Hayne" is especially evident in that section of the famous deliberative address where Webster imagines the "practical application" of Hayne's doctrine, as armed secessionists prepare to seize federal property. "Here would ensue a pause: for they say that a certain stillness precedes the tempest." Some from among Hayne's "military array," would "request of their gallant commander in chief to be informed a little upon the point of law. . . . They would inquire whether it was not somewhat dangerous to resist a law of the United States." The followers of Hayne would properly ask "shall we swing for it? We are ready to die for our country, but it is rather an awkward business, this dying without touching the ground! After all, that is a sort of hemp tax worse than any part of the tariff" ("Reply to Hayne," in *Great Speeches and Orations of Daniel Webster,* 267). What Webster says here to ridicule Hayne, he asserts with conviction in the fictional speech against Independence: "It will be upon us, if, failing to maintain this unseasonable and ill-judged declaration, a sterner despotism, maintained by military power, shall be established over

our posterity, when we ourselves, given up by an exhausted, a harassed, misled people, shall have expiated our rashness and atoned for our presumption on the scaffold" ("Adams and Jefferson," 257).

74. Burke, "Four Master Tropes," 516.
75. Ibid., 516.
76. Webster, "Adams and Jefferson," 255.

WEBSTER'S EULOGY AND THE TROPES OF PUBLIC MEMORY

Stephen H. Browne

O n July 4, 1826, the bells of Boston rang in celebration of an American Jubilee; six days later, they rang again for the passing of Adams and Jefferson. By that time, word of the remarkable deaths had drifted south to Jefferson's ancestral county; there the news was met by a skeptical Republican with the verdict that it was all "a damned Yankee trick." I mention this bit of apocrypha as a reminder that while for many the event was, as Professor Farrell says, "a coincidence of providential proportions," others were rather less certain as to its interpretation. Adams's legacy especially could strain the invention of even the most earnest orator. As one witness put it: "Not half an age has roll'd its winter o'er,/Since hate of Adams's spread to every shore,/Now how rever'd in love they seem to melt,/And feign an adoration they never felt!."[1]

That Webster authentically admired Adams, and that he chose to interpret his death as he did, tells us as much about the orator's politics as his vaunted craft. I would like to examine in further detail Professor Farrell's suggestion that the one can be read through the figures of the other. In particular, I hope to show that if we are to read Webster's address in such a fashion, we ought to foreground synecdoche as its governing trope. As the dominant and enabling trope of the text, synechdoche asserts itself by negotiating a movement between general principle and exemplifying particular, between, that is, the Whig conception of history and the figural presence of John Adams.

I

Professor Farrell's own work convincingly demonstrates how difficult it was for Adams to determine his place in the incipient mythology he helped create.[2] If ever there was a figure certain of an American future, and doubtful that he would be remembered properly in it, surely that was Adams; the same, perhaps, could be said of Webster, who continues to be shadowed by the twin legacies of ambition and failure. There is one certainty about Webster, however, on which we can rely: in Farrell's words, he "reinforced those tenets of the national mythology upon which later eulogists [would] found their commemoration of Daniel Webster."

In retrospect, at least, no one was more perfect for the job. By the year of Jubilee, Webster had become an architect of American memory at a time when that art was still unabashed. "The apotheosis of 1826," Merrill Peterson writes, "joined this piety of remembrance to the idea of an eternally valid heritage from the founders. In the "'age of commemoration,' the imagery of The Signers, The Heroes and Sages of the Revolution, the Founding Fathers was a fixture of the American mind."[3] Webster helped enormously to make it so, and he did it by exploiting the rich stores of Whig history and by mastering the idiom by which it was given expression.

The vocabularies of identity are seldom stable and never exhaustive; they are, nevertheless, essential as a way of making sense of one's presence in political life. Citizens of the early republic, Daniel Walker Howe suggests, had available to them two such vocabularies, roughly distinguishable along party lines.[4]

Both functioned in important ways to interpret the meaning of the revolution and consequently the meaning of American political life. Whereas Democrats clung ominously to a contractual theory of government, Whig spokesmen drew from and extended a highly developed discourse of inheritance, a language of tradition by which commitments were secured, values transmitted, and precedents respected. Experience, they never ceased to claim, was their guide into and through the progressive stages that were sure to mark American growth. The institutions of culture, which helped instill responsibility and protect against those who would, with their abstractions and self interest, rip the bonds of Union, were at their best but formal expressions of private virtue—itself defined as a type of devotion to the principles of republican government.

We have in Webster's oratory a literal compendium of the topoi structuring this Whig vision and voicing its aspirations. Webster knew, too, that, in the words of Jean Matthews, "to constitute oneself a member of the party of memory was neither mere nostalgia nor disgruntled reaction—it was a political act."[5]

Webster's rhetorical art is accordingly indistinguishable from its political referent, and on this basis we are able, as Farrell asks us, to read in the eulogy a configuration of appeals at the very heart of Whig history. Like all histories, moreover, it required a principle of transmission to keep it compelling, and in Webster's oration we discover that what is being transmitted is, more than anything, cultural knowledge. This act of transmission I take to be Webster's distinctive contribution to the Whig tradition, for in rehearsing its principles he made dramatic and plausible the forms of knowledge by which the Union could be made perpetual.

I need now to be more specific about what is meant by cultural knowledge, and to detail its relationship to Webster's address. For immediate purposes, Lyotard's description of narrative tradition will help focus the point. Such a telling, Lyotard writes, "is also the tradition of the criteria defining a three-fold competence—"know-how," "knowing how to speak," and "knowing how to hear" (*savoir-faire, savoir-dire, savoir entendre*) through which the community's relationship to itself and its environment is played out. "What is transmitted through these narratives," Lyotard stresses, "is the set of pragmatic rules that constitutes the social bond."[6]

Webster's legacy is precisely the legacy of these rules, and his description of Adams may be understood as a kind of *ethopoeisis* by which they are given rhetorical force. These rules, moreover, are recognizable in classical and scriptural lore as injunctions to act wisely, to speak well, and, to quote Proverbs, "get wisdom."

To treat each of these formations in turn: Know-how (*savoir faire*) is familiar as a symbolically constructed standard of action; it stresses and celebrates those individuals who seem able to move well and quickly. It is in this sense a practical wisdom, an ability to read a situation and respond to it with the full force of experience. It thus requires judgment of a particular type, beholden neither to rules nor to sheer intuition. Know-how is thus displayed as a quality of character as much as of mind, and is evident in the actor's successful negotiation between principle and expedience. It is the sign of prudence.

Webster's set piece on eloquence further draws our attention to the centrality of speech to cultural knowledge. "Knowing how to speak," Lyotard's description, presumes a particular type of competence and entails a set of standards that ensures its own transmission. That Webster casts this know-how in heroic terms is of course entirely consistent with the tradition; they are explicable only as they are associated with what Edward Said calls a "beginning-individual." That figure, Said notes, "must fulfill the requirements of an exacting and, as it were, inaugural logic in which the creation of authority is paramount—first, in the requisite feat of having done something for the first time, an original achievement that gains in worth, paradoxically, because it is so often repeated thereafter."[7]

Webster's celebration is thus in part a celebration of the orator-as-hero, a figure who in speaking inaugurates a logic that will be sustained in the coming time. Here, too, eloquence is taken to be an attribute of character, meaningful to the degree that it is embodied and as it gives to great action its fitting expression. Webster understood that the revolution could continue to live only as it was spoken, knew, in the words of Bruce James Smith, that "Only through speech can the deed remain entire and intact, distinguishable from and undissolved by the multitude of its consequences. Without speech to memorialize, says Arendt, there can be no remembrance."[8]

Knowing how, and knowing how to speak, specify those forms of knowledge requisite to the production of cultural identity. As such, they get passed down through the narratives of achievement by which communities make sense of themselves and their past. Webster was able to enrich this tradition by insisting on a third type of competence: *savoir entendre* (knowing how to listen). Literally every ceremonial address and most of his deliberative orations articulate a principle of reception, the need, that is, for citizens to actively study and learn from the past. I think we greatly underestimate Webster's craft and politics if we ignore this almost obsessive concern. Webster was for this reason highly sensitive to the needs of public education. He sought thereby to establish the optimal conditions of readiness, to inculcate republican virtue by teaching citizens to listen properly. In doing so, he hoped to provide through his own eloquence a model not only of one who acts and speaks well, but one who knows how to listen. On this point I think Professor Farrell is exactly right. As Webster commemorates Adams he in effect celebrates himself, at least as an exemplar of republican competence, and teaches others that in listening well the good citizen learns to remember. In remembering, he or she learns to regard. Thus Webster's message: get wisdom, speak it, and act on it.

With these observations in place, we can ask how that message gets textualized in the form of Webster's eulogy. As I have indicated, the most promising option is to foreground one of Farrell's tropic appropriations, and examine how synecdoche works to link the Adams speech with the cultural narrative it celebrates. It does this work, I will suggest, by inscribing the tenets of Whig tradition into itself and by putting on display the competencies defining that tradition. The figural move here is dynamic: synecdoche functions not just to draw the greater into the lesser, but in having done that to project back out a more dramatic version of itself. This emphasis seems to preserve the figural basis of the Adams speech, even as it provides for its rhetorical force. It allows us to see, moreover, how the text constructs for itself a world in which its values can be publicly confirmed and passed on. To the extent that such remembering is textually explicit, it may be read through its synecdochic representations.

II

Turning at last to the Adams speech: it is, again, a figural exemplification, a *characterismus*, designed to celebrate the forms of knowledge commanded by the speaker and basic to the tradition he represents. Adams is accordingly displayed as a man of action, of know how. Webster is able to draw on a range of commonplaces at once familiar and enduring: Adams, this speaker of words and doer of deeds, "knows" whether to act; he knows when to act; and he knows how to act. The first involves the relationship between principle and expedience, and the extent to which either is sufficient as a rationale for action. We know, of course, how these things turn out: Adams is willing to "sink," "die," *and* "perish" for the principle of the matter, but is happy to relate that, there being a "Divinity which shapes our ends," such commitment is rewarded with international prestige, enhanced commercial prospects, and a stronger hand at the bargaining table. Adams is revealed, further, to have acted in a timely and appropriate fashion: the Americans had been patient, but once pushed to the wall, must fight resolutely and immediately. "The injustice of England has driven us to arms; and, blinded to her own interest for our good, she has obstinately persisted, till independence is now within our grasp. We have but to reach forth to it, and it is ours. Why then should we defer the declaration?"[9] Adams is shown, finally, to know how to act, how, that is, to invest his decision with the greatest possible symbolic meaning.

"In acts of commemoration," writes Edward Casey, "remembering is intensified by taking place through the interposed agency of a text . . . and in the setting of a social ritual. . . . The remembering is intensified still further by the fact that both ritual and text become efficacious only in the presence of others, with whom we communicate in a public ceremony."[10] This convergence of memory, site, and ritual describes precisely the sense of "speaking well" at work in Webster's eulogy. As Professor Farrell points out, there is a mirroring effect by which Webster's eloquence is at once reflected by and projected onto Adams. And if, as Farrell also suggests, the voices become harmonically blurred, the principle being celebrated remains distinct enough. Adams is eloquent because he speaks the ancient truths; and those who, like Webster, would wish also to be eloquent, must rehearse those truths in the rituals of enlightened citizenship. This, then, is what it means to speak well: to know that the "clear conception, outrunning the deductions of logic, the high purpose, the firm resolve, the dauntless spirit, speaking on the tongue, beaming from the eye, informing every feature, and urging the whole man onward, right onward to his object—this, this is eloquence; or rather, it is something greater than all eloquence, it is action, noble, sublime, godlike action."[11]

Webster thus portrays Adams as exemplifying not only know-how, but the knowledge of how to speak what one knows. What Adams knows, of course, are the terms by which America will assume its place and play out its destiny. He comes to this knowledge as Webster would have his audience come to it: by selectively listening to the lessons of the past and the shared commitments it sanctions. This type of know-how, this *savoir entendre*, completes the image and dri-ves the Adams speech to its predestined conclusion. It is a type of knowledge which demands not only that Adams listen, but that he is listened to; and it is through this injunction that Webster's eulogy finds its ultimate rationale. Thus what Adams says of the Declaration might well stand as Webster's own: "We shall make this a glorious, an immortal day. When we are in our graves, our children will honor it. They will celebrate it, with thanksgiving, with festivity, with bon-fires, and illuminations. On its annual return they will shed tears, copious, gush-ing tears, not of subjection and slavery, not of agony and distress, but of exultation, of gratitude, and of joy. Sir, before God, I believe the hour is come."

III

In accounting for the legacy of the Adams speech, Professor Farrell stresses its "capacity to 'contain' the whole message," and "to 'represent' the eulogy and the eloquence of the Revolution." If I would add anything to this insight, it is by way of extension: I find synecdoche to govern the internal action of the text as well as its system of referents. It thus bears out Burke's point that synecdochic represen-tation "stresses a relationship or connectedness between two sides of an equation, a connectedness that, like a road, extends in either direction."[12] In this trope we locate the means by which Webster was able to simultaneously concentrate and expand the Whig claim to an American birthright. Its force is mnemonic, its effect to remind his audience of the knowledge requisite to the proper conduct of republican life. It is, finally, a way of reading the narratives by which people artic-ulate their past and fix their commitments. In rehearsing that narrative through the mouth of John Adams, Webster proved himself not only a spokesman of the Whig tradition but its most talented ventriloquist.

NOTES

1. Merill D. Peterson, *The Jefferson Image in the American Mind* (New York: Oxford University Press, 1960), 4, 6.
2. James M. Farrell, "John Adams' Autobiography: The Ciceronean Paradigm and the Quest for Fame," *New England Quarterly* 62 (1989): 505-28.
3. Peterson, 8; Stephen H. Browne, "Reading Public Memory in Daniel Webster's Plymouth Rock Oration," *Western Journal of Communication* 57 (1993): 464-77.
4. The summary is based on the analysis of Daniel Walker Howe, *The Political Culture of the American Whigs* (Chicago and London: University of Chicago Press, 1979), 69-95; see also James Jasinski, "The Feminization of Liberty, Domesticated Virtue, and the Reconstitution

of Power and Authority in Early American Political Discourse," *Quarterly Journal of Speech* 78 (1992): 146-64.

5. Jean V. Matthews, "Whig History: The New England Whigs and the Search for a Usable Past," *New England Quarterly* 51 (1978): 196.

6. Jean-Francois Lyotard, *The Postmodern Condition: A Report on the State of Knowledge*, trans. Geoff Bennington and Brian Massumi (Minneapolis: University of Minnesota Press, 1984), 21.

7. Edward Said, *Beginnings: Intention and Method* (New York: Basic Books, 1975), 32.

8. Bruce James Smith, *Politics and Remembrance: Republican Themes in Machiavelli, Burke, and Tocqueville* (Princeton, N.J.: Princeton University Press, 1985), 19.

9. Daniel Webster, "Adams and Jefferson," 2 August 1826, in *The Papers of Daniel Webster: Speeches and Formal Writings, Vol. 1, 1800-1833*, ed. Charles M. Wiltse (Hanover: University Press of New England, 1986), 1:240.

10. Edward S. Casey, *Remembering: A Phenomenological Study* (Bloomington: Indiana University Press, 1987), 218.

11. Webster, 240.

12. Kenneth Burke, *Grammar of Motives* (1945; reprint Berkeley: University of California Press, 1969), 509.

THE IRONY OF "EQUALITY" IN BLACK ABOLITIONIST DISCOURSE: THE CASE OF FREDERICK DOUGLASS'S "WHAT TO THE SLAVE IS THE FOURTH OF JULY?"

John Louis Lucaites

[H]ow is it with the American slave? . . . He is said to be happy; happy men can speak. But ask the slave—*what* is his condition?—*what* his state of mind?—*what* he thinks of his enslavement? and you had as well address your inquiries to the *silent dead*. There comes no *voice* from the enslaved, we are left to gather his feelings by imagining what ours would be, were our souls in his soul's stead.

Frederick Douglass[1]

True irony, humble irony, is based upon a fundamental kinship with the enemy, as one *needs* him, is *indebted* to him, is not merely outside him as an observer but contains him *within*, being consubstantial with him.

Kenneth Burke[2]

The word "equality" is an essential marker in the lexicon of American political discourse. By most contemporary accounts it ranks with "liberty" and "property" as one of a troika of terms constituting the discursive boundaries of legitimate political behavior in America's democratic republic. Most U. S. citizens premise the establishment of "equality" as a central component of the American credo on the "self-evident" claim expressed in the Declaration of Independence, that "all men are created equal." According to the narrative of American history that emanates from this premise, the newly constituted nation did not immediately live up to the ideal of its founding principle. Gradually, however, the courageous efforts of northern, white abolitionists motivated the nation to affirm its egalitarian ideals, first in the Emancipation Proclamation, and shortly thereafter in the Thirteenth, Fourteenth, and Fifteenth Amendments to the Constitution.[3] This affirmation required a protracted and costly civil war, but that, too, found a hallowed place in the story of American equality, framed as a trial by combat that resolved the issue once and for all under the sanctioning gaze of an approving and egalitarian Christian God.[4] In the twentieth century the story evolved into a tale concerning how the nation's initial commitment to equality led almost as if by necessity to the extension of political rights to a variety of minority groups, including most notably women and blacks. The moral of this rather traditional story is clear: America's distinction is its egalitarian commitment to treat all of its people the same, "regardless of religion, race, sex, or previous condition of servitude." And more, underlying this moral is the conventional belief that the meaning of equality was established as an ideal, self-evident principle at the time of the nation's founding.

Celeste Michelle Condit and I take these orthodoxies to task in *Crafting Equality: America's Anglo-African Word*, arguing that the traditional rhetorical narrative of American equality is neither the most inclusive nor necessarily the most compelling account of the facts of the case. In its place we offer an alternate narrative. In our story the word "equality" is not a self-evident political ideal, its meaning established and set in stone at the moment of the nation's assertion of independence. Rather, it is a symbolic, rhetorical foundation of America's collective identity, its meaning expanding and retracting in political usage as a result of the efforts of public advocates seeking to manage the tension between the nation's abstract political commitments and its material needs and socio-political practices.[5]

Our purpose in writing *Crafting Equality* was to account for some of the ways in which the word "equality" has been rhetorically negotiated in the experience of American public discourse from the time of the revolution to the present. The telling of this story is no simple task, for it not only requires reorienting how we think about equality conceptually, rooting it in the context of specific historical usages, but it also necessitates accounting for the significant rhetorical influence of a large body of public discourse that has been ignored or minimized by those who write about America's egalitarian roots, including the efforts of a very large cast of black American journalists, pamphleteers, and orators, writing and speaking in a wide range of public forums.[6] In the period from 1776 to 1860 alone, such forums included local, state, and national abolitionist and anti-colonizationist meetings, state and national Negro Conventions, the Lyceum circuit, town hall meetings, black church pulpits, local annual celebrations, and a large number of white and black abolitionist and black pan-Africanist newspapers and weeklies.

Because we focus on how the word "equality" circulated in public discourse over the course of American history, we tend to direct attention away from the efforts of specific speakers and writers and toward the rhetorical forms and func-

tions of particular linguistic usages. This leads us to underplay the rhetorical significance of individual agents as representatives of public consciousness and
arbiters of social and political change. That is not our intention, as our studies
indicate that individual rhetors can and do have important and wide ranging
influences upon the collective life of a community, just as individual speeches frequently are significant tokens of a social and political consciousness. A prime
example that bears directly on the crafting of an American "equality" in the latter
half of the nineteenth century is Frederick Douglass's "What to the Slave is the
Fourth of July?," a speech delivered on 5 July 1852 at the Corinthian Hall in
Rochester, N.Y.[7]

Frederick Douglass was without a doubt one of the most important
spokespersons for the burgeoning African-American identity in the antebellum
period, his reputation as a powerful orator ranking him with the likes of Wendell
Phillips and Daniel Webster among whites and H. H. Garnet among blacks.[8]
Given this reputation, it is striking that our bibliographies of nineteenth-century
public discourse generally fail to account for the rhetorical significance or com-
plexities of his leadership and public speaking in anything but passing fashion.[9]
There has been a great deal of critical analysis of the rhetorical dimensions of his
three autobiographies, as well as some consideration of his journalism, but on his
oratory there is almost nothing.[10] Of particular note is the virtual absence of consideration of "What to the Slave is the Fourth of July?," a speech characterized by
one of Douglass's biographers as "perhaps the greatest antislavery oration ever
given."[11]

The purpose of this essay is to begin to rectify this condition. In what follows
I argue that the rhetorical significance of this speech is a function of the ways in
which Douglass employed an ironic framework to craft a usage of equality that
would reconstitute the national public forum as a dialogue between past, present,
and future, and thus enact a legitimate public space for the articulation of a
uniquely *African-American* political voice. To that end I first characterize the
rhetorical problem that black abolitionists faced in constituting a collective identity for black Americans, locating it specifically in the symbolic environment of
the antebellum debates over the status of slavery in the U. S. Constitution. I then
direct attention to the ways in which Douglass configures and negotiates an ironic
tension between the problem of defining an African-American identity and competing interpretations of the Constitution as an egalitarian doctrine in his Fifth
of July oration. In the end, I speculate on the relevance of treating his ironic construction of equality in this oration as a representative anecdote for the rhetorical problem of racial equality in contemporary American political discourse.

THE RHETORICAL PROBLEM OF ANTEBELLUM BLACK AMERICAN COLLECTIVE IDENTITY

There is a popular propensity to conclude that because most of the slave population brought to the New World came from Africa, American slaves therefore shared a common cultural heritage and socio-political identity. In point of fact, however, neither the culture nor the nationality of the individuals enslaved in America were technically African. Many slaves came from the West Indies, and even those brought from Africa typically identified themselves in terms of their tribal affiliations and kin-groups, not their continent of origin.[12] Slaves from many different culture groups were frequently mixed with one another on the plantations such that, at least in the beginning, America's slave population possessed no sense of a common culture, let alone a collective or national identity.[13] However, in the wake of the growth of post-revolutionary free black communities in the north, these various groups gradually merged to constitute a separate and unique African-American people.[14]

The development of this collective identity was a slow and fragile process. Despite the growing number of black freemen in the years following the War for Independence, America's colored people did not always agree on a common set of social, political, and economic interests. In some measure, this was a function of the fact that most early efforts at social and political action emanated from within the black church and with an eye towards locally oriented change. The emergence of the American Colonization Society in 1817 stimulated local black groups in Philadelphia, Brooklyn, Boston, Richmond, and elsewhere to organize a national response to the Society's argument to colonize free blacks in Africa, and thus provided the springboard for a collective political identity. That identity began to crystallize in the form of a legitimate national political voice over the next fifteen years through the development of black newspapers, such as *Freedom's Journal* in 1827; nationally distributed pamphlets, such as David Walker's militant *Appeal to the Coloured Citizens of the World*; and national conferences, such as the first National Negro Convention held in Philadelphia in 1830.[15]

Constituting a legitimate collective voice and guaranteeing that it will be heard as equal to other political voices by the prevailing social and political order are two very different things, however, and it was this latter problem which occupied the attention of African-American orators, journalists, and pamphleteers from approximately 1830 until the final ratification of the Civil War amendments in 1870. The key issue initially facing such advocates was whether free blacks were included with and "equal" to the "people" identified in the preamble to the Constitution. For those socialized to the traditional narrative of American equality, this sounds like a *non sequitur*, if not an inherent contradiction. How could the American people reasonably commit themselves to the universal enlightenment principle that "all men are created equal," and then deny "equal liberties" to free blacks, let alone the massive slave population that provided the labor force for the nation's southern plantations?

The answer to this question is contained in the fact that the status of equality as a legal, constitutive commitment of American political society was not settled at the time of the revolution, nor even at the time of the constitutional conventions. Equality did appear as a radical foundation of the Declaration of Independence, but as important as that document was to become in defining the American national character, it did not legally constitute the United States of America. Once the Revolution was completed, the Declaration functioned in white public discourse to do little more than to articulate the relationship between "liberty" and "property" as a doctrine of natural rights warranting the colonists' violent resistance to the intolerable despotism of King George III; it thus served primarily to imply their authority to establish themselves as a self-governing society. This they accomplished in the Constitution and the Bill of Rights, but in doing so they failed to grant anything like legal status to the universal claim that "all men are created equal." Indeed, examination of the constitutional convention debates make it clear that the concept of equality was at best a vague and implicit consideration in the overall negotiations that functionally preserved the liberty and property of the men who had "freely" entered the social compact, and, in so doing, repressed the potential contradiction between "liberty" and "slavery" by agreeing that slaves could exist simultaneously as "people" and "property."[16]

This should not be taken to suggest that the word "equality" was absent from the public vocabulary of the new nation. Indeed, its presence in public discourse was abundant, a point commonly noted by historians who conclude that such usage indicates the degree to which the ideal of equality "lay at the heart of republicanism."[17] What such interpretations of the historical record typically ignore, however, is that the profusion of references to the word "equality" in the constitutional and early national periods were not to an ideal or natural right that persisted *after* the enactment of the social compact. Rather, they most frequently referred to a minimum list of rights, typically expressed as "equal liberties" or "equal representation," earned specifically by those who freely constituted the new nation.[18] Some public advocates, such as free blacks and white abolitionists, did attempt to transcend these usages with appeals to a universalistic conception of equality expressed under the rubrics of "equal liberty for all" and "equal citizenship," but prior to the twentieth century there was no public consensus on these more inclusive usages.[19]

The lack of public consensus notwithstanding, it was precisely the appeal to a concrete, universalistic conception of equality that stood at the core of the public efforts of black abolitionists to legitimize their collective identity and voice as citizens of the United States. The chief rhetorical problem facing these advocates was to craft a publicly acceptable heritage for American democracy that mediated the constitutional tension between the collective commitments to liberty and property through the regulative agency of equality. To do that they needed to revise the received view of the relationship between the Declaration of Independence and the Constitution so as to authenticate the legal or constitutive standing of equality as a founding principle of governance. In the 1840s, such efforts crystallized in the debate concerning the status of the Constitution as a pro-slavery or anti-slavery document.[20] In order to understand how black abolitionists took advantage of this situation, we need to consider the dynamics of that debate as it unfolded within the white abolitionist community.

The institutionalization of the abolitionist crusade began in the early 1830s with the publication of William Lloyd Garrison's *Liberator* and the formation of the New England Anti-Slavery Society in 1831, and the New York and American Anti-Slavery societies in 1833. This is not to say that abolitionists were all of one mind on the various issues confronting them. Throughout the 1830s there was a great deal of debate and factionalization among abolitionists concerning whether emancipation should be gradual or immediate, whether the emancipation of slaves should take precedence over other pressing needs for reform such as women's rights, whether or not the Bible treated slavery as a sin, and whether abolitionists should promote their cause through moral suasion and government non-resistance or through political action.[21] A formal schism occurred in 1840 at the annual American Anti-Slavery Society meeting over the issue of female participation, leading Lewis Tappan, a self-proclaimed misogynist, to form the American and Foreign Anti-Slavery Society.[22]

The tensions and bickering within the abolitionist community intensified in the 1840s as the newly formed Liberty and Free Soil Parties became increasingly vocal on the need for some kind of direct political action to effect emancipation, and the Garrisonians reinforced their position for moral suasion by demanding "no union with slaveholders." When Congress rejected the Wilmot Proviso, an effort to prohibit slavery in the territories acquired during the Mexican War, it became increasingly apparent to northern abolitionists of all stripes that a southern "Slave Power" wielded significant influence in the government.[23] The key question, of course, was whether that power was inherently and appropriately derived from the Constitution. In the context of justifying their positions the prevailing abolitionist factions began to debate the status of the Constitution as a pro-slavery or anti-slavery document.

Garrisonians maintained that at its core the Constitution legally represented the interests of the Slave Power. In Garrisons' own words, it was "a covenant with death and an agreement with hell," and any attempt to operate within its structure was to do the Devil's work.[24] As evidence of the Constitution's pro-slavery proclivities, Garrison and his supporters pointed to the fact that when the nation was constituted slavery "existed in all the states except Massachusetts," and then underscored those portions of the Constitution representing the slave interest. They were particularly fond of pointing to the 3/5s compromise in Art. 1, sect. 2; the failure to prohibit foreign slave trade under the federal commerce clause in Art. 1, sect. 8, further conceding authority in this area to the states in Art. 1, sect. 9; and the granting of total ownership rights over those "held to service or labor" in Art. 4, sect. 2.[25] The protection of slavery, it seemed, was carefully coded into the many compromises of the Constitution, and in the words of those like Wendell Phillips and William Bowditch, anybody who so much as voted or held office under a government thus established was no less a slaveholder than those who directly reaped the profits of slave labor:

> Slave-owners are not the only slaveholders. All persons who voluntarily assist or pledge themselves to assist in holding persons in slavery are slaveholders. *In sober truth, then, we are a nation of slaveholders!* for we have bound our whole national strength to the slave-owners, to aid them, if necessary, in holding their slaves in subjection![26]

From such a perspective it was literally the physical power afforded by the North and legitimized by a pro-slavery Constitution that sustained the peculiar institution of slavery. Garrison himself had arrived at this position by 1842, at which time he committed himself and the American Anti-Slavery Society to what he believed was the only viable alternative: disunion and secession.[27]

To maintain that the Constitution was an inherently pro-slavery document required denying the constitutive status of the Declaration of Independence, for to do otherwise implied the prior legal status of human equality as a natural right. If such were the case, one might argue that the Declaration of Independence superseded the Constitution, and is thus the legal form through which the latter should be interpreted in ambiguous or contested circumstances. As such, the burden of proof would rest on those claiming that the Constitution was a pro-slavery document to demonstrate that it hàd literally established slavery as a legal institution, not merely that it passively countenanced slavery's existence. This was the primary position taken by those who argued that the Constitution was an anti-slavery document. The chief architect of this argument was Lysander Spooner, and the vehicle of his argument was a pamphlet entitled *The Unconstitutionality of Slavery*.[28] First published in 1845, it became the handbook for those in the Liberty Party and others who later sought to invoke the Constitution as both the moral warrant and technical mechanism for effecting abolition.

Spooner's pamphlet is interesting, both for its attempt to establish the rules for interpreting legal discourse through what today we would call rhetorical hermeneutics, as well as for its weaving of a diachronic analysis of American constitutional history that systematically denied the *legality* of slavery from the time of the Articles of Confederation through the Declaration of Independence and beyond. In the end, at least by some contemporary accounts, the pamphlet was tortured by Spooner's "ponderous" and unrelenting lawyer's logic, which failed to account for the rhetorical appeal of the narrative, shared alike by Garrisonians and southern slaveholders, that the simplest and most direct evidence clearly indicated the pro-slavery nature of the Constitution.[29] As Garrison pointed out in an editorial in the *Liberator*, the "logic" of Spooner's argument is "ingenious . . . unanswerable," *but* logic does not undermine "fact," and here the facts of the case are "the bargain itself."[30]

Garrison was only half-right. Read in 1846 in the context of the defeated Wilmot Proviso and growing northern perceptions of the invisible hand of the Slave Power, Spooner's analysis struck many white abolitionists—at least those outside of the Liberty Party—as both counterfactual and logically counter-intuitive. How exactly to interpret "the bargain itself" was another matter. Regardless of how illogical Spooner's argument may have seemed, it was strong enough to require a more than passing response and defense from those who maintained that the Constitution was a pro-slavery document. That response, and the subsequent counter-responses that it in turn elicited, *ad infinitum*, created a loud and contentious public debate within the white abolitionist community. Black abolitionists had been interpreting the Constitution as an anti-slavery document for years, but their audiences were small and as public advocates they were generally treated as either non-persons or as part of the lunatic fringe.[31] For nominally free African-Americans desperately searching for a way to legitimize their collective voice through an egalitarian rhetoric that revised the relationship between the Declaration of Independence and the Constitution in a public forum that would have a much larger audience, the opportunity could not have been much better. The only question was how to exploit it to maximum effect? To answer that question we need to look to Frederick Douglass's "What to the Slave is the Fourth of July?," a speech delivered in 1852, but clearly in the making since 1847.

FREDERICK DOUGLASS AND THE PROBLEM OF IDENTITY

Eighteen hundred and forty seven is an important date for the abolitionist movement in general, and the cause of African-American identity in particular, for in November of that year Frederick Douglass returned from a two year speaking tour of the British Isles and moved his home from Lynn, Massachusetts to Rochester, New York, where he founded and became the publisher of the *North Star*. Almost all of Douglass's biographers point to this event in his life as a personal declaration of independence, for it marked his first step away from the patronizing influence of Garrison and toward the active and independent political abolitionist he would become.[32] That transformation did not occur immediately, but by 1849 it was clear that Douglass had begun publicly to question the strict pro-slavery interpretation of the Constitution and its implications for political action.[33] Rochester was a hotbed of anti-Garrisonian political abolitionists, and over the next two years Douglass flirted with the anti-slavery interpretation of the Constitution as expressed by radicals like Gerrit Smith. Finally, in May of 1851, he announced his full conversion to an anti-slavery interpretation of the Constitution, demanding that it be used "in behalf of emancipation."[34] The following month, almost as if to emphasize his divorce from the Garrisonians as a political rebirth, he changed the name of his paper from the *North Star* to *Frederick Douglass's Paper*.

Douglass's public conversion entailed important consequences for the status of the collective identity of African-Americans. African-Americans had long argued that American democracy was a hypocritical institution, but as long as the Constitution was held to be an inherently pro-slavery document, that hypocrisy was systemic, and the weight of its charge could not be leveled at any particular individual. In an important sense then, this interpretation of the Constitution absolved contemporary white, northern abolitionists of any moral complicity in the nation's hypocrisy. The shift in interpretation changed that condition, for if the Constitution was truly an anti-slavery document, then white northern abolitionists were inherently responsible for finding ways to make the nation live up to its legally constituted foundations. Douglass, however, was after more than just abolition, and in his post-conversion public discourse America's hypocrisy was not simply the political failure to enact vague egalitarian principles, but the wholesale failure to acknowledge the citizenship of African-Americans as a unique and independent voice in American democracy.

As a nominally free black in America who had experienced both political freedom and basic human respect on his extended speaking tour of the British Isles, Douglass came to recognize the latent, if well-intentioned, racist paternalism that underscored the efforts of many white abolitionists like Garrison.[34] He thus came relatively quickly to the conclusion that the social and political implications of such racism were even more significant than the problem of slavery, for they pervaded not only the plantation, but the world of the free black as well. In shifting his allegiance to an anti-slavery interpretation of the Constitution then, Douglass was looking for the opportunity to legitimize the difference between the collective identity of African-Americans and white Americans, and it was in the expression of the political authenticity of that difference that he crafted a more concrete and inclusive conception of American equality than theretofore had been articulated by either white or black abolitionists. The most complete version of this development occurred in "What to the Slave is the Fourth of July?"

When Douglass was invited by the Rochester Ladies' Anti-Slavery Society to deliver a Fourth of July oration he must have been struck by the irony of the request. Or at least so we might conclude when we consider that from beginning to end Douglass delivered a speech fraught with bitter and sarcastic ironies which he systematically called to the attention of his audience. So, for example, there is the irony that England had better learned the lessons of the Declaration of Independence than the sons and grandsons of the men who forged such insights at the time of the revolutionary war.[35] Or even more striking, the irony of establishing criminal laws that in one stroke acknowledged the slave's "moral, intellectual, and responsible being," and refused to affirm his "equal manhood" (369-70). Or the irony of a society that "invites to its shores the fugitives of oppression from abroad," and then passes a law that allows slave owners to "advertise, hunt, shoot, and kill" fugitive slaves in the United States (382).

The irony of this speech, however, goes much deeper than these and a plethora of other relatively simple and direct examples might indicate. In the classical tradition, irony was treated as a "figure of thought," which meant that its use frequently extended "beyond the sentence to larger units of discourse."[36] As both an inventional topos and a dispositional scheme, irony often served to configure dialectical tensions within a text, or between a text and its context, so as to give the orator an opportunity to embody and enact the union of wisdom and eloquence by managing or resolving the apparently problematic oppositions in a given situation. Treated from this perspective, "What to the Slave is the Fourth of July?" constitutes an ironic embodiment and enactment of an inclusive conception of equality as a necessary component to a vitalized democratic republic.

The speech is organized in three major sections, corresponding to the past, present, and future of American independence as seen from a slave's point of view. What marks the ironic disposition of the text, however, are not the parts themselves, but the dialectical tensions Douglass creates and manages between and among them as a dialogue on the relationship between the Declaration of Independence and the Constitution. That dialogue emerges in two stages. In the first stage, Douglass identifies a tension between the nation's glorious historical past and its bleak present as a means of enacting both the audience's complicity in the hypocrisy of American democracy, as well as the public voice of a unified African-American community. In the second stage, he enacts an ironic reversal by reconstituting America's lived present in an egalitarian future (through a vitalized past) that embodies cultural differences as an essential element of a free and open society. I will consider each of these stages as a means of directing attention to the implications of Douglass's speech for the rhetorical problem of equality, both in his time and in our own.

TENSION BETWEEN PAST AND PRESENT

As with most group anniversaries, America's Fourth of July is a formal occasion for celebrating the community's historical past in the lived present as a prelude to an even rosier and more optimistic, collective future. In "What to the Slave is the Fourth of July?" Douglass subverts this expectation by celebrating the past as a standard against which to vilify the present.

The speech begins in a rather conventional manner. Douglass humbly disclaims his ability to speak before such an audience on such a hallowed occasion, and expresses his gratitude for the opportunity. This is done subtly, in a way that forecasts the ironic tone that pervades the complex, dialogic structure of the speech itself. Rather than to seek complete identity with his audience in a way that would warrant his speaking for them as a community, as would be customary in a speech of this sort, he carefully distinguishes himself from them as an outsider: First, he calls attention to "the distance between this platform and the slave plantation, from which I escaped," thus underscoring his continuing identity as a former slave—as one whose freedom had been denied by the duly constituted laws of the United States. Second, he highlights the cause for "this celebration" as "the birthday of *your* National Independence, and of *your* political freedom" (360). Taken together, these two passages establish the terms of an ironic, dialogic tension between those who have cause to celebrate their political freedom, and those who must always question the status of their freedom. Douglass thus puts himself in the position of speaking *to* his audience as a dialogical other, rather than to speaking for them as a duly constituted member of their community.

Having established the initial terms of difference, he proceeds to what appears as a rather standard narration of the events leading to the Declaration of Independence, careful to praise the "eternal principles" and patriotic virtues that motivated the Founding Fathers' selfless and courageous behavior (359-64). It is precisely at this point, where the audience ought to anticipate a bold characterization of the glorious specifics of that behavior, that Douglass introduces his first ironic reversal by abruptly shifting the time frame of the speech. "My business," he notes, "if I have any here to-day, is with the present. The accepted time with God and his cause is the ever-living now." After quoting a stanza from Longfellow's "A Psalm of Life" he goes on:

> We have to do with the past only as we can make it useful *to the present and to the future*. To all inspiring motives, to noble deeds which can be gained from the past, we are welcome. But *now* is the time, the important time. Your fathers have lived and must die, and you must do your work. *You have no right to enjoy a child's share in the labor of your fathers, unless your children are to be blest by your labors*. You have no right to wear out and waste the hard-earned fame of your fathers to cover your indolence. (366)

This passage is important, for it provides an explicit statement of Douglass's intention to subvert the conventions of the occasion. The nation's past will not be blindly and optimistically read into the present or the future as an automatic entitlement of all who live and breathe. Rather, as Douglass emphasizes, if the "hard-earned fame" of the past is to have any relevance to the present or the future, it must be earned again and again, *actively* revived in the labors of each subsequent generation. To celebrate the past without regard for how it is activated in the "ever-living now" is to "eulogize the wisdom and virtues of [one's] fathers, [only] to excuse some folly or wickedness of their own" (366).

To be an authentic celebration of the Fourth of July, then, the speech must represent a dialogue between the nation's past on the one hand, and its present and future on the other. As Douglass moves to this task, however, he confronts a serious problem. To speak in the present implies a legitimate, public voice; but it is precisely that legitimacy which the *present* enactment of the Constitution denies the African-American community. Earlier in the speech, Douglass described himself, almost in passing, as an "escaped slave," but here it becomes clear that in the gaze of contemporary America, "slavery" is *the* condition of African-Americans writ large, whether bound on a southern plantation or nominally free in the north. And as such, it raises questions as to Douglass's authority to speak in praise of the lived relationship between the nation's past and its present: the past defined in the terms of the Declaration of Independence, which he characterizes as the "RING-BOLT to the chain of [the] nation's destiny," and the present dominated by the legal enactments of the Constitution.

The passage in which these doubts are expressed, one of the two most often cited from the speech, marks a sharp change in Douglass's tone, and in so doing completes the first ironic reversal begun in his shift in focus from the past to the present. I quote it here in full:

> Fellow-citizens, pardon me, allow me to ask, why am I called upon to speak here to-day? What have I, or those I represent, to do with your national independence? Are the great principles of political freedom and of natural justice, embodied in that Declaration of Independence, extended to us? and am I, therefore, called upon to bring our humble offering to the national altar, and to confess the benefits and express devout gratitude for the blessings resulting from your independence to us?
>
> Would to God, both for your sakes and ours, that an affirmative answer could be truthfully returned to these questions! Then would my task be light, and my burden easy and delightful. For *who* is there so cold, that a nation's sympathy could not warm him? Who so obdurate and dead to the claims of gratitude, that would not give his voice to swell the hallelujahs of a nation's jubilee, when the chains of servitude had been torn from his limbs? I am not that man. In a case like that, the dumb might eloquently speak, and the "lame man leap as a hart."
>
> But, this is not the state of the case. I say it with a sad sense of the disparity between us. I am not included within the pale of this glorious anniversary! Your high independence only reveals the immeasurable distance between us. The blessings in which you, this day, rejoice, are not enjoyed in common. The rich inheritance of justice, liberty, prosperity and independence, bequested by your fathers, is shared by you, not by me. The sunlight that brought life and healing to you, has brought stripes and death to me. The Fourth [of] July is *yours* not *mine*. *You* may rejoice, *I* must mourn. To drag a man in fetters into the grand illuminated temple of liberty, and call upon him to join you in joyous anthems, were inhuman mockery and sacrilegious irony. Do you mean, citizens, to mock me, by asking me to speak to-day? If so, there is a parallel to your conduct. And let me warn you that it is dangerous to copy the example of a nation whose crimes, towering up to heaven, were thrown down by the breath of the Almighty, burying that nation in irrecoverable ruin!

Following a brief passage from *Psalms 137: 1-6*, he continues:

> Fellow-citizens; above our national, tumultuous joy, I hear the mournful wail of millions! whose chains, heavy and grievous yesterday, are, to-day, rendered more intolerable by the jubilee shouts that reach them. If I do forget, if I do not faithfully remember those bleeding children of sorrow this day, "may my right hand forget her cunning, and may my tongue cleave to the roof of my mouth!" To forget them, to

pass lightly over their wrongs, and to chime in with the popular theme, would be treason most scandalous and shocking, and would make me a reproach before God and the world. My subject, then fellow-citizens is AMERICAN SLAVERY. I shall see, this day, and its popular characteristics, from the slave's point of view. Standing, there, identified with the American bondman, making his wrongs mine, I do not hesitate to declare, with all my soul, that the character and conduct of this nation never looked blacker to me than on the 4th of July! Whether we turn to the declarations of the past or to the professions of the present, the conduct of the nation seems equally hideous and revolting. America is false to the past, false to the present, and solemnly binds herself to be false to the future. (367-69)

In the introduction to the speech, Douglass had subtly foreshadowed the hypocrisy of American democracy when he commented on the "distance" between the "platform" from which he spoke and the "plantation" from which he had escaped. Following the announcement of his true subject as "American Slavery," the obvious irony of the speech is no longer veiled, and the metonymic "distance" of the introduction becomes the legally enacted, political difference between white and black in a self-proclaimed free and democratic society. The long middle portion of the speech is thus given over to demonstrating America's hypocrisy as a condition of the lived, constitutional present, and the national failure both to remember and engage a dialogue with its authentic past founded in the "ring-bolt" of the Declaration of Independence. In paragraph after paragraph Douglass ridicules and reproaches those who question the slave's humanity or the black man's morality, returning over and again to the multitude of inconsistencies embodied in the practices of the nation's political and religious leadership.

Throughout this attack one claim surfaces over and again as that which configures the hypocrisy in its most vicious and debilitating form: the culturally and legally sanctioned absence of a publicly viable African-American voice. One finds it subtly implied in Douglass's depiction of the cold and heartless "man drovers" who are totally oblivious to the weeping and wailing of a thirteen year old girl torn from her mother's arms or in his mistresses' apparent inability to hear the slaves except through the "rattle of the chains" (373-74). It is more explicit in his description of the Fugitive Slave Law which treats the "black man's" testimony as "nothing" in deciding if he should be sent into the "remorseless jaws of slavery," legally binding judges "*to hear only his accusers!*" (375-76). It surfaces again in his attack on the "bulwark of American slavery," the Christian church, which refuses to speak on the slave's behalf as a means of enacting its true mission of "ameliorating, elevating, and improving the condition of mankind" (376-81). Finally, it reaches an apogee in his expression of indignation over those who "shed tears over fallen Hungary, and make the sad story of her wrongs the theme of your poets, statesmen and orators, till your gallant sons are ready to fly to arms to vindicate her causes against her oppressors, but in regard to the ten thousand wrongs of the American slave, you would enforce the strictest silence" (382-83).

To this point in the speech, the dialogue between past and present that Douglass stages inscribes the voice of the American slave into the public discussion of the state of the nation. And in that context, it serves to engage white America's failure to live up to the "eternal principles" of the Declaration of Independence. But there, of course, is the rub, for the key question concerns the status of the dialogue between the Declaration and the Constitution, and whether or not slavery is a legitimate condition of that interaction. To address this question, Douglass effects a second ironic reversal as he directs attention from the nation's bleak present to what he characterizes as its hopeful future.

DESCRIBING THE PRESENT IN THE FUTURE

Although a dialogic tension between the Declaration of Independence and the Constitution pervades Douglass's speech, virtually from the beginning, that tension is never explicitly articulated in terms of specific principles. Of particular note is the *almost* complete absence of any direct consideration of the word "equality" until the very end of the speech.[38] Today, of course, it is almost impossible to think of the Declaration of Independence *without* affiliating it with the word "equality," but that really reflects the eventual hegemony of Lincoln's rewriting of American history in the "Gettysburg Address."[39] In 1852 Lincoln's speech had yet to be given, and the constitutional relevance of the commitment to equality was a highly contested notion. Nevertheless, as Douglass concludes his litany of American hypocrisies near the very end of the speech, the one he saves for last, and the one that immediately precedes his characterization of America's republicanism, humanity, and Christianity as, in order, a "sham," a "base pretence [sic]," and a "lie," derives directly from the nation's failure to live up to its declaration that "all men are created equal"(383).

How might we understand this? Douglass's main problem was not only to effect abolition, but to find a way to constitute the public legitimacy of an African-American voice in American politics. The word "equality" was obviously suited to this task, but not as it had been minimized and restricted in the Constitutional Conventions or in subsequent state and national legislation. Thus, he needed to establish the grounds for redefining equality in more inclusive terms as a kind of "equal citizenship." To succeed, however, he needed to avoid sounding like a revolutionary attempting to level all social and cultural difference, or appearing to supplant the national commitments to liberty and property with an expanded notion of equality.

Although there is no explicit reference to such a redefinition of equality in this speech, the premises leading in that direction underscore the entire discussion of American hypocrisy in the middle sections. Such an ending, however, would have been insufficient for several reasons. First, while the engagement of past and present highlights the tension between the Declaration of Independence and the Constitution, it does nothing to resolve it, and the ironic figuration of the speech demands some such resolution. Second, and perhaps more to the point, without such a resolution the legitimacy of the African-American voice would remain, at best, a contested possibility. Douglass needed more than that. He needed to demonstrate that from the African-American perspective the tensions literally placing the Union at risk were rooted in no more than an *interpretation* of the Constitution as a pro-slavery document, and an incorrect interpretation at that. To resolve that tension required opening the debate to the widest possible range of voices contained within "the people."

It is thus in the conclusion of the speech that Douglass effects his second ironic reversal. When Douglass initially established the ironic disposition of the speech at the end of his introduction, he maintained that the present must be understood and judged in its dialogue with a particular reading of the past. And speaking as the voice of the American slave, he provided one interpretation of that relationship. To stop there, however, would have been rhetorically dissatisfying, if not altogether dysfunctional. To begin with, it would have destabilized the prevailing ideology without offering a viable substitute for future living. In Douglass's view this was the Garrisonian alternative, a stagnant and elitist morality that selfishly ignored the possibilities of *activating* social and political progress. Additionally, and perhaps more important, it was only one voice, and as Douglass recognized, locating the truth in a single voice implicitly denies the condition of equality as a meaningful relationship, for it precludes the possibility of a world of legitimate differences.

As an alternative, Douglass vaguely suggests a second, more hopeful, dialogue which incorporates and transcends the tension between past and present as constructed through the voice of the slave in the earlier part of the speech. Here, the American national identity is reinterpreted through the engagement of past (the Declaration of Independence) and present (the voice of the African-American slave) in a reconstituted America that perpetually defines itself through the very absences present in the Constitution. Drawing upon Spooner's second rule of interpretation, which claims that the "intention of the Constitution must be collected from its words,"[40] Douglass implores his listeners to identify the place at which slavery is *constituted*:

Read its preamble, consider its purposes. Is slavery among them? Is it at the gateway? or is it in the temple? It is neither. While I do not intend to argue this question on the present occasion, let me ask, if it be not somewhat singular that, if the Constitution were intended to be, by its framers and adopters, a slave-holding instrument, why neither *slavery, slaveholding,* nor *slave* can anywhere be found in it. (385)

This is of course not the *only* interpretation of the Constitution, though Douglass does emphasize that it is the "plain reading" and how it "ought" to be read. More important, it is a viable interpretation that efficiently accommodates the larger dialogue of past and present within the parameters of the right of "every American citizen . . . to form an opinion of the Constitution, and to propagate that opinion, and to use all honorable means to make his opinion the prevailing one"(385). When read this way, the Constitution is plausibly an anti-slavery document, for the failure to mention slaves in the text itself functions as an absence that opens a space for the "equal" inclusion of a legitimate African-American voice.

In the end, the equality that Douglass implies will be born of a continuing national dialogue that "draws its encouragement from the Declaration of Independence" (the nation's glorious past) and "the genius of American institutions" (a living and vitalized Constitution). But more than that, it is rooted in what he characterizes as the "obvious tendencies of the age," a new world in which the physical "distance" between cities and nation-states no longer entails an exclusionary, political or cultural difference that precludes the desirability of open and active commerce. "Oceans no longer divide," he notes, "but link nations together. . . . Space is comparatively annihilated. Thoughts expressed on one side of the Atlantic are distinctly heard on the other" (387). And so, in an important sense Douglass comes full circle, resolving the problem of distance that created the conditions for the irony of the speech in the first place, for read in this context, the political equality that he crafts is a potentially flexible and regulative principle that both accommodates and thrives on difference.

THE IRONY OF "EQUALITY"

The ironic construction of equality that emerged from Douglass's Fifth of July oration underscored the importance of adding the voice of African-Americans to what we have come to call the dialogue of American public address. The immediate impact of that construction was of course limited, but it was to be repeated over and again by Douglass and others in the ensuing years leading to the Civil

War and beyond, and eventually it contributed to the usages of "equality" that emerged in the wake of the reconstructed Constitution. Those usages emphasized the *differences* between white and black Americans as a prelude to the cultural necessity for "equality under the law." And, in point of fact, it was the Pharisaic-like interpretation of such usage that led eventually to the hegemonizing effect of the "separate but equal" doctrine that dominated the first half of the twentieth century.

In an important sense, then, Douglass's construction of equality turned out to be ironic in ways that perhaps he did not entirely foresee. While it constituted an ideological space from within which the American slave could legitimately speak as an African-American, it simultaneously invited the institutionalization of what W. E. B. DuBois would later call the "double-consciousness" or "two-ness" of the American Negro, "two souls, two thoughts, two unreconciled strivings; two warring ideals in one dark body."[41] Many of the advocates of American racial equality have since treated this "two-ness" as the primary problem facing the cultural assimilation of the black person into American culture. Such complaints notwithstanding, Douglass's conception of equality as an inherently ironic ideological commitment might yet well prove to be an instructive representative anecdote for the problems of social and political equality that we face in our own times.

America, of course, is a nation founded on "difference." The search to legitimize difference in the form of religious liberty brought our original founding fathers and mothers to the new world, and the desire to legitimize our political identity as different from Great Britain led to the expression of "equality" as a rhetorical foundation for the new nation in the Declaration of Independence. As a liberal-democratic commitment of community, the word "equality" acknowledges the existence and legitimacy of competing and oppositional voices. Indeed, it is the special irony of this equality that it preserves the legitimate difference of such opposition, even as it strives to achieve a metaphorical social and political parity or identity. In the absence of such difference, where there is only one legitimate voice, equality becomes an unnecessary if not altogether meaningless political concept. Unfortunately, especially in recent times, the hegemonic conception of American "equality" has been displaced from its ironic configuration, statically reified as a condition of social and political identity or one-ness. To be equal is literally to be the same; to speak one's difference is to deny one's metaphorical identity with the national culture and thus to exist outside the boundaries of equality. In such a world, the perpetual dialogue between self and other so important to the sustenance of equality as a principle of democratic life risks dissolution.

In Frederick Douglass's usage, equality is an ironic relationship in precisely the way that Kenneth Burke describes irony as a master trope. As Burke notes:

Irony arises when one tries, by the interaction of terms upon one another, to produce a development which uses all the terms. Hence, from the standpoint of this total form (this "perspective of perspectives"), none of the participating "sub-perspectives" can be treated as either precisely right or precisely wrong. They are all *voices* [emphasis added], or personalities, or positions, integrally affecting one another. When the dialectic is properly formed, they are the number of characters needed to produce the total development.[42]

In antebellum America the missing voices necessary to that development were those of the African-American community. By entering the voice of that community in a dialogue between the nation's past, present, and future, Douglass sought to legitimize the presence of a unique African-American identity and, in so doing, to vitalize America's commitment to equality as a flexible but pivotal foundation for the nation's enlightened political identity.

The key to seeing Douglass's ironic crafting of equality as a representative anecdote for contemporary America is to recognize with Douglass that political identity is a protean phenomenon, subject to the demands of the ever changing relationships between past, present, and future. To be whole as a nation we must continually negotiate and renegotiate those relationships with an eye to the multiple tensions between past and present, as well as between present and future, for each is motivated by the insertion of continually new and different voices in the dialogue. And therein lies the value of an ironic construction of equality that by its rhetorical form and function necessitates the presence of cultural and political difference, even as it seeks to award all such differences common dignity and legitimacy. In the 1990s the missing voices belong to a multicultural rainbow of needs and interests, not just the concerns of African-Americans, but the central principle implicit in Douglass's Fifth of July oration remains the same: In order to fulfill its potential as a vibrant democracy, America's political identity must become an enactment in the "ever-living present" of the promise of liberty as a dialogue that acknowledges the continual necessity to interpret and determine the ever-changing meaning of the terms of the nation's collective existence. This does not mean that every demand by every interest group must be acceded to, but it does mean that all citizens must be guaranteed an equal voice in the dialogue without being *forced* to sacrifice the legitimacy of their difference in the bargain.

NOTES

1. "Slavery and Slave Power: An Address Delivered in Rochester, New York, on 1 December 1850," *The Frederick Douglass Papers; Series One: Speeches, Debates, and Interviews, 1847-*

54, ed. John W. Blassingame, 5 vols. (New Haven, Conn.: Yale University Press, 1982), 2:259 (this collection is hereafter cited as *Douglass Papers*).

2. Kenneth Burke, *A Grammar of Motives* (1945; reprint, Berkeley: University of California Press, 1969), 514.

3. For the most recent rendition of this narrative see Gordon Wood, *The Radicalism of the American Revolution* (New York: Alfred A. Knopf, 1992) and Wood's review of Garry Wills, *Lincoln at Gettysburg: The Words That Remade America* in *The New Republic* 207 (2 July 1992): 40.

4. See Martha Solomon, "'With firmness in the right': The Creation of Moral Hegemony in Lincoln's Second Inaugural," *Communication Reports* 1 (1988): 32-37.

5. Celeste Michelle Condit and John Louis Lucaites, *Crafting Equality: America's Anglo-African Word* (Chicago: University of Chicago Press, 1993).

6. See, e.g., J. R. Pole, *The Pursuit of Equality in American History* (Berkeley: University of California Press, 1978); Terry Eastland and William J. Bennett, *Counting by Race: Equality from the Founding Fathers to Bakke and Weber* (New York: Basic Books, 1979); Charles Redenius, *The American Ideal of Equality* (Port Washington, N.Y.: Kennikat Press, 1981); and Kenneth L. Karst, *Belonging to America: Equal Citizenship and the Constitution* (New Haven, Conn.: Yale University Press, 1989). For a recent and excellent volume to the contrary see Donald G. Nieman, *Promises to Keep: African-Americans and the Constitutional Order, 1776 to the Present* (New York: Oxford University Press, 1991).

7. *Douglass Papers*, 2:359-88.

8. Among his contemporaries see N. P. Rogers, "Herald of Freedom, Dec. 3, 1841," *Newspaper Writings* (Concord, N.H.: John R. French, 1847): 203-4; William G. Allen, "Orators and Orations, An Address Before the Dialexian Society of New York Central College, June 22, 1852," *The Liberator* (Boston), October 29, 1852; James Gregory, *Frederick Douglass: The Orator* (Springfield, Mass.: Willey and Co., 1893), esp. 8-12; and Thomas Wentworth Higginson, *American Orators and Oratory* (Cleveland: Imperial Press, 1901), 87-89. The point has been repeated as an article of faith by numerous biographers. See, e.g., David W. Blight, *Frederick Douglass' Civil War: Keeping Faith in Jubilee* (Baton Rouge: Louisiana State University Press, 1989): 4; and Waldo E. Martin, Jr., "Frederick Douglass," ed. Bernard K. Duffy and Halford R. Ryan, *American Orators Before 1900: Critical Studies and Sources* (New York: Greenwood Press, 1987), 139-45.

9. See, e.g., the typical treatments in Frederick May Holland, *Frederick Douglass: The Colored Orator* (New York: Haskell House Pub., 1891); and James M. Gregory, *Frederick Douglass: The Orator* (1893; reprint, Chicago: Afro-Am Press, 1969). In more recent works his role as an "orator" has been treated as more or less epiphenomenal to his role as an "intellectual." See, e.g., the otherwise excellent study by Waldo Martin, *The Mind of Frederick Douglass* (Chapel Hill: University of North Carolina Press, 1984).

10. For consideration of the rhetorical dimensions of Douglass's narratives, albeit with a literary focus, see Harold Bloom, ed., *Frederick Douglass's Narration of the Life of Frederick Douglass* (New York: Chelsea House Pub., 1988); Eric J. Sundquist, ed., *Frederick Douglass: New Literary and Historical Essays* (New York: Cambridge University Press, 1990); and

William L. Andrews, ed., *Critical Essays on Frederick Douglass* (Boston: G. K. Hall, 1991). For an excellent study that considers the larger socio-rhetorical functions of Douglass's narrative see Gregory Jay, "American Literature and the New Historicism: The Example of Frederick Douglass," *Boundary 2*, no. 17 (1990): 210-42. There are a few exceptions to the larger claim that Douglass's public speaking has been ignored, but they do not mitigate the larger point that relatively little attention has been focused on the relationship between the rhetorical forms and functions of his public speaking situated within particular historical contexts. See, e.g., John Blassingame's Introduction to the *Douglass Papers*, 1:xxi-lxx which provides an informative overview of Douglass as a public speaker. See also Gerald Fulkerson, "Exile as Emergence: Frederick Douglass in Great Britain, 1845-1847," *Quarterly Journal of Speech* 16 (1974): 69-82. Two works that discuss Douglass's public discourse in a larger socio-rhetorical framework are Blight; and David Howard-Pitney, *The Afro-American Jeremiad: Appeals for Justice in America* (Philadelphia: Temple University Press, 1991), 17-52.

11. William S. McFeely, *Frederick Douglass* (New York: Norton, 1991), 173. Two recent studies that I became aware of only after having completed this essay are Neil Leroux, "Frederick Douglass and the Attention Shift," *Rhetoric Society Quarterly* 21 (1991): 36-46; and Bernard W. Bell, "The African-American Jeremiad of Frederick Douglass's Fourth of July 1852 Speech," Paul Goetsch and Gerd Hurm, eds., *The Fourth of July: Political Oratory and Literary Reactions, 1776-1876* (Tübingen: Gunter Narr Verlag, 1992), 139-54.

12. See, e.g., "The Life of Olaudah Equiano or Gustavus Vassa, The African, as Written by Himself," in *Great Slave Narratives*, ed. Arna Bontemps (Boston: Beacon Press, 1969), esp., 26.

13. Several scholars have traced out cultural similarities between and among these various groups, but such similarities do not guarantee a collective or national political identity. See Mechal Sobel, *The World They Made Together: Black and White Values in Eighteenth Century Virginia* (Princeton, N.J.: Princeton University Press, 1987); Roger Bastide, *African Civilizations in the New World*, trans. Peter Green (New York: Harper and Row, 1971); Sterling Stuckey, *Slave Culture: Nationalist Theory and the Foundations of Black America* (New York: Oxford University Press, 1987), 3-97; John W. Blassingame, *The Slave Community: Plantation Life in the Antebellum South* (New York: Oxford University Press, 1979); Lawrence W. Levine, *Black Culture and Black Consciousness: Afro-American Folk Thought from Slavery to Freedom* (New York: Oxford University Press, 1977); Donald R. Wright, *African Americans in the Colonial Era: From African Origins Through the American Revolution* (Arlington Heights, Ill.: Harlan Davidson, 1990), esp. 6-115; and Molefi K. Asante, *The Afrocentric Idea* (Philadelphia: Temple University Press, 1987).

14. Leon F. Litwack, *North of Slavery: The Negro in the Free States, 1790-1860* (Chicago: University of Chicago Press, 1961), and Benjamin Quarles, *Black Abolitionists* (New York: Oxford University Press, 1969). The first petition to claim a direct right to freedom was also the first in which the petitioners identified themselves directly as a people, i.e., "a free-born Pepel [sic]." See "Petition to Massachusetts House of Representatives," 25 May 1775, in Herbert Aptheker, ed., *A Documentary History of the Negro People in the United States*

(New York: Citadel Press, 1951), 1:9-12. Later they identified themselves as "black people" and by 1808 "colored people." See also the debate over the names controversy in Stuckey, 193-244.

15. To suggest that there was a growing national, black political identity is not to suggest that it was univocal. While all blacks opposed the inhumanity and degradation of slavery and racial prejudice, many emphasized their African roots and sought the establishment of a separate black nation; others, underscoring their American origins promoted assimilation with the dominant, white, Anglo-American society. These various tensions are character-ized well in the introduction to *The Black Abolitionist Papers*, ed. C. Peter Ripley, et al., 5 vols. (Chapel Hill: University of North Carolina Press, 1991), 3:4-71. A useful condensa-tion of this discussion plus a sampling of documents is contained in idem, *Witness For Freedom* (Chapel Hill: University of North Carolina Press, 1993).

16. See Celeste Michelle Condit and John Louis Lucaites, "The Rhetoric of Equality and the Expatriation of African-Americans, 1776-1826," *Communication Studies* 42 (1991): 1-21; and *Crafting Equality*, 6-100.

17. Wood, 232-35.

18. See Condit and Lucaites, "The Rhetoric of Equality," 5-9.

19. Wood, 236.

20. The public debate over the constitutionality of slavery is characterized in some detail in Aileen S. Kraditor, *Means and Ends in American Abolitionism: Garrison and His Critics on Strategy and Tactics, 1834-1850* (1969; reprint Chicago: Elephant Paperbacks, 1989), 178-234.

21. See Louise Filler, *The Crusade Against Slavery, 1830-1860* (New York: Harper, 1960); and Herbert Aptheker, *Abolitionism: A Revolutionary Movement* (Boston: Twayne, 1989). Many of the issues separating and dividing the abolitionists, especially in the early years, were mostly tactical. See Kraditor.

22. See Lewis Tappan to Theodore Weld, May 26, 1840 in Tappan Manuscripts, *Weld Grimke Letters*, 2:836 as reprinted in *Slavery Attacked: The Abolitionist Crusade*, ed. John L. Thomas (Englewood Cliffs, N.J.: Prentice Hall, 1965), 85-86.

23. David Brion Davis, *The Slave Power Conspiracy and the Paranoid Style* (Baton Rouge: Louisiana State University Press, 1969).

24. These words come from a resolution passed at the Eleventh Annual Meeting of the Massachusetts Anti-Slavery Society Meeting in 1843. Garrison subsequently used them as the heading for his editorial columns in *The Liberator*. See *The Liberator*, 17 March 1843.

25. See William Ingersoll Bowditch, *Slavery and the Constitution* (Boston: Robert F. Wallcutt, 1849), esp. 120-26; and Wendell Phillips, "Can Abolitionists Vote or Take Office Under the United States Constitution?" *The Anti-Slavery Examiner*, no. 13 (New York: American Anti-Slavery Society, 1845).

26. Bowditch, 126.

27. See "The Annual Meeting at New-York," *The Liberator*, 22 April 1842, and "Repeal of the Union," *The Liberator*, 6 May 1842. The AASS did not officially take up the position until its annual meeting in 1844.

28. Lysander Spooner, *The Unconstitutionality of Slavery* (1845; reprint, New York: Burt Franklin, 1860). See also William Goodell, *Views of American Constitutional Law, in Its Bearing upon American Slavery* (Utica, N.Y.: Jackson & Chaplin, 1844).

29. Thomas, *Slavery Attacked: The Abolitionist Crusade*, 115. See also Wendell Phillips, *Review of Lysander Spooner's Essay on the Unconstitutionality of Slavery* (Boston, 1847). On the received view of the relationship between the Constitution and the Declaration of Independence see Philip Detweiler, "The Changing Reputation of the Declaration of Independence: The First Fifty Years," *William and Mary Quarterly* 19 (1962): 557-58.

30. "Slavery Unconstitutional," *The Liberator*, 22 August 1845.

31. See Nieman, 30-49.

32. See Waldo Martin, "Frederick Douglass: Humanist as Race Leader," in *Black Leaders of the Nineteenth Century*, eds. Leon Litwack and August Meier (Urbana: University of Illinois Press, 1988), 67-69; and McFeely, 168-69.

33. See *North Star*, 9 February 1849; and "Resolved, That The Constitution of the United States, in Letter, Spirit, and Design, is Essentially Antislavery: A Debate Between Samuel Ringgold Ward and Frederick Douglass in New York, New York, on May 11, 1849," in *Douglass Papers*, 2:193-7.

34. See "Change of Opinion Announced," *North Star*, 23 May 1851.

35. Martin, *The Mind of Frederick Douglass*, 26-27. The point generally is made regarding white abolitionist attitudes toward interracial marriages, but in Douglass's case there was a strong feeling of being patronized by white abolitionists who did not want him to start his own newspaper.

36. "What to the Slave is the Fourth of July?," *Douglass Papers*, 2:362. Subsequent page references to this speech will be cited in the text.

37. Michael C. Leff, "Burke's Ciceronianism," in *The Legacy of Kenneth Burke*, eds. Herbert W. Simons and Trevor Melia (Madison: University of Wisconsin Press, 1989), 120.

38. There are two exceptions. The first occurs in his affirmation of the "equal manhood of the negro race" (370). The second occurs in his charge that the nation's celebration of "liberty and equality" bring forth a "hollow mockery" (371).

39. See Garry Wills, *Lincoln at Gettysburg: The Words that Remade America* (New York: Simon and Schuster, 1992), 38-40.

40. Spooner, 161.

41. W.E.B. DuBois, "Of Our Spiritual Strivings," in *The Souls of Black Folk* (1903; reprint, New York: New American Library, 1969), 45.

42. Burke, 512.

REARTICULATING HISTORY IN EPIDEICTIC DISCOURSE: FREDERICK DOUGLASS'S "THE MEANING OF THE FOURTH OF JULY TO THE NEGRO"

James Jasinski

Men make their own history, but they do not make it just as they please; they do not make it under circumstances chosen by themselves, but under circumstances directly encountered, given and transmitted from the past. The tradition of all the dead generations weighs like a nightmare on the brain of the living.

Karl Marx, "The Eighteenth Brumaire of Louis Bonaparte" (1852)[1]

The principles of the American Revolution may be said to have been as various as the thirteen states that went through it, and in some sense almost as diversified as the individuals who acted in it.

John Adams to Mercy Warren, 20 July 1807[2]

Over the past decade, rhetoric's status as a temporal art has received considerable attention.[3] There now appears to be a consensus that public discourse, the practical and aesthetic product of rhetorical art, plays a pivotal role in creating, sustaining, and revising a political community's sense of itself as a temporal phenomenon.[4] Public discourse articulates a political community's relationship with its past, shapes its understanding of the temporal topography of the present (the experience of duration, a feeling of urgency), and structures its possibilities for the future.[5]

John Lucaites's essay on Frederick Douglass, although organized around the problems of voice, identity, legitimacy, and equality, nevertheless recognizes and contributes to the ongoing project of clarifying the manner through which public address structures temporal experience. Lucaites's analysis of Douglass's 1852 oration identifies the central "dialectical tensions" among past, present, and future that Douglass attempts to negotiate through "an ironic embodiment and

71

enactment of an inclusive conception of equality." One moment in this ironic performance, Lucaites argues, is Douglass's "dialogue with the past," especially Douglass's reading of the relationship between the Declaration of Independence and the U. S. Constitution. But a singular emphasis on Douglass's dialogic relationship with the past elides Douglass's participation in an ongoing public dialogue over the meaning of America's past. Starting in the post-ratification period, public advocates "articulated" a particular understanding of America's revolutionary experience.[6] By the 1850s the dialogue on the nation's past had narrowed and was dominated by a rather conservative interpretation of the American revolution. The revolution was "domesticated" and this articulation of the revolution, enacted discursively in Fourth of July orations among other vehicles, significantly constrained reformers like Douglass. In order for Douglass to, as Lucaites puts it, "deconstruct the prevailing ideology" that gave at least tacit support to slavery, it was necessary to destabilize the reified, sedimented, and hegemonic *tradition* in order to recover America's revolutionary *heritage*.[7]

My project is not a counterreading of Douglass's oration in opposition to Lucaites's analysis. Rather, what I hope to do is advance further a specific aspect of Lucaites's discussion insufficiently developed because of the constraints imposed by his larger project. I begin by reviewing some of the dominant articulations of America's revolutionary experience developed in the late eighteenth and early nineteenth centuries. While these articulations do not constitute a completely unified or coherent narrative, they nevertheless reveal a debilitating paradox: various efforts to both fix the meaning and preserve the memory of the revolution were fostering a forgetfulness that threatened America's present and future. Douglass's principal task, in my view, is to confront this paradox; he does so by appropriating the epideictic genre and rearticulating the forgotten heritage of the revolution. Douglass "denaturalizes" the revolution by removing its aura of inevitability, thereby restoring moments of choice and contingency; he radicalizes the revolution by recovering its audacity and its neglected principles. This rearticulation prepares for Douglass's most significant objective: constructing an understanding of the revolution as a continuing project.[8]

Articulating the Revolutionary Experience in the Late Eighteenth and Early Nineteenth Centuries

Discussing early nineteenth-century America, Gordon Wood notes that "to be an American could not be a matter of blood; it had to be a matter of common belief and behavior. And the source of that common belief and behavior was the American Revolution: it was the Revolution, and only the Revolution, that made them one people. Therefore Americans' interpretation of their Revolution could never cease; it was integral to the very existence of the nation."[9] As Wood suggests, interpreting the Revolution, articulating its meaning as a historical event and as a guide for political action, is a central feature of American public life. In order to develop an understanding of this process, scholars must investigate the rhetorical forms that are its driving force.

In their monograph tracing the revolutionary tradition in American rhetoric, Kurt Ritter and James R. Andrews describe the essentially "conservative nature of the Revolutionary heritage." They conclude that "from our Revolutionary heritage . . . it was even possible to construct, as did Warren Harding, a repudiation of revolution itself."[10] This articulation of the Revolution emerged over time, was inscribed in a number of rhetorical forms, and was, in part, a response to historically specific situational exigencies (such as the problem of legitimating the Constitution, the need to suppress social and political agitation like the Virginia and Kentucky resolutions, the South Carolina secessionist movement, or the Dorr rebellion in Rhode Island). To better understand Douglass's participation in the discursive struggle for America's past, we need to look more closely at how the conservative articulation was constructed as well as how it was contested.[11]

The revolutionary experience was a topic of contention both during and after the ratification dispute. Federalists articulated the revolution into their rationale for ratification by arguing that a principal goal of the revolutionary movement was the creation of a strong national government. A New York Federalist writing as "Caesar," for example, claimed that patriots "fought to obtain liberty for no particular State, but for the whole Union, indissolubly connected under one controling and supreme head." Along similar lines, Madison (in *Federalist* #45) asked his readers in 1788: "Was, then, the American Revolution effected, was the American Confederacy formed, was the precious blood of thousands spilt, and the hard-earned substance of millions lavished, not that the people of America should enjoy peace, liberty, and safety, but that the governments of the individual States, that particular municipal establishments, might enjoy a certain extent of power and be arrayed with certain dignities and attributes of sovereignty?" Federalists like Madison and "Caesar" suggested that an energetic national government was an inherent, and central, goal of the revolutionary movement.[12]

Conservative interpretations of the aims of the American Revolution continued into the nineteenth century. During the debate on Constitutional reform in Massachusetts in 1820, Webster maintained that "the disastrous revolutions which the world has witnessed, those political thunder-storms and earthquakes which have shaken the pillars of society to their deepest foundations, have been revolutions against property." Fortunately, Americans of the revolutionary period adopted the English model: "The English Revolution of 1688 was a revolution in favor of property . . . and our own immortal Revolution was undertaken, not to shake our plunder property, but to protect it. The acts of which this country complained were such as violated rights of property."[13]

The relationship between the Revolution and Constitution was taken up in the immediate aftermath of the ratification controversy. Despite its ratification, some Americans felt that the Constitution had not been fully legitimated. One way supporters attempted to realize this objective, according to Michael Lienesch, was to make the Constitution appear "old." For example, historians like David Ramsey reconfigured the narrative boundaries of the American Revolution by situating the Philadelphia Constitutional convention and ratification as the culminating final act of the revolution. Reviewing the efforts of Ramsey and others, Lienesch concludes that the new "Constitutional historians made the Revolution look distinctly less revolutionary than before. That is, their arguments tended to place the Revolutionary War within a sequence of events culminating in the Constitutional convention, effectively picturing a violent revolt as a deliberate reform. . . . This was a radical reinterpretation, through which a theory of politics inspired by Revolutionary passion became in retrospect an idea of government informed by Constitutional reason."[14] In the post-ratification period, the Constitution was legitimated and its status as the organizing force in American politics secured by placing it at the end of a rationalized revolution.[15] Once rationalized, the Revolution could be celebrated without endangering the Constitutional order or communal stability.

Even ratification era efforts to keep the revolutionary spirit alive contributed to a conservative understanding of the revolutionary experience. Benjamin Rush began his 1787 address to the people of the United States by noting, "there is nothing more common, than to confound the terms of *American Revolution* with those of *the late American war*. The American war is over: but this is far from being the case with the American revolution. On the contrary, nothing but the first act of the great drama is closed. It remains yet to establish and perfect our new forms of government; and to prepare the principles, morals, and manners of our citizens, for these forms of government, after they are established and brought to perfection." Rush's conclusion exhorted his readers to listen to the feminized voice of America: "Hear her proclaiming, in sighs and groans, in her governments, in her finances, in her trade, in her manufactures, in her morals, and in her manners, 'THE REVOLUTION IS NOT OVER!'"[16] Rush's address anticipated the efforts of historians like Ramsey who inserted the Constitution into the revolutionary drama as its ultimate telos. More importantly, Rush redirected the idea that the Revolution may be a continuing project into what would, in the nineteenth century, become a preoccupation with cultural independence and social improvement. In reminding his readers that revolutionary tasks were left unfinished, Rush emphasized largely apolitical objectives. When Rush maintained that the nation needed to establish economic and cultural autonomy, political struggle was pushed to the margins of public life as a relic of the past. Rush's continuing Revolution was organized around a decidedly domesticated agenda.

THE DOMESTICATED REVOLUTION AND THE SECOND PARTY SYSTEM

The partisan political disputes that broke out in Washington's first administration reached a climax in the late 1790s and early 1800s. These disputes abated after the War of 1812 but were resuscitated in the aftermath of the 1824 presidential election. By mid-century a second party system was entrenched and in its wake came rival readings of America's revolutionary experience. Daniel Walker Howe argues that "both [Whigs and Democrats] rejoiced in the American Revolution, of course, but they interpreted it differently. For Democrats, it represented liberation from history; for Whigs, it was the climax of history."[17] While these competing articulations of the Revolution help explain the intensity of party politics in antebellum America, they also mark an infrequently noticed common ground that constituted a traditional understanding of the revolutionary experience shared by many Americans in the nineteenth century. Whigs and Democrats were fundamentally ambivalent about America's revolutionary experience. To be sure, orators affiliated with each party helped celebrate that experience every July 4th and on other ceremonial occasions. But these celebrations evolved into rigid, formulaic rituals that, despite a certain degree of tension, reified the nation's memory of the revolution.

As Howe notes, Jacksonian Democrats embraced the disruptive quality of the revolutionary experience. The Revolution inaugurated a new epoch in politics by liberating the nation from the cycles of corruption and decline.[18] Ironically, Jacksonians remembered the Revolution for removing the burden of history and memory.[19] The Jacksonian version of the paradox was reflected in John O'Sullivan's 1837 essay for the *United States Magazine and Democratic Review*. "The American Revolution was the greatest of experiments, and one of which it is not easy at this day to appreciate the gigantic boldness. Every step in the onward march of improvement by the human race is an experiment, and the present is most emphatically an age of experiments. The eye of man looks naturally *forward*; and as he is carried onward by the progress of time and truth he is far more likely to stumble and stray if he turns his face backward, and keeps his looks fixed on the thoughts and things of the past."[20] What begins as a celebration of revolutionary boldness, something that is increasingly difficult to appreciate, ends with a figurative admonishment to forget. The Revolution's disruptive nature is inscribed in the metaphor of the experiment. The success of the earlier experiment freed Americans to continue experimenting in the present. But in O'Sullivan's metaphoric configuration, experiments past and present are disconnected; there is nothing of substance in the past that might guide or inform present practices.[21] As Tocqueville noted, in early nineteenth-century America "the woof of time is every instant broken and the trace of generations effaced. Those who went before are soon forgotten; of those who will come after, no one has any idea." He continued: "The mind of each member of the community is therefore unattached to that of his fellow citizens by tradition or by common habits . . . for amongst democratic nations each new generation is a new people." Jacksonians idolized the past, and particularly the Revolution, because of its irrelevance to the present. Historical memory was articulated in celebrations but it had a meager substantive function.[22]

Whigs resisted the Jacksonian's attempt to escape the past. J. V. Matthews argues that the Whig preoccupation with memory "was neither mere nostalgia nor disgruntled reaction—it was a political act."[23] While the Whigs articulated an understanding of history and the Revolution that contested the Jacksonians' version, they also manifested a similar profound ambivalence toward the revolutionary experience. Matthews maintains that Whig narrative and figurative structures assigned the revolution "the status of one event in a logical development." There existed in the nineteenth century, Matthews contends, a "tendency among educated Americans, when they thought about their own past, to convert history, with its chances, struggles, defeats, and paths not taken, into *natural* history, with the inevitable unfolding and development of the mature result from the tiny seed." Whig orators like Webster, Choate, and Edwards frequently constructed their historical narratives in such a way that the revolution was merely the culmination of a process begun centuries before. In Whig narratives, the truly active agents were often the Puritans.[24] Choate combined narrative and figurative structures in an 1834 address that illustrates this tendency:

The Declaration of Independence, the succeeding conduct of the war of Independence, the establishment of our local and general governments, and the splendid national career since run,—these are only the effects, fruits, outward manifestations! The seed was sown, the salient living spring of great action sunk deep in that long, remote, less brilliant, less regarded season,—the heroic age of America that preceded. The Revolution was the meeting of the rivers at the mountain. . . . But the colonial period is the country above, where the rivers were created. You must explore that region if you would find the secret fountains where they began their course, the contributory streams by which they grew, the high lands covered with woods, which, attracting the vapors as they floated about them, poured down rain and melted snow to swell their currents, and helped onward the momentum by which they broke through the walls of nature and shook the earth to its centre.[25]

In Choate's address, narrative and figurative structures fuse to articulate the "naturalness" and inevitability of the Revolution.

The effects of the Whig narrative were paradoxical. They memorialized the Revolution by articulating it into a narrative structure that diminished its importance. "This kind of historical 'placing,'" Matthews suggests, "inevitably deprived individual events of much decisive importance." The Whig narrative "both justified and defused [the Revolution] as a vital force in contemporary life; the Revolution was natural, legitimate—and over."[26]

Choate exemplifies the Whig double gesture of memorialization and banishment. Early on in a July third 1845 address at Harvard law school, Choate acknowledges that reforms and reformers are needed at certain moments in history. Such was the case in 1776. But America's task in the mid-nineteenth century is conservation: "With us the age of this mode and this degree of reform is over; its work is done." Later in the address Choate blends his metaphors in acknowledging but then repressing one of the principal legacies of the revolutionary era:

> it is the right of the people, at any moment of its representation in the legislature, to make all the law, and by its representatives in conventions, to make the Constitution anew. It is their right to do so peaceably and according to existing forms, and to do it by revolution against all forms. This is the theory. But I do not know that any wise man would desire to have this theory every day, or ever, acted upon up to its whole extent, or to have it eternally pressed, promulgated, panegyrized as the grand peculiarity and chief privilege of our condition. . . . True wisdom would advise to lock up the extreme medicine till the attack of the alarming malady. True wisdom would advise to place the power of revolution, overturning all to begin anew, rather in the background, to throw over it a politic, well-wrought veil, to reserve it for crises, exigencies, the rare and distant days of great historical epochs. These great, transcendental rights should be preserved, must be, will be. But perhaps you would place them away, reverentially, in the profoundest recesses of the chambers of the dead, down in deep vaults of black marble . . . [where] wise and brave men may go down, in the hour of extremity, to evoke the tremendous divinities of change from their sleep of ages.[27]

In this speech, Choate effectively dissociates the legacy of the revolution. The "theory" or guiding principles of the revolution are exposed as mere appearances: no one really wants to act on them; they have been transformed into ornaments. These ornamental principles are retained, safely locked away for their, and our, safety, while the work of conserving and perpetuating the (real) institutional legacy of the revolution (the law) continues. Matthews aptly describes the doubleness of this address: while celebrating the memory of the Revolution, Choate "banished [the Revolution] from the forefront of the American consciousness, even the stimulus of its principles as an impetus to political or social reform would be paradoxically a betrayal of its achievements."[28]

Jacksonian and Whig ambivalence toward the revolutionary experience continued the conservative articulation begun in the ratification era. By the middle of the nineteenth century, a reified tradition had been constructed. This tradition was not internally consistent but its underlying vision of the Revolution was clear: the Revolution was rational, inevitable, natural, orderly, and conservative; the Revolution had become, in a word, domesticated. The domesticated Revolution merited remembrance because this memory could function as a source of national unity. The vehicle for remembering the domesticated Revolution was the Fourth of July oration. "The message of numerous Whig Fourth-of-July orations," Matthews notes, "was that the Revolution had not been particularly revolutionary, but was a grand historic event inspiring patriotism and devotion rather than a set of living principles directly applicable to current problems." In Whig Fourth of July oratory the Revolution was revealed as an object "worthy of pious recollection." Edward Everett summarized the norm that came to structure traditional Fourth of July oratory in an 1835 fourth of July address: "I would devote this day, not to the discussion of topics which divide the people, but to the memory of the events and of the men which unite their affections."[29] This was the reified tradition that Douglass set out to destablize and rearticulate in his 1852 address.

REARTICULATING HISTORY IN EPIDEICTIC DISCOURSE

Ritual and epideictic discourse are commonly considered to be tools for promoting cultural continuity and social hegemony. Recently, scholars have begun to attend to the subversive potential of ritual behavior generally and epideictic discourse specifically.[30] The efforts of radical reformers in the nineteenth century provide numerous examples. Labor agitators were among the first to appropriate the Fourth of July and transform ceremonial oratory into social critique.[31] Abolitionist agitation is another example of how ritualized forms can be appropriated for social critique. As early as the 1820s, moderate anti-slavery reformers generated controversy when they used fourth of July oratory as a forum for soliciting contributions for the colonization movement.[32] In the late 1820s and continuing into the 1830s, abolitionists like Garrison attempted to rearticulate the Declaration of Independence and appropriate Independence Day celebrations as part of their campaign for immediate abolition.[33] Douglass's 1852 address can be considered an exemplary instance of this trend.[34]

Part of the force of Douglass's historical rearticulation resides, as Lucaites suggests, in the radical juxtaposition between Douglass, the former slave, and the events he will narrate. Cox observes that critical "memory is always *mediated* by the experience of a historical, material people. Though dominant groups may lay claim to the authority of a tradition, theirs is not the only story." Douglass is able to engage America's tradition critically because he is able to use his own historical, material existence—as someone who is part of (as "fellow citizen") yet radically separated from the American mainstream—to mediate the nation's history.[35]

Douglass discloses the mediated quality of his memory in the passage introducing the true subject of the speech: slavery. He announces:

> Fellow citizens, above your national, tumultuous joy I hear the mournful wail of millions, whose chains, heavy and grievous yesterday, are today rendered more intolerable by the jubilee shouts that reach them. If I do forget, if I do not faithfully remember those bleeding children of sorrow this day, "may my right hand forget her cunning, and may my tongue cleave to the roof of my mouth!" To forget them, to pass lightly over their wrongs and to chime in with the popular theme would be treason most scandalous and shocking and would make me a reproach before God and the world. My subject, then, fellow citizens, is American slavery.[36]

This passage, coming after Douglass's opening account of the American Revolution, rearticulates history through mediated memory. The suffering of black Americans, in Douglass's hands, becomes a vehicle for destabilizing the reified tradition and recovering suppressed historical possibilities.

Lucaites notes that Douglass opens his address "in a rather conventional manner. Douglass humbly disclaims his ability to speak before such an audience, expresses his gratitude for the opportunity, and then proceeds to what initially appears as a rather standard narration of the events leading to the Declaration of Independence." The qualification is important because Douglass's narrative is far from standard. But the focus of Lucaites's project precludes an exploration of the strategies Douglass employs in constructing his counternarrative. Such an exploration is necessary if we are to understand in more detail the way Douglass destabilizes the received tradition and rearticulates a revolutionary heritage.

Douglass's opening apology, while consistent with generic expectations,[37] takes on added significance through his explicit reflection on the norm. Douglass concludes his apology by commenting: "I know that apologies of this sort are generally considered flat and unmeaning. I trust, however, that mine will not be so considered" (107). In the very first paragraph of the address, Douglass engages in a complex process of generic subversion and reconstitution: he acknowledges the generic norm, calls its authenticity into question, but then affirms a reconstituted version of the norm. This opening move adumbrates Douglass's double gesture and presages his larger strategy of generic subversion. As an alternative to the hegemonic gesture of celebration coupled with banishment, Douglass sets out to balance or blend subversion with reaffirmation. He will engage the ritualized norms and reified tradition that structure America's independence day celebration but these norms will be challenged, or destabilized, so that his audience can be provided with a more authentic and participatory way of remembering its revolutionary heritage.

In the paragraph that opens the body of the address, Douglass weaves together two rather standard metaphors: the nation as person (that ages) and as river. In each case, Douglass subverts the metaphor's more customary usage in order to recover latent possibilities that are currently dormant. When America was metaphorically conceptualized in nineteenth-century public discourse as a person that ages, the nation is usually described as mature and as an adult. Choate, for example, employs the metaphor when he refers to the colonial era as America's "infancy and youth," the revolutionary period as her coming of age, and the present time as one of adulthood.[38] Douglass reconfigures the metaphor in order to claim that America is "still lingering in the period of childhood" (107). Understood in the context of customary usage, it seems that Douglass is accusing Americans of being childish. Douglass's metaphorical shift contains such a critical or subversive moment but its larger purpose is more constructive. Reconceptualizing the age of the nation allows Douglass to recover or reaffirm "hope." Douglass tells his audience that he is glad the nation is still young: "I repeat, I am glad this is so. There is hope in the thought, and hope is much needed under the dark clouds which lower above the horizon" (107-8).

The end of this sentence begins a slow shift of metaphorical terrain. Douglass moves from age to nature, with the conclusion of the paragraph linking the two metaphors:

There is consolation in the thought that America is young. Great streams are not easily turned from channels worn deep in the course of ages. They may sometimes rise in quiet and stately majesty, and inundate the land, refreshing and fertilizing the earth with their mysterious properties. They may also rise in wrath and fury, and bear away on their angry waves the accumulated wealth of years of toil and hardship. They, however, gradually flow back to the same old channel and flow on as serenely as ever. But, while the river may not be turned aside, it may dry up and leave nothing behind but the withered branch and the unsightly rock, to howl in the abyss-sweeping wind, the sad tale of departed glory. As with rivers, so with nations. (108)

It is instructive to contrast Douglass's river metaphor with Choate's. Choate's metaphor reflected a common assumption about the American revolution: it was, like any natural event, inevitable. This way of articulating the revolutionary experience tended to marginalize contingency, agency, and choice. But Douglass's reconfigured metaphor of a "young river" restores these qualities to American life. Great streams may move inexorably toward their destination but America need not be constrained by "the same old channel." Alternative possibilities are within the nation's grasp. This metaphorical reconstruction of America's age prefigures Douglass's more direct assault on the reified revolutionary tradition.

This assault begins in an early digression. Douglass notes that his views on the legitimacy of the Revolution "would not be worth much to anybody" (108). But the issue merits further reflection. Douglass continues:

> To say now that America was right and England wrong is exceedingly easy. Everybody can say it. . . . It is fashionable to do so; but there was a time when to pronounce against England and in favor of the cause of the colonies tried men's souls. They who did so were accounted in their day plotters of mischief, agitators and rebels, dangerous men. To side with the right against the wrong, with the weak against the strong, and with the oppressed against the oppressor—here lies the merit, and the one which, of all others, seems unfashionable in our day. The cause of liberty may be stabbed by the men who glory in the deeds of your fathers. But, to proceed. (109)

It seems evident that Douglass is drawing an implicit parallel between the revolutionary generation and present day abolitionists. The force of the argument depends, however, on Douglass's re-articulation of the revolutionary experience. Given its narrative structure of naturalness and inevitability, the reified tradition marginalized agency and choice and rendered the issue facing the colonists exceedingly simple. Most histories of the revolution written in the late eighteenth and early nineteenth centuries ignored the problem posed by the presence of loyalists and implied that all colonial Americans supported the movement for independence.[39] But Douglass reminds his audience that the issue was complex and contested. He revoices the words of Paine to emphasize that the decision for revolution was incredibly difficult: it "tried men's souls." The "merit" of the revolution can be found, Douglass asserts, in the courage to choose, to stand up and be counted. Unfortunately for America, these virtues are now "unfashionable."

A few paragraphs later, Douglass returns to the courage of the revolutionary generation: "With brave men there is always a remedy for oppression. Just here, the idea of a total separation of the colonies from the Crown was born! It was a startling idea, much more so than we at this distance of time regard it. The timid and the prudent . . . of that day were, of course, shocked and alarmed by it" (109). Time has made the Revolution seem less audacious, but Douglass insists on recalling the novelty of the undertaking. In this passage, Douglass's recollections appear to parallel those of John O'Sullivan, who recalled the boldness of the revolutionary experiment but whose recollection was overshadowed by a general neglect of the past. Douglass, however, rearticulates the audacity of the revolutionary generation in order to further disrupt the reified tradition and critique the political practices of the present.

Douglass amplifies this theme by contrasting revolutionary advocates with the "timid and prudent" who opposed their efforts. "Such people," Douglass asserts, "lived then, had lived before and will, probably, ever have a place on this planet; and their course, in respect to any great change (no matter how great the good to be attained, or the wrong to be redressed by it), may be calculated with as much precision as can be the course of the stars. They hate all changes, but silver, gold and copper change! Of this sort of change they are always in favor" (109-10). Why do we need to remember the prudent moderates and timid Tories who opposed revolution and independence? One reason is that by recalling the moderate and Tory opposition Douglass can continue his assualt on the inevitability of the Revolution. Re-articulating the opposition into the narrative helps reestablish the contingency of the Revolution. The colonists had multiple options and faced difficult choices. The Revolution was not a natural event, not a river flowing out of the mountains, but the result of practical choices made in the face of an "earnest and powerful" (110) opposition.[40]

Toward the end of the narrative, Douglass elaborates on the qualities of the revolutionary leadership. "They were," Douglas remarks, "peace men; but they preferred revolution to peaceful submission to bondage. They were quiet men; but they did not shrink from agitating against oppression. They showed forbearance, but that they knew its limits. They believed in order, but not in the order of tyranny. With them, nothing was 'settled' that was not right" (111). The presence of the domesticated tradition in this passage is clear: the Revolution was conducted by men of reason who were committed to order and stability. But

Douglass reconfigures the tradition by recalling that the leadership's commitment to order and stability was not absolute and did not prevent them from destabilizing the political order in their pursuit of political ideals. The revolutionary generation should be remembered, Douglass suggests, for its willingness to act on behalf of its radical beliefs as well as for its commitment to order and stability.

One final element in Douglass's assault on the tradition, a dissociation between products and principles,[41] merits attention. Matthews notes that in the traditional view of the nineteenth century "fidelity to the Revolution . . . mean[t] loyalty to its offspring: the nation, its institutions, the Union."[42] In other words, the memory of the revolution could be honored by a commitment to its domestic "products": the Constitution and the Union. This is the general effect of Choate's dissociation. Douglass subverts this commitment by locating a more authentic legacy: the revolution's principles. Douglass maintains "that the Declaration of Independence is the ringbolt to the chain of your nation's destiny; so indeed, I regard it. The principles contained in that instrument are saving principles. Stand by those principles, be true to them on all occasions, in all places, against all foes, and at whatever cost" (110). The principles of the Declaration, not mere institutional structures, constitute the real revolutionary heritage which Douglass through disassociation attempts to reclaim.

But reclamation alone is insufficient. The principles of the Revolution must be brought into the present and not locked up in a "deep vault" as Choate urged. The key passage in the oration is the one Lucaites notes. Douglass calls upon his audience to stop employing celebrations of the past as a substitute for acting in the present: "But now is the time, the important time. Your fathers have lived, died, and have done their work, and have done much of it well. You live and must die, and you must do your work. You have no right to enjoy a child's share in the labor of your fathers, unless your children are to be blest by your labors. You have no right to wear out and waste the hard-earned fame of your fathers to cover your indolence. Sydney Smith tells us that men seldom eulogize the wisdom and virtues of their fathers, but to excuse some folly or wickedness of their own. This truth is not a doubtful one" (113). Douglas has destabilized the received tradition along with its generic rhetorical form and has rearticulated the revolutionary heritage as an active commitment to more egalitarian principles. In this passage, Douglass will not repeat the Whig gesture and banish Fourth of July celebrations even though they are commonly used to "excuse some folly or wickedness" perpetrated in the memory of the fathers. Remaining true to the revolution, Douglass suggests, requires more than allegiance to, or perpetuation of, institutions and products or pious recollection of men and events. In order to truly remember the Revolution and follow in the footsteps of the revolutionary generation, Americans must continue it through "work" and "labor" on behalf of its guiding principles.

Douglass's rearticulation of the revolutionary experience works on at least three levels. In addition to negotiating the debilitating paradox that marked most nineteenth-century Americans' memory of the Revolution, Douglass's rearticulation situates the abolitionist movement as the true heirs of the revolutionary generation and does so without getting entangled in Garrison's generational anxiety. This allows Douglass to claim legitimacy not only for a black American "voice" but for the abolitionist movement as a whole. Finally, Douglass's recovery of a radical revolutionary heritage helps preempt a potentially divisive hermeneutic struggle over the relationship between the Declaration and the Constitution. Douglass's rearticulation effects, as Lucaites suggests, a reversal: instead of reading the Constitution as the final act of a conservative revolution, as proponents of the domesticated tradition were inclined to do, Douglass reads the Constitution as the first act of a continuing revolution.[43] Conceptualized in this way, the Constitution could not be a pro-slavery document. It merely institutionalizes the egalitarian principles of the Revolution.

CONCLUSION

J. Robert Cox suggests that in the modern world "the possibility of continued argument . . . requires some transformative practice—interpretation of a tradition in ways that fundamentally alter our understanding of the original principle or norm."[44] Douglass's 1852 address exemplifies this kind of transformative practice: a domesticated revolution that was severed from the present was rearticulated and a vibrant revolutionary heritage recovered. Such practices are not guaranteed to succeed. Indeed, scholars disagree on how effective the abolitionist movement was in helping end slavery in the south. But the continued presence of a radical revolutionary heritage into the twentieth century suggests that the efforts of Douglass and others like him to rearticulate the revolution were at least partially successful. Perhaps most importantly, the fact that the practice of public address has the potential to rearticulate temporal experience so as to recover lost or suppressed possibilities may give us reason for hope, and that may constitute our common ground with Frederick Douglass.

NOTES

1. In *Surveys from Exile: Political Writings*, ed. David Fernbach, tran. Ben Fowkes (New York: Random House, 1973), 146.
2. In *Correspondence Between John Adams and Mercy Warren*, ed. Charles F. Adams (New York: Arno Press, 1972), 338.
3. Among the important contributions to this trend, see: Thomas B. Farrell, "Knowledge in Time: Toward an Extension of Rhetorical Form," in *Advances in Argumentation Theory and Research*, eds. J. Robert Cox and Charles A. Willard (Carbondale: Southern Illinois University Press, 1982), 123-53; Michael Leff, "Rhetorical Timing in Lincoln's 'House Divided' Speech," Van Zelst Lecture in Communication, May 1983 (Evanston: Northwestern University, 1984); Leff, "Textual Criticism: The Legacy of G.P. Mohrman," *Quarterly Journal of Speech* 72 (1986): 377-89; G. Thomas Goodnight, "Generational Argument," in *Argumentation Across the Lines of Disciplines: Proceedings of the Conference on Argumentation*, ed. Frans H. Van Eemeren, et al. (Dordrecht: Foris Publishing, 1987), 129-44; and Randall A. Lake, "Between Myth and History: Enacting Time in Native American Protest Rhetoric," *Quarterly Journal of Speech* 77 (1991): 123-51.
4. J.G.A. Pocock, *The Machiavellian Moment: Florentine Political Thought and the Atlantic Republican Tradition* (Princeton: Princeton University Press, 1975); Pocock, *Politics, Language and Time: Essays on Political Thought and History* (New York: Atheneum, 1971).
5. See James Jasinski and Dennis Davis, "Political Communication and Politics: A Theory of Public Culture," American Political Science Association Conference, September, 1990.
6. The concept of articulation, as employed in this essay, assumes that texts and events lack full or complete "positivity": that is, they do not possess an intrinsic or inherent meaning. Texts and events are constituted by what Laclau and Mouffe term "elements" that can be investigated objectively (for example: did "x" exist?; did "y" happen?). But these elements do not possess inherent meaning and cannot supply an objective meaning for the larger text or event. Applied to the case of the American revolution, the concept of articulation maintains that there is no objective meaning to be discovered.

   Articulation refers to the largely discursive process by which elements are shaped, con-figured, crafted into "nodal points" ("partial fixations" that establish a contingent mean-ing for a text or event), deconstructed or destabilized, and eventually reconstructed. Discursive articulations typically exhibit a double structure in that elements are brought together, or made to cohere, in order to fix the meaning of a text or event so that this artic-ulated meaning can be further articulated to a position in an ongoing controversy or, in other words, so that articulated meanings can be deployed strategically in rhetorical advo-cacy. Frederick Douglass, in my view, participates in the struggle to determine the mean-ing of the American Revolution. Douglass's speech is a specific manifestation of that struggle. In it he labors to construct or articulate a particular understanding of the mean-ing of America's Revolution that can be further articulated to the abolitionist struggle.

   My sense of articulation is informed by a number of contemporary theorists. While their positions do not always coincide, see: Ernesto Laclau and Chantal Mouffe, *Hegemony and*

Socialist Strategy: Towards a Radical Democratic Politics (London: Verso, 1985); Stuart Hall, "On Postmodernism and Articulation: An Interview with Stuart Hall," *Journal of Communication Inquiry* 10 (1986): 45-60; Lawrence Grossberg, *We Gotta Get Out Of This Place: Popular Conservatism and Postmodern Culture* (New York: Routledge, 1992).

7. The Heideggerian distinction between tradition and heritage is developed by Cox in a number of important essays on the relationship between rhetoric and critical memory. See J. Robert Cox, "'Against Resignation': Memory and Rhetorical Practice," International Communication Association Conference, May 1986; Cox, "Cultural Memory and Public Moral Argument," Van Zelst Lecture in Communication, May 1987 (Evanston: Northwestern University, 1988); Cox, "Argument and Usable Traditions" in *Argumentation Across the Lines of Disciplines*, 93-99.

8. Studying Douglass's articulation of the revolutionary heritage calls into question Andrew Ross's claim that the "politics of appropriation" traditionally has been "the discursive preserve of the colonizer." Ross, "Introduction" in *Universal Abandon? The Politics of Postmodernism*, ed. A. Ross (Minneapolis: University of Minnesota Press, 1988), xi.

9. Gordon Wood, *The Radicalism of the American Revolution* (New York: Knopf, 1992), 336.

10. Kurt W. Ritter and James R. Andrews, *The American Ideology: Reflections of the Revolution in American Rhetoric* (Annandale, Va.: Speech Communication Association, 1978), 101, 48.

11. Ritter and Andrews do devote part of a paragraph to Douglass and "competing visions of the past" (45). On the discursive construction of the American Revolution during the late eighteenth and early nineteenth centuries, see Carolyn Sue Weddington, "The Image of the American Revolution in the United States, 1815-1860," (Ph.D. diss., Louisiana State University, 1972); Arthur H. Shaffer, *The Politics of History: Writing the History of the American Revolution 1783-1815* (Chicago: Precedent Publishing, 1975), esp. 103-59; and Michael Kammen, *A Season of Youth: The American Revolution and the Historical Imagination* (1978; reprint, Ithaca: Cornell University Press, 1988), esp. 33-75.

12. "Caesar" II, [NY] *Daily Advertiser*, 17 October, 1787 (reprinted in *The Documentary History of the Ratification of the Constitution: Commentaries on the Constitution*, eds. John P. Kaminsky and Gaspare J. Saladino [Madison: State Historical Society of Wisconsin, 1981], 398); James Madison, *The Federalist Papers*, ed. Clinton Rossiter (New York: New American Library, 1961), 289.

13. Daniel Webster, "The Basis of the Senate," 15 December 1820 in *The Writings and Speeches of Daniel Webster* (Boston: Little, Brown and Co., 1903), 5:15-16.

14. Michael Lienesch, *New Order of the Ages: Time, the Constitution, and the Making of Modern American Political Thought* (Princeton: Princeton University Press, 1988), 166-67. See also Shaffer, 143-59.

15. See David Zarefsky and Victoria J. Gallagher, "From 'Conflict' to 'Constitutional Question': Transformations in Early American Public Discourse," *Quarterly Journal of Speech* 76 (1990): 247-61

16. Benjamin Rush, "Address: To the People of the United States," Philadelphia, 1787 (reprinted in Hezekiah Niles, *Principles and Acts of the American Revolution* [New York: A.S. Barnes and Co., 1876], 234-36).

17. Daniel Walker Howe, *The Political Culture of the American Whigs* (Chicago: University of Chicago Press, 1979), 70.

18. It should be noted that while Democratic discourse abandons certain assumptions of republican political thought, their discourse nevertheless continued to employ many central republican categories. On the relationship between Jacksonian democracy and the republican tradition, see Russell L. Hanson, *The Democratic Imagination in America: Conversations with Our Past* (Princeton: Princeton University Press, 1985), 92-154; Harry L. Watson, *Liberty and Power: The Politics of Jacksonian America* (New York: Noonday Press, 1990), 42-72.

19. See also Michael Kammen, *Mystic Chords of Memory: The Transformation of Tradition in American Culture* (New York: Alfred A. Knopf, 1991), 40-61.

20. [John L. O'Sullivan], "Introduction" *Democratic Review* 1 (October 1837): 10.

21. Paul Kahn argues that the metaphor of "experiment" has a particular function in the founder's conceptual world, a world organized around the idea of "making." This world, Kahn suggests, disappears in the early nineteenth century and is replaced by one ordered by the idea of maintenance. Hence the possible meanings of the metaphor change in the nineteenth century. See Paul W. Kahn, *Legitimacy and History: Self-Government in American Constitutional Theory* (New Haven: Yale University Press, 1992), esp. 9-64.

22. Alexis de Tocqueville, *Democracy in America* (New York: The Colonial Press, 1899), 1:252; 2:61-62.

23. J. V. Matthews, "'Whig History': The New England Whigs and a Usable Past," *New England Quarterly* 51 (1978): 196.

24. Webster, in the speech marking the completion of the Bunker Hill monument in 1843, maintained that the American Revolution "was but the full development of principles of government, forms of society, and political sentiments, the origin of which lay back two centuries in English and American history." *Great Speeches and Orations of Daniel Webster* (Boston: Little, Brown and Co., 1879), 142. On the Puritan motif in Webster's oratory, see Paul D. Erickson, *The Poetry of Events: Daniel Webster's Rhetoric of Constitution and Union* (New York: New York University Press, 1986), 63-78; on the Whig use of Puritan history, see Matthews, 200-1; Howe, 88-9.

25. Rufus Choate, "The Colonial Age of New England" 16 August 1843 (in *The Works of Rufus Choate*, I [Boston: Little, Brown and Co., 1862]: 350-51). Even radical abolitionists like Wendell Phillips employ this imagery. In 1852, Phillips insists: "Revolutions are not made: they come. A revolution is as natural a growth as an oak. It comes out of the past. Its foundations are laid far back. . . . The beginning of great changes is like the rise of the Mississippi. A child must stoop and gather away pebbles to find it. But soon it swells broader and broader, bears on its ample bosom the navies of a mighty republic, fills the Gulf, and divides a continent." Phillips, "Public Opinion" (speech delivered on 28 January 1852) in *Speeches, Lectures, and Letters* (Boston: Walker, Wise, and Co., 1864), 36-7.

26. Matthews, 201-2.

27. Choate, "The Position and Functions of the American Bar," 3 July 1845 (in *Works*, I: 419-20, 433). Choate would probably have been pleased when the Declaration of Independence

was removed from public display in 1894 and locked in a safe until 1924. See Kammen, *Season*, 62.

28. Matthews, 203.

29. Ibid., 206; Edward Everett, "The Youth of Washington" 4 July 1835 (in *Orations and Speeches* I [Boston: Little, Brown and Co., 1870]: 573-74). See also Weddington, esp. 1-59, as well as Cedric Larson, "Patriotism in Carmine: 162 Years of July 4th Oratory," *Quarterly Journal of Speech* 26 (1940): 12-25; and Howard H. Martin, "The Fourth of July Oration," *Quarterly Journal of Speech* 44 (1958): 393-401.

30. On the subversive potential of ritual, see David L. Kertzer, *Ritual, Politics, and Power* (New Haven: Yale University Press, 1988) and Peter Shaw, *American Patriots and the Rituals of Revolution* (Cambridge: Harvard University Press, 1981). On epideictic discourse, see Cox, "Against Resignation"; Mark Pollock, "Hannah Arendt's Critical Reappropriation of the Past," Speech Communication Association Convention, Chicago, 1990; and Michael P. Sipiora, "Heidegger and Epideictic Discourse: The Rhetorical Performance of Meditative Thinking," *Philosophy Today* 35 (1991): 239-53.

31. See Staughton Lynd, *Intellectual Origins of American Radicalism* (Cambridge: Harvard University Press, 1968), 140; *We, the Other People: Alternative Declarations of Independence by Labor Groups, Farmers, Woman's Rights Advocates, Socialists, and Blacks, 1829-1975*, ed. Philip S. Foner (Urbana: University of Illinois Press, 1976); and Kammen, *Season*, 45.

32. See Henry Hawken's account of Leonard Bacon's 1824 and 1825 Fourth of July orations in *Trumpets of Glory: Fourth of July Orations, 1786-1861* (Granby, Conn.: Salmon Brook Historical Society, 1976), 47-56.

33. [William Lloyd Garrison], "Declaration of Sentiments of the National Anti-Slavery Convention" *The Abolitionist* 1 (December 1833): 178-80 (reprinted in *The Antislavery Argument*, ed. William H. Pease and Jane H. Pease [Indianapolis: Bobbs-Merrill, 1965], 65-71). Throughout the early section of the "Declaration," where he most directly engaged the revolutionary tradition, Garrison evinces a rather common "anxiety of influence" (see George B. Forgie, *Patricide in the House Divided: A Psychological Interpretation of Lincoln and His Age* [New York: Norton, 1979] and Kammen, *Season*, 49-50). Garrison seems worried that abolitionists, while invoking the memory of the revolution, will appear inferior to the revolutionary generation. He expends considerable energy trying to demonstrate the superiority of present day abolitionists. Douglass (perhaps because of his status as an outsider) appears unaffected by such anxiety. For examples of Garrison's Fourth of July oratory, see his 1829 and 1838 orations in *Selections from the Speeches and Writings of William Lloyd Garrison* (New York: Negro Universities Press, 1968), 44-61, 188-200.

34. In addition to the epideictic context of fourth of July oratory, Douglass's speech can be located within the tradition of the African American jeremiad. On the general nature of this tradition, see David Howard-Pitney, *The Afro-American Jeremiad: Appeals for Justice in America* (Philadelphia: Temple University Press, 1990); on Douglass's speech as an instance of this tradition, see Bernard W. Bell, "The African-American Jeremiad and Frederick Douglass' Fourth of July 1852 Speech" in *The Fourth of July: Political Oratory and Literary Reactions, 1776-1876*, ed. P. Goetsch and G. Hurm (Tubingen: Gunter Narr Verlag, 1993),

139-53. Situating the speech within the jeremiad tradition illuminates an additional tension that supplements and extends the paradox of traditional fourth of July oratory. Extending on Sacvan Bercovitch's classic study *The American Jeremiad* (Madison: University of Wisconsin Press, 1978), Thomas Gustafson suggests that calls to renew the words and deeds of the revolutionary generation, a common feature of the secularized jeremiad, "is deeply problematic given what the words of the Revolution and Constitution underwrote and sanctioned, and given how that call transforms dissent into a ritual of consensus and how the language of the Revolution has been exploited by merchandisers of the word to sell middle-class goods" (in *Representative Words: Politics, Literature, and the American Language, 1776-1865* [Cambridge University Press, 1992], 4). Bell does not consider this "dark side" of the jeremiad in his analysis but Douglass helps illustrate an alternative to the either/or logic present in Bercovitch and Gustafson (that is, advocates must either reject the entire American tradition or, however indirectly, reaffirm it). Douglass's critical appropriation of the revolutionary tradition and his articulation of a neglected heritage works as a double gesture that both subverts *and* reaffirms this tradition, making stable innovation possible.

35. Cox, "Cultural Memory," 12. On the doubleness and ambivalence of Douglass's identity, see Priscilla Wald, *Constituting Americans: Cultural Anxiety and Narrative Form* (Durham: Duke University Press, 1995), esp. 14-105.

36. Frederick Douglass, "The Meaning of the Fourth of July to the Negro," 5 July 1852 (reprinted in *The Voice of Black America*, ed. Philip S. Foner [New York: Simon and Schuster, 1972], 115). Subsequent references will be made parenthetically in the text.

37. Martin, 399.

38. Choate, "Colonial Age," 350.

39. See Weddington, 20, 30-1, 50. See also Lincoln's 1838 claim that "at the close of that struggle, nearly every adult male had been a participator in some of its scenes." Abraham Lincoln, "The Perpetuation of Our Political Institutions: Address Before the Young Men's Lyceum of Springfield, Illinois," 27 January 1838 (in *Abraham Lincoln: His Speeches and Writings*, ed. Roy P. Basler [1946; reprint, New York: Da Capo Press, n.d.], 84).

40. As Jim Farrell points out in his study of Webster's eulogy to Adams and Jefferson (elsewhere in this volume), Webster includes the moderate voice in his account of the revolution to recall its "conservative" qualities. Douglass's inclusion has a more ironic and subversive function.

41. For an account of the relationship between dissociative arguments and critical memory, see Cox, "Cultural Memory" and "Usable Traditions."

42. Matthews, 206.

43. I do not believe that an alternative formulation, one that would interpret the Constitution as a kind of Thermidorian reaction to a radical revolution, was available to Douglass in the nineteenth century. While this interpretation was prefigured in some Anti-federalist discourse, it was not fully articulated until Beard's work in the early twentieth century.

44. "Usable Traditions," 95.

THE DYNAMICS OF INTERTEXTUALITY: RE-READING THE DECLARATION OF INDEPENDENCE

Martha Solomon Watson

The title of Garry Wills's recent, highly praised work suggests its argument: *Lincoln at Gettysburg: The Words that Remade America.*[1] Among Wills's arguments is that Lincoln imposed a new meaning on the Constitution, drawing his inspiration and support from the Declaration of Independence.[2] Wills contends that in 272 words Lincoln imposed a new interpretation on the key phrase from the Declaration, "all men are created equal" and, in so doing, changed the meaning of the Constitution. His romantic view of the impact of that speech is worth quoting.

> Everyone in that vast throng was having his or her intellectual pocket picked. The crowd departed with a new thing in its ideological luggage, that new constitution Lincoln had substituted for the one they brought there with them. They walked off, from those curving graves on the hillside, under a changed sky, into a different America. Lincoln had revolutionized the Revolution, giving people a new past to live with that would change their future indefinitely.[3]

Certainly, Wills's assessment of the Gettysburg Address and his description of it are provocative. However, his view overlooks important rhetorical antecedents of Lincoln and, at least to some extent, ignores the dynamic nature of our public discourse. Rather than creating a new interpretation of the Declaration of Independence and imposing that onto the Constitution, Lincoln was reiterating and publishing more widely a viewpoint that had been articulated in hundreds of speeches and pamphlets by abolitionists and woman's rights advocates.[4] In part, the following study will explore how abolitionists and woman's rights advocates accomplished what Wills credits solely to Lincoln. Undoubtedly, Lincoln added power and even eloquence to their appeals but this essay will seek to demonstrate that the process of changing the meaning and status of the Declaration of Independence had begun long before in the rhetoric of these reformers.

Responding to Wills's book is, however, only incidental to this essay. My primary purpose is to join the ongoing debate in our field about the nature of texts and, in so doing, to offer what I think are important extensions and amendments to previous work. The research of Michael Calvin McGee and others on ideographs and Raymie McKerrow's essay on critical rhetoric spawned this discussion about the nature of texts and how rhetorical critics should constitute the works they study.[5] On one side, Michael Leff and Andrew Sachs argue for a traditional view of a text as an icon, the nature of which is violated if it is not considered as a discrete whole.[6] In contrast, McGee argues that the fragmentation of American culture has produced a reversal in roles, "making interpretation the primary task of speakers and writers and text construction the primary task of audiences, readers, and critics."[7] In the same special issue of the journal in which Leff, Sachs, and McGee debated this matter, various other persons joined the debate, not primarily to take sides but rather to consider the sources, similarities, and implications of each view.[8]

While I acknowledge the influence of McGee on my thinking, this essay will take issue with his claim that contemporary fragmentation of culture has altered rhetorical roles. In contrast to McGee, I will demonstrate that historically rhetors have been the interpreters of texts to their own strategic ends. In my view, rhetors have often construed the meaning of previous texts to their own advantage by constructing discourse that draws on those texts. In fact, I would argue that much public discourse is a struggle to fix the meaning of foundational texts in line with the interests of a particular group or cause. Using a case study, I will explore this process of text construction to explicate what I term the dynamics of intertextuality. The analysis that follows will demonstrate how texts interact with each other and how that interaction shapes their rhetorical impact. Scholars in other areas have long examined the influence of one text on others and the topic of intertextuality is a commonplace in literary criticism. However, since the concept has not been widely discussed in the discipline of communication studies,[9] a brief explanation is in order.

INTERTEXTUALITY

In his excellent, detailed survey of American literary criticism, Vincent B. Leitch locates the issue of intertextuality as central to deconstructive approaches.[10] Persons who advocated this concept were reacting most immediately to the structuralist and semiotic approaches in vogue at the time; but they were also in tension with the New Critics of an earlier period. Different as they are, structuralists, semioticists, and new critics all tended to view texts as discrete objects (much as Leff does), which can be fruitfully and meaningfully analyzed without extensive references to other works. As Christopher Norris wrote of poetic criticism, "The New Critics invented various ways of sealing the poem off within a timeless, self-sufficient realm of interlocked meaning and structure."[11]

In contrast, deconstructionists held that "A literary text is not a thing in itself, 'organically unified,' but a relation to other texts which are relations in their turn. The study of literature is therefore a study of intertextuality."[12] As Leitch explains: "For deconstructors *intertextuality* designated a text's dependence on and infiltration by prior concepts, figures, codes, unconscious practices, conventions, and texts."[13] In essence, "the ground of any text was always another text."[14] Arguing for the strongest form of this view, Harold Bloom asserted that "Poems did not exist— only 'interpoems' did."[15] Later deconstructionists enlarged the concept of intertextuality to encompass the "social text," arguing that even literary works refer not merely to the literary tradition but to other documents in cultural history as well.[16]

Some work in communication studies—genre studies and Michael Osborn's work on archetypal metaphors—may be tangentially related to intertextuality as it will be examined here. However, I wish to explore the two important dimensions of intertextuality that explain how texts interanimate each other: (1) rhetors, as audiences for previous texts, interpret those as a basis for their own products; and (2) these "new" products, in turn, reconstrue and alter the "meaning" of the texts on which they are based. My focus is not on persons who simply respond or react to other texts or use quotations from them in conventional ways. This study will focus on the process by which rhetors deliberately use previous texts as the model and basis for their own rhetorical action. The strategies by which they do so, the impact of this intertextuality on their efforts, and the *reciprocal* impact of the "new" text on the "old" text are the centers of interest here. The view of rhetorical texts advanced here is akin to that expressed by Terry Eagleton in his discussion of the post–structuralist ideas of Roland Barthes: "All literary texts are woven out of other literary texts, not in the conventional sense that they bear the traces of 'influence,' but in the more radical sense that every word, phrase or segment is a reworking of other writings which precede or surround the individual work. There is no such thing as literary 'originality,' no such thing as the 'first' literary work: all literature is 'intertextual.'"[17] In essence, this analysis will demonstrate and expand on McGee's rejection of our discipline's traditional iconic approach to texts.

To explore these concerns, the essay will examine two nineteenth-century texts that deliberately echoed the Declaration of Independence: the Declaration of Sentiments adopted by the 1833 American Anti-Slavery Society and the document of the same name adopted at the 1848 Seneca Falls Woman's Rights Convention.[18] Although these documents provide good materials for the process

I wish to investigate, they merit consideration in their own right. Each was the first important statement of principles of what became a major, national social movement in the nineteenth century and each was authored by persons who were the primary spokespersons for their movements (William Lloyd Garrison in the case of the 1833 document, Elizabeth Cady Stanton and Lucretia Mott, among others, for the 1848 statement). Despite their importance, the documents have received very little attention from scholars in communication studies.[19]

In brief, this essay will suggest that the two Declarations of Sentiments appropriated and exploited the rhetorical force embedded in the Declaration of Independence in different, but equally powerful ways. Moreover, it will argue that the interpretations of the Declaration of Independence provided in the two documents altered and shifted its meaning significantly. The goal of this argument is to demonstrate how in these two cases rhetors, who were an audience for the Declaration of Independence and for discussions of its meaning, constructed interpretations of that document into their works. Through such intertextuality, these seemingly iconic texts interanimate each other, mutually determining each other's meaning.

THE DECLARATIONS OF SENTIMENTS AS INTERPRETATIONS OF A FOUNDATIONAL TEXT

The reliance of the two Declarations of Sentiments on the Declaration of Independence is clear both from historical evidence and within the texts themselves. According to Ronald Reid, at the hastily called meeting to create the American Anti–Slavery Society, Garrison saw the strategic advantages of "identifying abolitionism with the American Revolution. He wished to hold the society's first meeting in the place where the Continental Congress had adopted the Declaration of Independence."[20] During one session, he slipped outside to pen this statement of principles, which was approved with little discussion by the persons at the meeting.[21]

Even more explicitly, Eleanor Flexner notes that when the women had decided to hold the Seneca Falls meeting, they turned directly to the Declaration of Independence for a model:

> Having drafted the notice [for the meeting], the women were at a loss as to how to proceed. Obviously what was required was some kind of declaration of sentiments, such as they were familiar with from their experiences with anti-slavery meetings. But what form it should take, they had no idea. When Mrs. Stanton began to read aloud from the Declaration of Independence, it seemed to lend itself to their purpose; the resulting paraphrase of the original, sentence by sentence and para-

graph by paragraph, became a Declaration of Principles that would serve three generations of women.[22]

One first step to understanding the intertextual dynamics among these documents is to consider the possible shade of meaning of the term "Sentiments," which in both stands in sharp, deliberate contrast to the "Independence" of the original document. At least according to modern definitions, "sentiments" are, in contradistinction to "opinion," judgments "arrived at as the result of deliberation and representing a rather fixed conviction . . . with a tinge of emotion about it."[23] In both cases, the Declarations of Sentiments use the values and principles of the Declaration of Independence as a *starting point* for their deliberations; the political philosophy and views they perceived in (or, as I prefer, read into) that document become indisputable "truths." Moreover, by using the Declaration of Independence in this way, the two statements, in effect, reframed its significance as a speech act. Originally, the Declaration of Independence was a speech act *justifying* an armed revolution; the statements in the preamble about the nature of governments were eighteenth-century commonplaces to introduce the rationale for rebellion. But the two Declarations of Sentiments focus on those generalizations in the preamble, somewhat distorting the focus of the document as a whole, and treat it as a speech act *proclaiming* a political philosophy. Significantly, in focusing on the Declaration of Independence in this light, the two statements are obscuring the role of the Constitution in establishing the framework of American government. This approach is not accidental. On the one hand, the Constitution is a much more complex document and is far less amenable to easy imitation. But, more significantly, the Constitution had approved and even codified some of the practices which the two groups rejected. In reframing the import of the Declaration of Independence, they are also "misconstruing" its place in American political life.

As they compare their perception of present circumstances to the principles outlined in that document, they assume a stance of moral fervor. They are aggrieved parties, just as the colonists perceived themselves to be. Jefferson's document may have inherently encouraged such an identification. At least one scholar has read the Declaration of Independence as a "slave narrative," a form popular in eighteenth-century political pamphleteering. According to Edwin Gittleman, "slavery" in this sense was a broad term that referred to a situation in which a person was forced to act or not act because of the will of another, rather than because of his/her own desire and conscience.[24] Gittelman also observes that in his initial draft, Jefferson included a strong statement at the climactic point in the list of grievances, which explicitly assailed the King for having encouraged and imposed the slave trade on the colonies. With this statement, which was deleted before the document was approved, Jefferson had moved from the metaphorical description of the colonists' position as slavery to a consideration of the real institution.[25] Thus, the fervor of the two Declarations of Sentiments, which arises from their perceptions of their own or others' "slavery" within the system, accords well with the underlying tenor of the earlier document. While Jefferson controlled the emotion of the Declaration of Independence to make a convincing argument to a "candid world" for the American Revolution, the other two statements give vent to the feelings implicit in his work.

If both statements of sentiments rely on the Declaration of Independence and incorporate features of it quite effectively, their techniques for exploiting it differ. Each case merits separate discussion.

DECLARATION OF SENTIMENTS, 1833

The Declaration of Sentiments of 1833 bears little overt resemblance to the Declaration of Independence. But close examination reveals how that document has interpenetrated into the 1833 Declaration substantively. Three areas merit mention: (1) the use of structural and space metaphors to link this document to the political work begun in the Declaration of Independence; (2) the clear connection established between the founding fathers and this group; and (3) the argumentative approach.

The abolitionists depict their text as an extension of a work of construction begun in the Declaration of Independence. For example, paragraph two alludes to Philadelphia as the place in which the Declaration of Independence was formulated. In one sense, Philadelphia serves as a sacred ground for Americans.[26] The next paragraph explicitly links this document to the former in various ways:

> The corner-stone upon which they founded the TEMPLE OF FREEDOM was broadly this—"that all men are created equal; that they are endowed by their creator with certain inalienable rights; that among these are life, LIBERTY, and the pursuit of happiness." . . . We have met together for the achievement of an enterprise, without which that of our fathers is incomplete, and which, for its magnitude, solemnity, and probable results upon the destiny of the world, as far transcends theirs as moral truth does physical force. (343)

The directly quoted phrases are from the preamble to the Declaration of Independence. Even though most scholars see those phrases as preliminary to the main argument of that document and almost incidental to its rhetorical purposes, by construing them as the foundation of the "Temple of Freedom" the abolitionists accord the Declaration of Independence great stature as a statement of the political philosophy of the country.[27] The abolitionist cause seeks to enlarge the "Temple of Freedom," which the Declaration allegedly produced.

The paragraph also begins a structural metaphor (cornerstone, temple, incomplete) which identifies the abolitionist cause with finishing a project begun earlier.[28] Later in the document, the structural metaphor recurs with some allusions to the sacred philosophical ground established through the Declaration of Independence. In this passage, the phrases "law of nature" and "social compact" also echo the language and ideas of the earlier document:

> That all those laws which are now in force, admitting the right of slavery, are there-fore before God utterly null and void; being an audacious usurpation of the Divine prerogative, a daring infringement on the law of nature, a base overthrow of the very foundations of the social compact, a complete extinction of all relations, endearments, and obligations of mankind, and a presumptuous transgression of all the holy commandments. (345)

The edifice (corner–stone, temple, overthrow of the foundations) images and those dealing with occupation of space (null, void, usurpation, infringement, transgression) clearly depict the actions and purposes of the abolitionists as an extension of the ideals contained in the Declaration of Independence. The abolitionists are not occupying new ground but are simply building on the foundations laid in the Declaration of Independence. They are, in essence, perfecting the order ordained in what they implicitly argue is *the* sacred political writ that established this nation. They have engrafted the principles they read into the Declaration of Independence into their own agenda.

This depiction is strategically shrewd because it seeks to transfer the prestige of and reverence which Americans were beginning to feel toward the Declaration of Independence to the abolitionist cause. Opponents might easily reject this linkage because the founding fathers, some of whom were slave-owners, clearly did not perceive slaves as citizens within the state. However, one must recall that this document is not intended for such hostile readers; it is, instead, a document which justifies and ennobles abolitionists' efforts within their own nascent community.

The drafters of the abolitionist declaration clearly link themselves to the founding fathers; they are the inheritors of the patriotic mantle of those persons. The second and third paragraphs of the document establish this theme:

> More than fifty-seven years have elapsed since a band of patriots convened in this place, to devise measures for the deliverance of this country from a foreign yoke. . . .

> We have met together for the achievement of an enterprise, without which that of our fathers is incomplete. . . . In purity of motive, in earnestness of zeal, in decision of purpose, in intrepidity of action, in steadfastness of faith, in sincerity of spirit, we would not be inferior to them.

Despite these important links between the abolitionists and signers of the Declaration of Independence, the next three short paragraphs develop two important contrasts between the abolitionists and the founding fathers. While the founding fathers used force and shed blood to achieve their goals, the abolitionists will not do so; they will rely solely on "the opposition of moral purity to moral corruption—the destruction of error by the potency of truth—the overthrow of prejudice by the power of love—the abolition of slavery by the spirit of repentance" (344). In other words, they will continue in the moral path established by the founding fathers, not their literal course of action. This distinction in means is extremely important and contextually significant. While the abolitionists are locating themselves in the revolutionary tradition of the signers of the Declaration of Independence, they are specifying the *kind* of revolution they seek and the means they will endorse to achieve it.[29] Carl Becker argues in his careful study of the Declaration of Independence that

> The nineteenth century, while progressively democratic, was on the whole anti-revolutionary. In the United States from the Revolution to the Civil War, the strongest political prepossession of the mass of men was founded in the desire to preserve the independence they had won, the institutions they had established, the "more perfect union" they had created.[30]

Thus, many persons were chary both of adopting too enthusiastically all the ideals we now accept in that document and of endorsing its revolutionary course. While they wished to incorporate many elements of the Declaration of Independence into their own statement, the abolitionists were also reacting and responding to fears of revolution which some persons still associated with the bold action of 1776 and the subsequent blood bath of the French Revolution.

The abolitionists insist that "*Their* grievances, great as they were, were trifling in comparison with the wrongs and sufferings of those for whom we plead." This statement serves not only to imply the seriousness of the abuses which they perceive but also to establish that they are acting for others, not for themselves.

Identifying themselves both as heirs of the founding fathers and as agents for others accomplishes an important rhetorical purpose. It enables supporters to assume the "we" persona which Hugh Dalziel Duncan labels "community guardians."[31] In that role, abolitionists become not a threat to the social order, as they were perceived by many of their opponents, but protectors of it. Duncan writes:

> the most common form of such address occurs when the guardians speak as protectors of the great principles of social order which sustain the community. In this guise, the guardians are the voice of tradition and custom, or of the utopias which lie ahead for all those who do their duty. In solemn and majestic speech . . . the guardians warn individual actors and the general public, of the doom that awaits those who violate the sacred principles of social order which uphold their communities.[32]

The abolitionists are able to assume this role because they are, by virtue of the Declaration of Independence and the Constitution, citizen-participants. They are inside the system they hope to perfect through their efforts. They can, thus, by following the lead of the signers of the Declaration of Independence, interpret and criticize that system. Significantly, they, unlike their forefathers, eschew military force in obtaining their demands. They will rely exclusively on moral suasion.

The assumption of this role plays into another strategic adaptation of the ideas of the Declaration of Independence. Working from the deistic conception of God in that document, the abolitionists move to a clear Judeo-Christian view: Jehovah (344). They "plant" themselves "upon the Declaration of our Independence, and upon the truths of Divine Revelation, as upon the EVERLASTING ROCK" and envision "a host coming up to the help of the Lord against the mighty" (346). With this stroke, they are able to unite the religious fervor, characteristic of the period and of many of their adherents, with patriotic zeal. In a real sense, they invoke American civil religion as the legitimizing force for their actions.

The abolitionists parallel the general argumentative strategy of the Declaration of Independence by listing the abuses the slaves have suffered and explaining the course of action they will pursue. Here too, close examination reveals that the apparently different problems of the slaves and the circumstances confronting the founding fathers have some underlying similarities. For example, "slaves are plundered daily of the fruits of their toil without redress"; the colonists are cut off from their "Trade with all parts of the world" and must pay taxes imposed "without their consent." Slaves "really enjoy no constitutional or legal protection from licentious and murderous outrages upon their persons"; the founding fathers deplored actions that permitted "swarms of Officers to harass our People, and eat out their substance" and quartered "large bodies of troops among us" who are protected "by a Mock Trial, from Punishment, for any Murders which they should commit on the Inhabitants of these States." The colonists are deprived "in many cases, of the benefits of Trial by Jury." If slaves "are ruthlessly torn asunder—the tender babe

from the arms of its frantic mother—the heart-broken wife from her weeping husband—at the caprice or pleasure of irresponsible tyrants," for the colonists the
King has "plundered our seas, ravaged our Coasts, burnt our towns, and destroyed
the lives of our people" even to the extent of "transporting large armies of foreign
mercenaries to compleat the works of death, desolation and tyranny, already
begun with circumstances of Cruelty and perfidy scarcely paralleled in the most
barbarous ages." It is worth noting that the vivid personal images used by the abolitionists—the "tender babe," "frantic mother," "heart-broken wife," and "weeping
husband"—may serve to bring home the cruelty of slavery to a somewhat
removed audience; in contrast, the Declaration of Independence could use less
concrete images in part because many members of the target audience shared a
perception of British injustices based upon their own experiences.

By listing the abuses suffered by slaves and exposing how actions repudiate the
founding principles of the nation, the abolitionists indict their opponents as the
colonists indicted the King. Here the authors draw a subtle but rhetorically
shrewd distinction between their slave-holding enemies and a political philosophy they deplore but are bound to accept for the time being. The abolitionists
focus their wrath on the slave–holders and planters, labeling them as thieves
(345–346); this attack resembles the colonists' identifying the actions of the King
as the basis for their action. The abolitionists explicitly recognize "the sovereignty
of each State, to legislate exclusively on the subject of slavery which is tolerated
within its limits" and "concede that Congress, *under the present national compact,*
has no right to interfere with any of the slave States, in relation to this momentous subject."

Their role is to do all in their power, through moral suasion and political
action, to end this situation. They list their intentions and actions, before vowing
to work until they "witness the triumph of JUSTICE, LIBERTY, and HUMANITY,
or perish untimely as martyrs in this great, benevolent and holy cause" (346). In
essence, they are, like the signers of the Declaration of Independence, trusting in
"Divine Providence," and by implication at least are "mutually pledg[ing] to each
other our Lives, our Fortunes and our Sacred Honor."

DECLARATION OF SENTIMENTS, 1848

If the earlier Declaration of Sentiments consciously engrafted ideas from the
Declaration of Independence, the declaration issued by the Seneca Falls convention drew on both earlier documents. Flexner notes that parts of this 1848 document are largely a paraphrase of the Declaration of Independence, with the
crucial substitution of "man" for "king" as the oppressor and women rather than

the male citizens of the American colonies as the oppressed. The first two paragraphs of the documents are virtually identical. Moreover, throughout, this document achieves its rhetorical force by deliberately and closely echoing the language and arguments of the Declaration of Independence.

Although the specific abuses listed in the two documents differ, they fall into similar general categories and follow a similar pattern of organization. The Declaration of Independence first lists ways in which the King has restricted the right of the colonists to participate in the legislative process and then indicates the consequences and implications of them. The Seneca Falls document begins with related claims: women are denied the ballot and have no voice in the making of laws to which they are subject. Then, like the Declaration of Independence, it indicates the abuses which flow from such denial: "Having deprived her of this first right of a citizen, the elective franchise, thereby leaving her without representation in the halls of legislation, he has oppressed her on all sides" (367). Women are deprived of the three inalienable rights averred in the Declaration of Independence:

civic *life*—they are, "if married, in the eye of the law, civilly dead";

liberty because "she is compelled to promise obedience to her husband, he becoming, to all intents and purposes, her master—the law giving him the power to deprive her of her liberty, and to administer chastisement"

the pursuit of happiness—she has no right to her children in divorce cases—"wholly regardless of the happiness of women"; has no access to "profitable employments," is denied "facilities for obtaining a through education," is subordinated even in religious affairs, and is the victim of "a false public sentiment" which severely penalizes her for actions excused in men.

Paralleling the treatment of and problems confronting women with the list of abuses suffered by the founding fathers and those endured by the slaves accomplishes two rhetorical tasks. In Burkean terms, it produces a new perspective by incongruity. Women, who had been acculturated into the notion of separate spheres of activity for the sexes, were encouraged to reconceptualize their status as contrary to the principles of the nation. For example, the statement "He has compelled her to submit to laws, in the formation of which she had no voice" clearly echoes the charge in the Declaration of Independence: "He [the King] has combined with others to subject us to a jurisdiction foreign to our constitution, and unacknowledged by our laws." The implicit argument is clear: if such offenses were sufficient cause for a revolution, they also constitute a powerful basis for women claiming a new role. This implied argument forces hearers to reconsider their comfortable political assumption because their ideals conflict with the stated principles of the political order.

This deliberate paralleling of oppressions also permits women to take advantage of the linguistic generality in the Declaration of Independence to assert their status as citizens. Significantly, the Declaration of Independence begins with the term "one people," repeatedly uses the pronoun "we," and concludes by designating the signers "Representatives of the United States." The then-generic "man" and "mankind" are easily accommodated into the larger sense of "the people." This is not mere wishful thinking. Since the Constitution did not contain the word "male" until the passage of the Fourteenth Amendment after the Civil War, women later could and would claim that this document and the Declaration of Independence did not in and of themselves exclude women from political life or at least from the franchise.

Since many of the women active in the woman's movement had long worked for the abolitionist cause (Lucretia Mott, Elizabeth Cady Stanton), it is not surprising that their document reflects the 1833 Declaration as well. Like the 1833 document, the Seneca Falls Declaration bases women's claims in the natural rights arguments of the Declaration of Independence as augmented with the religious warrants of the abolitionists. Man has, in the words of the women, "usurped the prerogative of Jehovah himself, claiming it his right to assign for her a sphere of action, when that belongs to her conscience and to her God" (367). Following the lead of the abolitionists, this document emphasizes the numbers of persons affected by the situation. While the abolitionist averred that "one-sixth part of our countrymen" suffered under the yoke of slavery, the women deplore "this entire disfranchisement of one-half the people of this country, their social and religious degradation" (368). Like the abolitionists, the women target a group of individuals—men—rather than the principles of the system as their enemy. Implicitly, they argue that persons with power within the system, in this case men, have perverted the principles of that system to their own selfish ends. Ending that abuse of the principles will produce "a more perfect union."

Like the founding fathers, the women pledge themselves to action, but that action follows in the peaceful path of the abolitionists: the employment of agents, the circulation of tracts, the petitioning of legislatures, the holding of conventions, and the enlisting of "pulpit and press in our behalf" (368). In short, women like the abolitionists will seek to change the system by working through it.

INTERANIMATION OF TEXTS

The two Declarations of Sentiments engrafted elements from the Declaration of Independence that worked strategically for the groups. But this intertextual "play" is not one–directional. The interpretations of and uses to which these groups put the Declaration of Independence worked to change the socially constructed meaning and implications of that text as well.[33] To understand their impact on the Declaration of Independence, one must know something of the earlier history and changing status of that document. In his excellent analysis of the first fifty years of the Declaration of Independence's history, Philip E. Detweiler declares that the document has usually been evoked in answer to some "current political or social question, with the result that the Declaration has had a different message at different times for different persons."[34] For at least the first two decades of its life, the document was seen as the instrument of revolution, and its preamble, which has since become its most signal part, received very little attention. Indeed, Detweiler notes that "In these years immediately following the Revolution it was still viewed primarily as the act of independence" and had not assumed "the character of 'a repository of magical and immortal phrases that burn in the mind and sing in the heart.'"[35] Moreover, the ideas and views expressed in the document were the subject of hot political debate between the Republicans and the Federalists; while its status depended almost entirely on one's political affiliations, no side accorded it the reverence we now accept as normal.[36]

But after the War of 1812 and particularly after the fiftieth anniversary of its signing, many Americans began to regard the Declaration of Independence with greater deference. This greater respect, however, did not produce uniform agreement about the meaning of the document, particularly its idealistic preamble. Indeed, some people drew a sharp distinction between the unalienable rights all persons had and their ability to enjoy the privileges—especially the franchise—which those rights might entail.[37] Moreover, from the beginning many persons had noted a tension between the guarantee of rights and the vagueness of the term "man." Becker notes that Thomas Hutchinson, in 1776 in exile in England, criticized the preamble precisely because it guaranteed rights to all men yet came from a country which deprived slaves of their rights.[38] Writers of the constitutions of some states in the Union addressed this problem by subtly altering its language to grant rights to "freed men" or to limit those rights to persons who formed "social compacts."[39] Others, while urging respect for the document, condemned its "glittering generalities" and construed its meaning to suit their political agendas. According to Becker, Rufus Choate pursued this path.[40] The details of these debates are not significant here. What is important is that the Declarations of

Sentiments of 1833 and 1848 represented one attitude toward the Declaration of Independence: acceptance of its ideas as "a living faith."[41] And they entered into a long-continuing debate about its "meaning," into which they injected their own construals of its ideas. If we study the "meanings" these Declarations found in the earlier document, we can perceive how they impressed their views onto it.

These two documents subtly but significantly enlarged the definition of citizen entailed in the Declaration of Independence. While both groups were receptive to limitations on the exercise of particular rights—the ballot, for example—they extended the concept of citizenship and its attendant general rights. The founding fathers' use of the term "the people" allowed these groups to insinuate women and slaves into citizenship, regardless of the intentions of the drafters of the document and regardless of the concept of citizenship under which they had worked. By assertion of their status as citizens, these groups enjoined a debate about how that concept was to be defined. In essence, they introduced "citizenship" as a contestable term and, in the final analysis, successfully imposed their meanings onto the Declaration of Independence.

Perhaps even more subtly, these documents asserted a preferred reading onto the first, key sentence in the preamble. Stephen Lucas, in his meticulous analysis of the Declaration of Independence, notes that the syntax of that sentence produces a strategic ambiguity.

> One way of interpreting "all men are created equal" in the Declaration is to read it as being modified by the succeeding clauses in sentence one of the preamble. Given this reading, "all men are created equal" would mean that all men are endowed equally by their creator with basic unalienable rights.... But the preamble need not be read this way. "All men are created equal" can also be taken as an independent clause whose meaning is not restricted by the succeeding clauses. In this case eighteenth-century readers would have interpreted "all men are created equal" in light of their own individual constructions of human equality.[42]

Lucas goes on to note that such construals might limit the meaning to simple equality of biological needs or the possession of an "innate moral sense that distinguishes them from the lower species." Lucas concludes that "part of the rhetorical brilliance of the Declaration of Independence is that it was written so people who differed on a wide range of particular political issues could accept the general ideas stated in the preamble."[43] Consciously or unconsciously, the persons who penned the 1833 Declaration of Sentiments exploited this ambiguity and the women at Seneca Falls reasserted that interpretation. In essence, by phrasing the sentence so that the assertion of human equality necessarily entailed equal rights, the

Declarations of Sentiments were selecting one preferred reading of the statement and deflecting attention from other interpretations less favorable to their cause.

They also shifted the rhetorical focus and purpose of the Declaration of Independence to accommodate their own needs and, in so doing, helped alter public perception of it. The Declaration of Independence is, in effect, a document which serves to justify an armed revolution; it relates the factors which compelled the signers to that drastic action.[44] Its focus was not a discussion of the rights of individuals. Lucas's analysis alludes to this when he discusses the colonist's reference to themselves as "one people" distinct from the British. This strategic labeling enabled the colonists to justify revolution which could, according to eighteenth-century principles, only be permitted in the most dire circumstances and then only by "the Body of the People" not "a handful of individuals."[45] More significantly, Lucas reads the second paragraph of the preamble as a series of five sequentially structured propositions of which the fifth, proclaiming the right of revolution, "is the most crucial in the overall argument of the Declaration."[46] Indeed, this often quoted preamble constitutes just over 20 percent of the entire document (273 words out of 1,322). As Lucas notes, the preamble was:

> debated but briefly by the Continental Congress, was given little heed by American loyalists or by English critics of the Declaration, and was all but ignored in America's early Fourth of July celebrations. For most people of the eighteenth century, it was an unobjectionable statement of commonplace political principles.[47]

The two Declarations of Sentiments, working from their particular interpretations of the preamble, assume as guaranteed to *individual citizens* the rights and privileges that the Declaration of Independence simply indicates as having been abridged by the King in his dealings with the colonies as a *unit*. This same confusion of individual rights vs. rights of citizens as a group informs our current debate over the right to bear arms.

Put in somewhat different terms, the writers of the two Declarations accepted as eternal truths statements that were very much bound up in eighteenth-century outlooks. Becker makes this point, without referring to the two Declarations of Sentiments, when he notes that in the nineteenth century the "self-evident" truths proclaimed in the document were "for the most part taken to be fallacies which common sense would reject. What seems but common sense in one age often seems but nonsense in another. Such for the most part is the fate which has overtaken the sublime truths enshrined in the Declaration of Independence."[48]

While they implicitly contested some of its concepts and altered its focus, the authors of these declarations also treated it as sacred text. They were part of a process that Lucas labels "the apotheosis" of the Declaration of Independence, which divorced it from the events of 1776.[49] These texts worked, in effect, to affirm the status of the Declaration of Independence as a philosophical foundation of American government rather than simply as the instrument of revolution.

Knowing the precise impact of these two documents in the social construction of the meaning of the Declaration of Independence is impossible. The process of redefining that document had certainly begun earlier. But the force of the abolition and woman's rights movements in American life in the nineteenth century is beyond dispute. And the ideas and attitudes encapsulated in the two Declarations of Sentiments became topoi in their public discourse. Moreover, because their advocates were among the most forceful and vocal during this period, these ideas were introduced to the public, regardless of their political sympathies. Elizabeth Cady Stanton wrote in her diary in 1888: "If I were to draw up a set of rules for the guidance of reformers . . . I should put at the top of the list: Do all you can, *no matter what*, to get people to think on your reform, and, then, if the reform is good, it will come about in due season."[50] In "due season," both the reforms sought by these groups succeeded and, thereby, they impressed their interpretation onto the Declaration of Independence and into our perception of it.

Because the Declarations of Sentiments affirmed the rather ambiguous principles of the introduction as beyond debate, those ideas as perceived by these groups became the starting points of argument for discussions of civic policy. The Declaration of Independence became an acid test for assessing the propriety of courses of action; American civic life became a process of striving toward and perfecting the ideals articulated in the Declarations. Abraham Lincoln's words in June of 1857 reflected the result of this process. He averred that the Declaration of Independence "set up a standard maxim for a free society, which would be familiar to all, and revered by all, constantly looked to, constantly labored for, . . . even though never perfectly attained."[51]

If Lucas's assessment is accurate, the framers of the Declaration of Independence had little sense of the role it was to play for succeeding generations of Americans. Noting that foreign readers paid little attention to it and that even in America "it was hardly treated with awe or reverence," Lucas quotes Merrill Peterson's conclusion that: "'neither Jefferson nor anyone else realized the far-reaching implications of the document.' Not until the burst of patriotic self-congratulation following the War of 1812 did Americans begin to regard the Declaration as a national treasure."[52] Indeed, in Lucas's eyes, the Declaration was intended to provide such a strong rationale for revolution that it would settle debate on that topic: "Seen in this way, the Declaration was not intended to be memorable but to be forgettable."[53]

In essence, these observations reflect exactly the process that McGee suggested has become typical in modern America. The authors of the two Declarations of Sentiments constructed their own texts within and upon the Declaration of Independence. Their documents were, in effect, made up of pieces of that previous text, and these documents, in turn, became bits of later texts. Thus, the political philosophy underlying Lincoln's Gettysburg Address as Wills has delineated it reflects the interpretation of that text that had been urged by abolitionists and woman's rights advocates for many years. Moreover, the metaphor of the Declaration of Independence as the foundation of an edifice is prominent in Martin Luther King, Jr.'s civil rights rhetoric.[54] Likewise, the abuses of women catalogued in the 1848 statement became commonplaces in the arguments for suffrage of women in the nineteenth century.

CONCLUSION

My goal in this essay has been to suggest how the study of the process of intertextuality can enrich our understanding of iconic texts. I have tried to show how rhetors engraft elements from previous texts and how this process enhances the force of their documents. Although it is beyond the scope of this essay, I have also suggested that the interanimative intertextual process sketched here does not end with these documents. In these cases, apparently iconic texts are involved in a dynamic intertextual play. This interanimation of texts may serve to provide at least the illusion of cultural coherence in a world of change; it may offer reassurance of the continuity of important principles even as they are being modified by changing needs and applications. To treat such texts as discrete units obscures this intertextual play and oversimplifies the complex character of our public discourse.

NOTES

1. Garry Wills, *Lincoln at Gettysburg: The Words that Remade America* (New York: Simon & Schuster, 1992).
2. Ibid., 38-39.
3. Ibid., 38.
4. Wills examines in some detail the influence of Theodore Parker on Lincoln's thinking, but does not consider the source of Parker's ideas. One paragraph Wills quotes from a speech by Parker suggests Parker's role as an intermediary between Lincoln and other abolitionist leaders:

> I think that the anti-Slavery men have not always done quite justice to the political men. See why. It is easy for Mr. Garrison and Mr. Phillips or me to say all of their thought. I am respon sible to nobody, and nobody to me. But it is not easy for Mr. Sumner, Mr. Seward, and Mr. Chase to say all of their thought; because they have a position to maintain, and they must keep that position. (Wills, 122)

5. Michael Calvin McGee "'The Ideograph': A Link Between Rhetoric and Ideology," *Quarterly Journal of Speech* 66 (1980): 1-16; and "Text, Context, and the Fragmentation of Culture," *Western Journal of Speech Communication* 54 (1990): 274-89. Raymie E. McKerrow, "Critical Rhetoric: Theory and Praxis," *Communication Monographs* 56 (1989): 91-111. Michel Foucault considers the problem of defining a "work" in "What Is An Author?" in *The Foucault Reader,* ed. Paul Rabinow (New York: Pantheon Books, 1984), 101-12.

6. Michael Leff and Andrew Sachs, "Words the Most Like Things: Iconicity and the Rhetorical Text," *Western Journal of Speech Communication* 54 (summer 1990): 252-73.

7. McGee, "Text, Context, and the Fragmentation of Contemporary Culture.

8. Dilip Parameshwar Gaonkar, "Object and Method in Rhetorical Criticism: From Wichelns to Leff and McGee," *Western Journal of Speech Communication* 54 (summer 1990):290-316; J. Robert Cox, "On 'Interpreting' Public Discourse in Post-Modernity," *Western Journal of Speech Communication* 54 (summer 1990): 317-29; Celeste Condit "Rhetorical Criticism and Audiences: The Extremes of McGee and Leff," *Western Journal of Speech Communication* 54 (summer 1990): 330-46; and John Angus Campbell, "Between the Fragment and the Icon: Prospect for a Rhetorical House of the Middle Way," *Western Journal of Speech Communication* 54 (summer 1990): 346-76.

9. Although I was not aware of it when I was writing this essay, Thomas W. Benson and Carolyn Anderson used an intertextual approach in their study of Frederick Wiseman's film *Missile*: "The Ultimate Technology: Frederick Wiseman's *Missile,*" *Communication and the Culture of Technology,* ed. Martin J. Medhurst, Alberto Gonzalez, and Tarla Rai Peterson (Pullman: Washington State University Press, 1990), 257-83. Their analysis of possible readings of the film develops an interesting and subtle model for considering the intertextuality of mediated discourse.

10. Vincent B. Leitch, *American Literary Criticism from the Thirties to the Eighties* (New York: Columbia University Press, 1988), 287-306.

11. Christopher Norris, *Deconstruction: Theory and Practice* (London: Methuen, 1982), 121-22.

12. J. Hillis Miller, "Stevens' Rock and Criticism as Cure, II," *Georgia Review* 30 (1976): 334. Quoted in Leitch, 287.

13. Leitch, 287.

14. Ibid.

15. Ibid., 287-88.

16. Ibid., 393.

17. Terry Eagleton, *Literary Theory: An Introduction* (Minneapolis: University of Minnesota Press, 1983), 138.

18. The text of the Anti–Slavery Society's document was printed in the *Liberator* of 16 December 1833 (198) and the Seneca Falls statement is available in the *History of Woman Suffrage* (I:70–73). However, for convenience, I will refer to the copies of these documents printed in Ronald F. Reid, *Three Centuries of American Rhetorical Discourse: An Anthology and Review* (Prospect Heights, Ill.: Waveland Press, 1988). Page numbers in parenthesis refer to this volume. The Seneca Falls Declaration is also available in Karlyn Kohrs Campbell, ed., *Man Cannot Speak for Her* (New York: Praeger, 1989), 2:33–37.

19. In the only extensive analysis I can locate of either document is Karlyn Kohrs Campbell's discussion of the 1848 declaration in *Man Cannot Speak for Her*, vol. 1 (New York: Praeger, 1989).

20. Reid, *Three Centuries of American Rhetorical Discourse,* "Commentary" on the Declaration of Sentiments, 341.

21. Gilbert Hobbs Barnes, *The Antislavery Impulse 1830-1844* (New York: D. Appleton-Century, 1933), 56. Garrison's control over the philosophy and even the wording of the 1833 declaration was largely due to circumstance. Originally, other persons interested in forming a national organization had abandoned the idea of meeting in late 1833, a date which would correspond with the important developments in England in regard to slavery. But Garrison insisted on proceeding with the meeting, which less than a hundred persons attended. Thus, Garrison was able to exert unusual power in establishing the principles that would guide the new American organization. The first national convention of the group was held in 1834, the date originally intended for the organizational meeting. Since more than 300 persons attended that meeting, Garrison would undoubtedly have had less control in drafting the statement of principles.

22. Eleanor Flexner, *Century of Struggle: The Woman's Rights Movement in the United States* (New York: Atheneum, 1971), 74.

23. *The Random House College Dictionary,* rev. ed., 1984.

24. Edwin Gittelman, "Jefferson's 'Slave Narrative': The Declaration of Independence as a Literary Text," *Early American Literature* 8 (winter 1974): 242.

25. Gittelman, 252-54. Becker, cited below (note 30), includes a copy of Jefferson's initial draft with this grievance listed as, apparently, do other writers.

26. For a discussion of sacred space, see Mircea Eliade, *The Sacred and The Profane: The Nature of Religion* (New York: Harcourt Brace Jovanovich, 1959), 20–65.

27. Stephen Lucas does argue convincingly, however, that the introductory paragraph was strategic rhetorically. See Stephen E. Lucas, "Justifying America: The Declaration of Independence as a Rhetorical Document," in *American Rhetoric: Context and Criticism,* ed. Thomas W. Benson (Carbondale, Ill.: Southern Illinois University Press, 1984), 74–82.

28. A modern reader cannot help being struck by how Martin Luther King, Jr. used this same structural metaphor as the basis for his "I Have a Dream" speech in 1963.

29. The questions of ends and means became points of dispute and, finally, disunion among abolitionists. For discussions of these disagreements, see: Aileen S. Kraditor, *Means and Ends in American Abolitionism: Garrison and His Critics on Strategy and Tactics, 1834-1850* (New York: Pantheon Books, 1969) and John Demos, "The Anti–Slavery Movement and the Problems of Violent 'Means,'" *New England Quarterly* 36 (1964): 501-26, reprinted in *Antislavery,* ed. Paul Finkelman (New York: Garland, 1989), 14:115-42.

30. Carl Becker, *The Declaration of Independence: A Study in the History of Political Ideas* (New York: Peter Smith, 1940), 237.

31. Hugh Dalziel Duncan, *Symbols in Society* (London: Oxford University Press, 1972), 98.

32. Ibid., 98.

33. See Owen Miller, "Intertextual Identity" in *Identity of the Literary Text,* ed. Mario J. Valdes and Owen Miller (Toronto: University of Toronto Press, 1985), 27-30, for an explanation of how later works may serve as an intertext for the interpretation of chronologically earlier texts.

34. Philip E. Detweiler, "The Changing Reputation of the Declaration of Independence: The First Fifty Years," *William and Mary Quarterly,* series 3 (October 1962): 557. For a careful explication of one "mis-reading" see: Barry Bell, "Reading and 'Misreading' the Declaration of Independence," *Early American Literature* 18 (1983): 71–83.

35. Detweiler, 564. Here he is quoting, Nathan Schachner, *Thomas Jefferson, a Biography* (New York, 1951), 1:129.

36. Ibid., 564-66.

37. A recent discussion of this viewpoint can be found in Paul Eidelberg, *On the Silence of the Declaration of Independence* (Amherst: University of Massachusetts Press, 1976).

38. Becker, 227.

39. Ibid., 240.

40. Ibid., 244-45.

41. Ibid., 240-41.

42. Lucas, 85-86.

43. Ibid., 85.

44. Ibid., 68, 88, 91. Becker (226) and Detweiler (558, 560, 564) support Lucas's assessments.

45. Ibid., 78.

46. Ibid., 88.

47. Ibid., 93, 72, and 90.

48. Becker, 233.

49. Lucas, 68.

50. Quoted in Ellen DuBois, "Women's Rights and Abolition: The Nature of the Connection," in Lewis Perry and Michael Feldman, eds., *Antislavery Reconsidered: New Perspectives on the Abolitionists* (Baton Rouge: Louisiana State University Press, 1979), 248.

51. Lucas, 68.

52. Ibid., 118.

53. Ibid., 120.

54. Martha Solomon, "Covenanted Rights: The Metaphoric Matrix in 'I Have a Dream,'" in *Martin Luther King, Jr. and the Sermonic Power of Public Discourse*, ed. John Louis Lucaites and Carolyn Calloway-Thomas (Tuscaloosa: University of Alabama Press), 66–84.

GARRISON AT PHILADELPHIA: THE "DECLARATION OF SENTIMENTS" AS INSTRUMENTAL RHETORIC

David Henry

I n the opening chapter of *Rhetorical Questions*, Edwin Black attends to the relationship between his most recent book and the path breaking *Rhetorical Criticism: A Study in Method.* "One conviction that influenced that old book," he writes, "has influenced also the present one, a conviction that the intervening twenty-five years have only strengthened. It is that almost all talk about criticism is sterile. Criticism lives only in acts of criticism, not in oracular abstractions about it. Goering once said," Black continues, "that when he heard the word 'culture,' he wanted to reach for his gun. I feel the same way about the prefix 'meta-.'"[1] Because this essay takes as its starting point Martha Solomon Watson's insightful critique of the Declarations of Sentiments issued by the American Anti-Slavery Society in 1833 and the Seneca Falls woman's rights convention of 1848, a meta-critical tack might well be in order. For Watson's proposition that the value of analyzing the texts resides largely in their interanimation of one another and of the Declaration of Independence, might well place critical theory at the center of discussion.

At least in the case of the American Anti-Slavery Society, however, proceeding to a conversation about critical method would be to miss an opportunity to right a serious disciplinary omission. For as Professor Watson herself observes,

> [a]lthough these documents provide good materials for the process I wish to investigate, they merit consideration in their own right. Each was the first important statement of principles of what became major, national social movements in the nineteenth century; and, each was authored by persons who were the primary spokespersons for their movements. . . . Despite their importance, the documents have received very little attention from scholars in communication studies.

Karlyn Kohrs Campbell's discussion of Seneca Falls in *Man Cannot Speak for Her*, Watson writes, is the only extensive analysis she could locate of either text.

While Watson's own examination of the documents' interdependence forms one perspective from which to posit a probative rhetorical-critical claim about the abolitionists' text, close reading of William Lloyd Garrison's Declaration of Sentiments on its own terms is at least equally illuminating. For in evidence is a rhetor who, as Watson contends, exploited the symbolic power of the Declaration of Independence and the founding fathers in propagating a course of action to correct past abuses. To disengage Garrison from that immediate context in search of a "larger" theoretical point, however, is to fail to appreciate the significance of such textual features for reaching multiple audiences at a particularly sensitive juncture in the early stage of the abolitionist movement.

Such disengagement is, as well, to risk missing masterful rhetorical artistry. Stephen Browne, in a highly praised work on Edmund Burke, articulates the dangers attendant to such a tack.[2] Browne writes that scholars who focus either on Burke's aesthetic value or his political philosophy, "too often reduce Burke to a set of propositions. The result is to lose sight of Burke as an artist, a fully embodied, three-dimensional master of rhetoric and oratory." To "read Burke rhetorically," he contends, "is to recall at every step that he was an orator—a public man who . . . was at once engaged and constrained by the expectations of the public mind."[3] Similarly, criticism of Garrison that situates his discourse in relation to context, audience, and subject reveals an exemplary practitioner of public argument.

This essay thus argues that full appreciation of the rhetorical genius embodied in the document Garrison crafted at Philadelphia hinges on examination of the American Anti-Slavery Society's Declaration of Sentiments as a study in instrumental rhetoric. Instrumental rhetoric is taken to mean (1) purposeful discourse, (2) shaped intentionally by a skilled rhetor, (3) for suasory effect on a target audience/s, (4) in response to immediate situational constraints. Such studies are neither necessarily superior nor inferior to analyses that seek the larger meaning/s of significant rhetorical experiences.[4] Rather, what may be termed "common sense" and "deconstructive" critical exercises can approach discursive events in different but mutually reinforcing fashion.[5]

The argument is guided by the conviction that what have often operated in the past as conflicting voices in an irresolvable debate, might be more productively approached as separate contributions to a potentially productive conversation.[6] In different terms, John Campbell proposes that neither extreme in the discussion need "win." Rather, the systematic study of rhetoric and criticism might be best served in constructing a "rhetorical house of the middle way." Instead of viewing disciplinary tensions as a permanent impasse, Campbell maintains that it "should be possible for rhetorical critics to analyze rhetorical objects at different levels of resolution (from micro to macro) and to move between episodes or epochs, as well as within them, in a natural yet methodologically rigorous way. A new kind of study—the longitudinal case study—would then emerge on the rhetorical horizon." What Campbell proposes, perhaps most appealingly, is "not only a program for peace but also for progress." The longitudinal case study aims to accommodate the best of both the ideological and textual critical projects, resulting in a

> different style of rhetorical analysis. This different style would be more historical than ideological—though sharing with ideological analysis a diachronic concern for the movement of constitutive transformative experiences across time. It would be more social than textual—though sharing with close reading a jealous concern for the integrity of the text and the situated art of the speaker.[7]

Where Professor Watson's exploration of the three Declarations works longitudinally to delineate textual interanimation, this essay provides an alternative reading, one focused on the "integrity of the text and the situated art of the speaker." Longitudinal elements are necessarily examined as well, however, albeit not in a manner that replicates Watson's critique. Instead, attention turns to how the abolitionists' Declaration of Sentiments evolved in the first of Garrison's four decades of anti-slavery advocacy during the nineteenth century, a period ripe for rhetorical-critical analysis.[8]

Ironically, the section of Professor Watson's essay in which she assesses the abolitionist text may stand on its own to exemplify the potential of iconic criticism for revealing the delicate interplay of a document's salient rhetorical features.[9] Watson argues that the Declaration of Independence influenced Garrison's drafting of the American Anti-Slavery Society's Declaration of Sentiments in three ways. The founders' work is evident in: "(1) the use of structural and space metaphors to link this document to the political work begun with the Declaration of Independence; (2) the clear connection established between the founding fathers and this group; and (3) the argumentative approach" employed in 1833. The irony rests with Watson's endorsement earlier in the paper of Christopher Norris's indictment of poetry's New Critics, who "invented various ways of sealing the poem off within a timeless, self-sufficient realm of interlocked meaning and structure." Despite Watson's disdain for the "sealing off" process, her attention to Garrison's work points to the data for an exceptionally valuable critique of the text as situated discourse carefully constructed by a facile rhetor to sway a diverse audience. Since Watson's reading of the American Anti-Slavery Society's Declaration of Sentiments is the stimulus for this essay, a brief summary of her evaluation's salient features precedes the alternative reading. The balance of this essay then delineates the instrumental features of the American Anti-Slavery

Society's Declaration of Sentiments, and concludes with a comment on the wisdom of scholarly engagement cast in the conversational mode.

GARRISON'S DECLARATION AS RHETORICAL FRAGMENT

In laying open the structural and space metaphors that link the Declaration of Sentiments to the Declaration of Independence, Watson shows how the abolitionists depicted their work as an extension of the task begun by the nation's revered founders. Literally, the abolitionists' selection of Philadelphia as their meeting place allowed them to call forth the suasory force attached to what had become a "sacred ground" for United States citizens. Metaphorically, the Declaration of Sentiments draws from key figurative wording of the Declaration of Independence, averring that the "corner-stone upon which [the nation's fathers] founded the TEMPLE OF FREEDOM was broadly this—'that all men are created equal; that they are endowed by their creator with certain inalienable rights; that among these are life, LIBERTY, and the pursuit of happiness.'"[10] This paragraph, Watson maintains, begins a clever use of structural metaphors that extends throughout the statement. Ultimately, by combining edifice images (corner-stone, temple, overthrow of the foundations) with images that deal with the occupation of space (null, void, usurpation, infringement, transgression), the founders of the American Anti-Slavery Society "engrafted the principles they read into the Declaration of Independence into their own agenda."

Watson next attends to a second parallel between the founders' principles and the abolitionists' appeal. Garrison and his adherents portrayed themselves as the "inheritors of the patriotic mantle of their forebears." Taking as their assignment completion of the work begun in 1776, they immodestly claimed that, "In purity of motive, in earnestness of zeal, in decision of purpose, in intrepidity of action, in steadfastness of faith, in sincerity of spirit, we would not be inferior to them" (343-44). Yet the abolitionists differentiated themselves from their predecessors in two distinct ways. First, as Professor Watson demonstrates, Garrison pledged the Anti-Slavery Society to nonviolence. Because force and bloodshed were essential to the revolution, the abolitionists recognized that the country feared a return to violence. Thus, they vowed to achieve their goals through the "opposition of moral purity to moral corruption—the destruction of error by the potency of truth—the overthrow of prejudice by the power of love—the abolition of slavery by the spirit of repentance" (344). This separation of the revolutionaries' means and ends, Watson illustrates, proved an essential feature of the abolitionists' rhetorical strategy.

A second feature of that strategy surfaced in anti-slavery leaders' casting of their relationship to those on whose behalf they worked. As they spoke not for themselves but for those prevented by law from voicing their own cause, the abolitionists assumed a "we" persona. Acting as "community guardians," they were thus able to become protectors of the social order, rather than the threat to that order that their detractors depicted in pro-slavery appeals. This movement eventuated in a further advantage. Exploiting the deistic conception of God evinced in the Declaration of Independence, the abolitionists subtly united their patriotic rhetoric with the religious fervor that defined the early nineteenth century.

The abolitionists' argumentative strategy constitutes the final parallel Watson discerns between the Anti-Slavery Society's manifesto and the Declaration of Independence. That strategy entailed enumerating the abuses suffered under slavery and providing a course of action to remedy the abuse. Although Watson's rendering of the parallels between the problems of the slaves and those of the patriots merits attention, her analysis of the abolitionists' rhetorical shrewdness in advocating a course of action is even more striking. On her reading, anti-slavery advocates separated the evils of the practice of slavery from the political philosophy that allowed that practice, concentrating their explicit attacks on the evils of the practice. This tactic permitted the abhorrent political philosophy that underlay the practice of slavery to be addressed indirectly. Abolitionists explicitly recognized State sovereignty, conceding that the "present national compact" precluded federal interference. Their goal, then, was to alter the national compact through "moral suasion and political action."

Watson's analysis of the abolitionists' rhetorical sleight of hand in separating adherence to current law from a philosophical disagreement with the law is telling. For she builds her case carefully and compellingly, relying almost exclusively on the texts of the Declaration of Sentiments and the Declaration of Independence in so doing. Intentionally or not, this concentration reinforces Black's conviction that the rhetorical critic's province lies in the evaluation of appearances, as those appearances are manifested in textual data.[11] The analysis also reveals the value of close textual analysis, whether the critic's concentration is on the text as a discrete field of rhetorical action, or, as is Watson's concern, on discourse as a resource of fragments for the [re]construction of meaning over time. Although there is much to commend her use of the data for her explicit analytical purposes, Watson's paper provides evidence as well of the value of critical pluralism. For in addition to its interanimative functions in relation to the Declaration of Independence and the woman's rights statement issued at Seneca Falls, the abolitionists' document operated instrumentally to unify disparate convention delegates at Philadelphia in 1833.

GARRISON'S TEXT AS INSTRUMENTAL RHETORIC

Early in her analysis, Professor Watson terms the American Anti-Slavery Society's Declaration of Sentiments the "first important statement of principles of what became [a] major, national social movement in the nineteenth century," a movement for which Garrison served as a "primary spokesperson." Both Garrison's text and the woman's rights Declaration at Seneca Falls, she adds, "merit consideration in their own right." John Campbell's notion of social-textual studies provides one perspective from which productive consideration proceeds. In the case of Garrison at Philadelphia, such a study entails examination of (1) the evolution and nature of Garrison's public advocacy, (2) the events of the summer and fall of 1833 that set the context from which the American Anti-Slavery Society document issued, and (3) the social-textual dynamics of the Declaration of Sentiments as situated rhetoric. Approached in this fashion, the present critique suggests the potential for mutually productive interaction between the practices of "ideological" criticism and the "close reading" of texts.

The dearth of rhetorical-critical analyses of William Lloyd Garrison's reform advocacy is striking, not least because Garrison's career spanned virtually half the century and ranged across myriad issues.[12] Abolition reigned supreme, but movements for temperance, women's rights, John Humphrey Noyes' doctrine of Perfectionism, and peace occupied his time and attention as well. Born in 1805, Garrison grew up poor, his father increasingly absent until deserting the family completely in 1808. Unable to care adequately for all of her children, his mother eventually apprenticed Garrison at age 13 to the printer of the Newburyport, Mass., *Herald.* The apprentice educated himself while spending seven years learning his trade.

In the process, Garrison's rhetorical character took shape, a character defined equally by a keen sense of audience and a penchant for powerful language. At the base of Garrison's rhetoric was the need for an audience, a need he began to fulfill by writing anonymous letters to the editor during his years in servitude. The presence of an audience, whether readers reviled or admired his claims, sustained Garrison throughout his career, even as he experienced incarceration, persecution, and death threats. "Anything," his biographer Walter Merrill writes, "so long as people would listen."[13] He acquired an audience for his reform views in 1829 when he accepted Benjamin Lundy's invitation to co-edit *The Genius of Universal Emancipation,* then located in Baltimore. Perhaps because of an upbringing characterized by poverty and a forced apprenticeship, Garrison sought to understand slavery from the slave's perspective. Wendell Phillips, a contemporary who knew Garrison as well as any of his associates, contended that the abolitionist cause owed its success to the "fact that he looked upon the great questions posed by the state and by the church as a Negro looked upon them."[14]

Garrison arrived at this perspective shortly into his editorship of *The Genius*, which carried Lundy's endorsement of the American Colonization Society. The Society favored colonization rather than emancipation as the ideal remedy to slavery. Influenced by events in Britain, however, where slavery in the West Indies was being combatted under the banner of "immediate emancipation," Garrison became increasingly strident in his rejection of the expatriation option. In the 13 November 1829 issue of *The Genius*, for example, he erroneously charged Francis Todd and Nicholas Brown, owner and captain of the *Francis*, with engaging illegally in the coastal slave trade. Garrison was prosecuted for libel the following spring, convicted, and sentenced to six months in jail. He served 49 days, during which time his commitment to immediate emancipation intensified. He left prison determined to establish an alternative voice to the *Genius*'s influential call for colonization.

Garrison intended initially to settle in Washington, D.C., but before he could do so Lundy moved *The Genius* to the nation's capital. So instead he returned to Boston, and on 1 January 1831 the nation heard the alternative voice for the first time. In the first issue of *The Liberator*, Garrison specified five groups that would define his audience. He anticipated emotional support from religious readers, financial relief from philanthropists, and shared love of country from patriots. A fourth group consisted in the "ignorant, the cold-hearted, THE TYRANNICAL," whom Garrison expected to instruct and to recruit to the cause of humanity's collective good. But above all, he addressed the "free colored," for "we know that you are now struggling against wind and tide."[15]

To aid in that struggle, Garrison promised an advocacy couched in severe language, but a language no harsher than the reprehensible institution that emancipationists sought to abolish. The first issue of *The Liberator* engaged the question of Garrison's suasory strategy in what has been termed the "most famous passage"[16] in all of his writings:

> I am aware, that many object to the severity of my language; but is there not cause for severity? I *will be* as harsh as truth, and as uncompromising as justice. On this subject I do not wish to think, or speak, or write, with moderation. No! no! Tell a man whose house is on fire, to give a moderate alarm; tell him to moderately rescue his wife from the hands of the ravisher; tell the mother to gradually extricate her babe from the fire into which it has fallen;—but urge me not to use moderation in a cause like the present. I am in earnest—I will not equivocate—I will not excuse— I will not retreat a single inch—AND I WILL BE HEARD. The apathy of the peo-

ple is enough to make every statue leap from its pedestal, and to hasten the resurrection of the dead.[17]

Garrison's combining of familial images with metaphors grounded in nature defined his advocacy for the two years between the establishment of *The Liberator* and the founding of the American Anti-Slavery Society. And his unyielding devotion to full emancipation resulted consistently in language designed "to sting and to rebuke." In concert with Campbell's notion of longitudinal case studies, the examination of discursive fragments is telling here for what it reveals about the evolution of the rhetorical strategy and tactics that undergirded the Declaration of Sentiments. Evident early on are Garrison's affinity for edifice metaphors and his characterization of slave owners and transporters as "manstealers," both of which Watson cites as central to her reading of the Declaration as a link in the chain of interanimation with the Declaration of Independence and the Seneca Falls text.

Both figures contribute as well, however, to the evolution of a suasory repertoire that would inform Garrison's instrumental rhetoric at Philadelphia. Consider, for instance, the abolitionist's "Address Before the Free People of Color," which he delivered at the Belknap-Street Church on 2 April 1833. It is not the edifice metaphor's presence alone that merits note. Rather, it is Garrison's strategic insinuation of the figure into his discourse, which reflects the careful use of language to dislodge an accepted or established image (or reality) in preparation for replacing it with a new image. Paul Ricoeur contends that the power to create a new reality by imposing a metaphor which "redescribes reality," is contingent first on "creating rifts in the old order." Such images work best, George Lakoff and Mark Johnson add, when cast in experiential terms.[18] On this view, Garrison's instantiation of the edifice metaphor as a recurring theme in his discourse depended on his ability initially to depict slavery in the most heinous and despicable terms, then to substitute for forced servitude a palatable experiential reality. The edifice metaphor comprised the desirable alternative, particularly when contrasted with the "whip" and "chain" that Garrison let stand metonymically for the peculiar institution:

> God will blow [slavery] into countless fragments, so that not the remnant of a whip or chain can be found in all the South, and so that upon its ruins may be erected the beautiful temple of freedom. I will not waste my strength in foolishly endeavoring to beat down this great Bastille with a feather. I will not commence at the roof, and throw off its tiles by piecemeal. I am for adopting a more summary method of demolishing it. I am for digging under its foundations, and springing a mine that shall not leave one stone upon another.[19]

In a tactic that recurred in his discourse, Garrison juxtaposed the anti-slavery advocates' desire to construct a "temple of freedom" with their opponents' "manstealing" practices. Alluding initially to his modest skill in expressing a forceful case, Garrison's words belied his professed limitations:

> I wish I could denounce slavery, and all its abettors, in terms equal to their infamy. But, shame to tell! I can apply to him who steals the liberties of hundreds of his fel-low-creatures, and lacerates their bodies, and plunders them all of their hard earn-ings, only the same epithet that is applied by all to a man who steals a shilling in his community. I call the slaveholder a thief because he steals human beings and reduces them to the conditions of brutes; and I am thought to be abusive! . . . I never will dilute or modify my language against slavery—against the plunderers of my fel-low-men—against American kidnappers.[20]

As his sense of audience matured, as his appreciation for the strategic and tac-tical powers of language evolved, Garrison's oratory and writing between 1829 and 1833 contributed to an emerging rhetorical character. And as his role as a public man developed, his notoriety grew at home and abroad. Invitations to for-eign travel and speaking engagements increased concurrently. His "Address Before the Free People of Color" in April 1833 was, in fact, part of a farewell tour that preceded Garrison's journey to England to raise funds for Boston's Manual Labor School. As summer progressed, he turned his attention from the original purpose to track the progress of Britain's policy of abolishing slavery in the West Indies. The British commitment to emancipation reinforced Garrison's conclu-sion that colonization constituted a misguided course. These events of the sum-mer of 1833 both solidified key dimensions of Garrison's public advocacy and portended the conflict that would create a unique rhetorical situation to be engaged at Philadelphia in December.

During his months in England, Garrison encountered Elliott Cresson, an agent for the American Colonization Society. Despite his own support for colo-nization early in his abolitionist advocacy,[21] Garrison had little tolerance for those who could not see the wisdom of emancipation, and he challenged Cresson to public debate. Cresson declined the invitation, but he followed Garrison's public appearances, giving particular attention to incidents that might help at home to portray the emancipationist as an unpatriotic radical. Garrison provided the materials for such a characterization on July 13, when he addressed an anti-colo-nization meeting in London. Introduced at Exeter Hall by British abolitionist George Thompson, Garrison announced himself a "citizen of the world," and recited a series of charges against the United States. His opening sentence echoed the phrase that had headed each issue of *The Liberator* from its inception on 1 January 1831: "*My country is the world and my countrymen are all mankind.*"[22] It "is true," he continued, "in a geographical sense, I am now in a foreign territory; but still it is a part of my country. I am in the midst of strangers; but still surrounded by my countrymen. There must be limits to civil governments and national domains."[23]

At one level, such an introduction might be interpreted simply as a skilled orator flattering the assembly. But Garrison's message functioned at other levels as well, not least of which was the apparent disparagement of his citizenship in a nation against which he held serious grievances. Although he declared a strong "love for the land of my nativity" and pride in "her civil, political, and religious institutions," Garrison averred that he had "some solemn accusations to bring against her." Nine successive paragraphs then began, "I accuse." Garrison's recitation of the charges reflected his propensity for appropriating the nation's founding documents for argumentative purposes, his finely honed talent for powerful language, and his use of familial images to equate the evils of slavery with the destruction of civilization:

> I accuse her, before all nations, of giving an open, deliberate and base denial to her boasted Declaration, that "all men are created equal; that they are endowed by their Creator with certain inalienable rights; that among these are life, liberty and the pursuit of happiness." . . .
>
> I accuse her of legalizing, on enormous scale, licentiousness, fraud, cruelty and murder. . . .
>
> I accuse her of stealing the liberties of two millions of the creatures of God, and withholding the just recompense of their labor; of ruthlessly invading the holiest relations of life, and cruelly separating the dearest ties of nature; of denying these miserable victims necessary food and clothing for their perishable bodies, and light and knowledge for their immortal souls; of tearing the husband from his wife, the mother from her babe, and children from their parents, and perpetrating upon the poor and needy every species of outrage and oppression.[24]

Such cues reflect the continuing evolution of Garrison's public voice, a voice understood most fully neither through the accumulation of fragmentary data nor from the Philadelphia manifesto in isolation, but from an appreciation for both as complementary dimensions of his advocacy. Elliott Cresson and American Colonization Society adherents ensured that Garrison's alleged lack of patriotism evident in that advocacy preceded his return across the Atlantic in the fall. Potential American Anti-Slavery Society supporters thus balked at the need to rush forward, particularly with the controversial Garrison in a central role. Yet

Garrison persevered, eschewing caution as a temporary victory for slavery proponents, and he proceeded to Philadelphia for the American Anti-Slavery Society
organizational meetings in early December. Once in residence, Garrison encountered an audience that constituted a demanding rhetorical challenge.

That audience merits consideration. Leaders of regional anti-slavery societies
scheduled a meeting for Philadelphia in the fall of 1833 to form a national organization. Under pressure from citizens of Philadelphia, Arthur and Lewis
Tappan, philanthropists and founders of the New York Anti-Slavery Society,
agreed to exercise their influence to postpone the national meeting to the spring
of 1834. Garrison, however, insisted on acting swiftly. With the backing of his
New England Anti-Slavery Society, Garrison's case carried the day, and a meeting was called for 5-6 December 1833, at Philadelphia. Although united by their
opposition to slavery, participants ranged from the moderate stance assumed by
the Tappans and their followers to the more radical posture of Garrison and his
supporters. Once assembled, delegates drafted a constitution, which proved to
be more a set of organizational guidelines than an inspirational document that
might generate fervor for the society's cause. Recognizing the need for such a
document, participants appointed a committee to prepare what would become
the Declaration of Sentiments, and a subcommittee selected Garrison to draft its
report. Garrison worked through the night, presenting his draft to the subcommittee the next morning. After debating—and ultimately deleting—a single
paragraph, the subcommittee and committee of the whole commended
Garrison's document to the assembled delegates.[25]

Professor Watson reads the abolitionists' use of structural and space
metaphors, the connections made between their cause and that of the founding
fathers, and the parallels between the argumentative approaches evinced in the
abolitionists' manifesto and the Declaration of Independence as evidence of the
texts' interdependence. Her analysis is at least equally valuable, though, for the
potential insight provided for a study that would attempt neither to isolate the
text, nor to "seal it off" from its context, but that would aspire to understand the
instrumentality of Garrison's manifesto.

As instrumental rhetoric, the Declaration of Sentiments is a critical marker in
the solidification of the nineteenth century anti-slavery movement. The meeting
at Philadelphia culminated early efforts to focus public attention on the slavery
controversy, and pitted moderates against radicals in the quest to define the next
stage of movement activism. This is a crucial phase in a social movement's life
cycle, as the goal shifts from establishing public awareness of a perceived ill to
adopting a document that identifies the problem's root causes and prescribes fitting remedies.[26] The advantage rests with leaders who can function as visionaries

as well as agitators, leaders possessed of the rhetorical facility to shape the form and content of the manifesto in which subsequent activism will be grounded.

Garrison proved such a leader in crafting the Declaration of Sentiments, a document that can be read as the culmination of four years of public advocacy for immediate emancipation. Watson's attention to the parallels between Garrison's work and the Declaration of Independence informs such a reading, but so does an appreciation for the manifesto's instrumental dimensions, beginning with structure. Although Watson acknowledges the importance of the broad organizational framework of the Anti-Slavery Society's text, with its movement from a recitation of grievances to a plan of action, she is less concerned with the importance of this tack for Garrison's convention audience. But it is the carefully constructed framework of the forty-four paragraph document that enabled Garrison to adapt antecedent tactics to immediate suasory purposes.

The first four paragraphs comprise Garrison's introduction, wherein the convention's Philadelphia setting and emancipatory purpose are linked to the founders' meeting fifty-seven years earlier. Paragraphs five through seven distinguish the abolitionists' means and ends from those of their forebears, with particular attention to the Revolutionary Fathers' willingness to employ violence to resolve grievances. Although averring the severity of those grievances, paragraphs eight and nine document the even more reprehensible circumstance of "TWO MILLIONS of our people," the enslaved who constitute one-sixth of the nation's population. "Hence we maintain," a single sentence paragraph ten, begins a series of six paragraphs specifying slavery as a violation of civil, religious, and natural right. Paragraph sixteen—"Therefore we believe and affirm"—initiates a second successive series of linked claims, declaring first that "there is no difference, *in principle*, between the African slave trade and American slavery," and announcing in conclusion that all laws "admitting the right of slavery" are "utterly null and void." Paragraphs twenty-two through thirty articulate the terms of a satisfactory resolution of the abolitionists' grievances: equality for all citizens, no compensation for slave owners, and nothing less than the "immediate and total abolition of slavery." The next four paragraphs engage the difficult issue of states' rights. Garrison acknowledges the sovereignty of each state to legislate on slavery, but he adds quickly that Congress has the right to abolish slavery where the Constitution prevails; more importantly, the "highest obligations" mandate that citizens of the free states "remove slavery by moral and political action."[27]

Their "views and principles" thus established, in signing the Declaration of Sentiments convention delegates pledged themselves to a sustained course of action:

We shall organize Anti-Slavery Societies, if possible, in every city, town, and village of our land.

We shall send forth Agents to lift up the voice of remonstrance, of warning, of entreaty and rebuke.

We shall circulate, unsparingly and extensively, anti-slavery tracts and periodicals.

We shall enlist the PULPIT and the PRESS in the cause of the suffering and the dumb.

We shall aim at a purification of the churches from all participation in the guilt of slavery.

We shall encourage the labor of freemen over that of the slaves, by giving a preference to their productions;—and

We shall spare no exertions nor means to bring the whole nation to speedy repentance.

Our trust for victory is solely in GOD. We may be personally defeated, but our principles never.[28]

A final paragraph pledged delegates "to overthrow the most execrable system of slavery that has ever been witnessed upon earth—to deliver our land from its deadliest curse—to wipe out the foulest stain which rests upon our national escutcheon."

Garrison arrived in Philadelphia directly from a controversial tour of England and a tumultuous return to the United States. Recognizing the diversity of his audience, yet committed to the radical cause of abolition, he adapted brilliantly to the situational constraints the convention presented. A master of strident language, he agreed to erase from his original draft the most controversial paragraph submitted to the subcommittee.[29] Remaining vociferous language was retained for its functional value, for its capacity to articulate the Anti-Slavery Society's grievances or to delineate remedies. The shock value of language that would "rebuke" was essential to focusing the nation's attention on slavery; a more refined prose would help convert that attention to action. Hence, when Garrison called forth the familial images that defined earlier discourse, the images served as means to an end rather than as ends in themselves. Consider the following:

... those for whose emancipation we are striving ... are ruthlessly torn asunder— the tender babe from the arms of its frantic mother—the heart-broken wife from her weeping husband—at the caprice or pleasure of irresponsible tyrants;—and for the crime of having a dark complexion, [they] suffer the pangs of hunger, the infliction of stripes, and the ignominy of brutal servitude.[30]

Garrison's style here contrasts sharply with the avowedly "harsh" and "uncompromising" tone characteristic of *The Liberator*'s first issue, as well as of much of Garrison's discourse in the intervening two years. Where severity was in order to dislodge the culture's dominant "reality," Garrison intuitively understood that moderation was more likely to accommodate a diverse audience convened to establish a national anti-slavery society. That he responded appropriately not only marked a critical juncture in the life of the abolitionist movement, but also in the evolution of Garrison's rhetorical character.[31]

TOWARD A CRITICAL CONVERSATION

Still four days shy of his twenty-eighth birthday on 6 December 1833, William Lloyd Garrison proposed for adoption a Declaration of Sentiments to serve as the founding document of the American Anti-Slavery Society. Textual and contextual evidence reveals that Garrison brought to the task a fervent commitment to immediate emancipation and a powerful rhetorical repertoire with which to advance the cause. Yet he was immensely sensitive to the competing sentiments of his audience, a gathering not fully convinced of the superiority of emancipation over colonization, and a public averse to his alleged lack of patriotism before British audiences. The Declaration of Independence and reverence for the founding fathers thus formed integral features of an instrumental rhetoric aimed at swaying doubters and sustaining the emancipationist cause. On this reading, Garrison's structural and stylistic tactics thus evinced immediate suasory purposes outside the explanatory scope of an interanimationist analytical project.

Clearly such a reading centers on traditional analytical *topoi* of context, audience, rhetor, and text. But it does not do so with an eye toward "privileging" one tack over another. Attention to text is offered instead as a contribution to discussion and debate about the place of public address studies in the larger scholarly conversation. Projects that feature text not only inform but in some ways define the uniqueness of the discipline's contribution. In Martin Medhurst's view, for example, rhetorical-critical studies will influence intellectual engagements when projects eventuate in scholarship that "makes a difference." Interest "in the functioning of texts is the *sine qua non* of making a difference," he contends, "for it is in the explication of the rhetorical dynamics of the text that public address scholars are (or ought to be) most expert."[32] This is not to demean the place of context in scholarship but rather, as Stephen Lucas advises, to urge an appreciation for the "rhetorical artistry" of important texts.[33] And Dilip Gaonkar emphasizes the interdependence of text and context when he notes that the "pressing task, for which 'textual studies' are ideally suited, is to offer an understanding of 'contexts' (non-discursive formations) through a reading of texts (discursive formations) while allowing the text to retain its integrity as a field of action."[34]

In her critical project, Martha Watson finds a focus on a text's "integrity as a field of action" too confining. Her interest in the abolitionists' and suffragists' Declarations of Sentiments stems from the extent to which the texts "appropriated and exploited the rhetorical force embedded in the Declaration of Independence in different, but equally powerful ways." More importantly, she argues, "the interpretations of the Declaration of Independence provided in the two documents altered and shifted its meaning significantly." Professor Watson's readings of the documents commend the vitality of public address scholarship. Her attention to textual detail, probing argument, analytical insight, and persuasive prose urge careful reading and contemplation of her thesis. Watson's explanation and application of intertextuality promises a valuable addition to the rhetorical critic's inventory of analytical approaches.

Textual and contextual evidence in this examination of the Declaration of Sentiments crafted by Garrison confirms Watson's contention that the principles of the Declaration of Independence and the achievements of the founding fathers informed Garrison's suasory strategy and tactics. Moreover, to the extent that her analysis reveals the interanimation of these texts in combination with the woman's rights Declaration of Sentiments, she achieves, in John Campbell's terms, a productive and instructive "act of criticism." Yet the critique need not be viewed as incompatible with a reading of the abolitionists' text as an immediate call for action, designed to unify a disparate audience.[35] Rather, Watson's analysis may combine with a textual-social assessment to provide an even larger understanding of the texts themselves. As divergent, yet complementary, voices in a scholarly conversation, the interanimationist and textual-social perspectives operate together to yield a more comprehensive understanding of the promise and prospect of rhetorical-critical studies than does either voice speaking in isolation.

NOTES

1. Edwin Black, *Rhetorical Questions: Studies of Public Discourse* (Chicago: University of Chicago Press, 1992), 17-18.
2. James R. Andrews, review of Stephen H. Browne, *Edmund Burke and the Discourse of Virtue* (Tuscaloosa: University of Alabama Press 1993) in *Quarterly Journal of Speech* 81 (1995): 253-54.
3. Stephen H. Browne, *Edmund Burke and the Discourse of Virtue* (Tuscaloosa: University of Alabama Press, 1993), 2, 4.

4. The idea that "rhetorical experiences" constitute the critic's focus of study is borrowed from Wayne Brockriede, "Rhetorical Criticism as Argument," *Quarterly Journal of Speech* 60 (1974): 165-74.

5. Malcolm O. Sillars, *Messages, Meanings, and Culture* (New York: HarperCollins, 1991), 10-11.

6. See, for example, the "dialogue" in the "Forum" of the *Quarterly Journal of Speech* 78 (1992): Michael Leff, "Things Made By Words: Reflections on Textual Criticism," 223-31, and Barbara Warnick, "Leff in Context: What is the Critic's Role?", 232-37.

7. John Angus Campbell, "Between the Fragment and the Icon: Prospect for a Rhetorical House of the Middle Way," *Western Journal of Speech Communication* 54 (1990): 347, 368.

8. Recent works indicating the prospective value of such inquiry are Gregory Clark and S. Michael Halloran, *Oratorical Culture in Nineteenth Century America: Transformations in the Theory and Practice of Rhetoric* (Carbondale: Southern Illinois University Press, 1993), and Kenneth Cmiel, *Democratic Eloquence: The Fight over Popular Speech in Nineteenth-Century America* (Berkeley: University of California Press, 1990).

9. The notion of "iconic criticism" as approached by Watson and in this essay is exemplified in Michael Leff and Andrew Sachs, "Words the Most Like Things: Iconicity and the Rhetorical Text," *Western Journal of Speech Communication* 54 (1990): 252-73.

10. American Anti-Slavery Society, "Declaration of Sentiments," 6 December 1833, *Three Centuries of American Rhetorical Discourse*, ed. Ronald F. Reid (Prospect Heights, Ill.: Waveland, 1988), 343. I follow Martha Watson's lead in using this version of the document, further references to which are cited in the text of this paper. An alternative text includes an additional paragraph, which would be inserted between paragraphs 31 and 32 of this version. That text is in Wendell Phillips Garrison and Francis Jackson Garrison, ed., *William Lloyd Garrison: The Story of His Life* (1885; reprint, New York: Negro Universities Press, 1969), 408-12.

11. Black, *Rhetorical Questions*, 9.

12. Rudimentary background, but limited analytical detail, is provided in Robert T. Oliver, *History of Public Speaking in America* (Boston: Allyn and Bacon, 1965), 229-32; Lloyd Rohler, "William Lloyd Garrison: Abolitionist," *American Orators Before 1900*, ed. Bernard K. Duffy and Halford R. Ryan (New York: Greenwood Press, 1987), 183-89; and D. Ray Heisey, "Slavery: America's Irrepressible Conflict," *America in Controversy: History of American Public Address*, ed. Dewitte Holland (Dubuque, Iowa: Wm. C. Brown Publishers, 1973), 103-21. Remarkably, but a single journal article touches on Garrison, and in that Loren Reid examines Garrison as the rhetor's subject rather than as rhetor: "Bright's Tributes to Garrison and Field," *Quarterly Journal of Speech* 61 (1975): 169-77.

13. Walter M. Merrill, *Against Wind and Tide: A Biography of William Lloyd Garrison* (Cambridge: Harvard University Press, 1963), 46.

14. Truman Nelson, ed., *Documents of Upheaval: Selections from William Lloyd Garrison's The Liberator, 1831-1865* (New York: Hill and Wang, 1966), xv. Celeste Michelle Condit and John Louis Lucaites, in a masterful scholarly enterprise, similarly credit Garrison's capacity for empathy. On their reading, however, white abolitionists owed an equal or greater debt to the public rhetorical efforts of African Americans. See: *Crafting Equality: America's Anglo-African Word* (Chicago: University of Chicago Press, 1993), 69-72 passim.

15. Merrill, *Against Wind and Tide*, 47-48.

16. Ibid., 45.

17. William Lloyd Garrison, "To the Public," *The Liberator*, 1 January 1831, reprinted in Garrison and Garrison, ed., *William Lloyd Garrison*, 225. See also: *Three Centuries of American Rhetorical Discourse*, ed. Reid, 321-23.

18. Paul Ricoeur, *The Rule of Metaphor*, trans. Robert Czerny (1975; reprint, Toronto: University of Toronto Press, 1977), 22; George Lakoff and Mark Johnson, *Metaphors We Live By* (Chicago: University of Chicago Press, 1980), 153-57.

19. Garrison and Garrison, eds., *William Lloyd Garrison*, 335.

20. Ibid., 336.

21. Perhaps the most complete statement of Garrison's brief endorsement of colonization is his 4 July 1829 address at Boston's Park Street Church, ibid., 127-37.

22. *The Liberator* carried the motto, "Our Country is the World—Our Countrymen are Mankind" on the masthead of each issue, ibid., 219, 233.

23. William Lloyd Garrison, "Address at London's Exeter Hall," 13 July 1833, ibid., 369.

24. Ibid., 372-73.

25. Delegates representing ten of the union's twelve free states participated; sixty-three delegates signed the final document. For accounts of Garrison's role in pushing for the society's formation, drafting the document, and securing the Declaration's adoption, see: Russel B. Nye, *William Lloyd Garrison and the Humanitarian Reformers* (Boston: Little, Brown, 1955), 68-72; John L. Thomas, *The Liberator* (Boston: Little, Brown, 1963), 171-76; Garrison and Garrison, eds., *William Lloyd Garrison*, 397-419; and Merrill, *Against Wind and Tide*, 76-80.

26. Charles J. Stewart, Craig Allen Smith, and Robert E. Denton, Jr., *Persuasion and Social Movements*, 3d ed. (Prospect Heights, Ill.: Waveland Press, 1994), chap. 4.

27. American Anti-Slavery Society, "Declaration of Sentiments," 343-46.

28. Ibid., 346.

29. Garrison and Garrison, eds., *William Lloyd Garrison*, 400.

30. American Anti-Slavery Society, "Declaration of Sentiments," 344.

31. Subsequent abolitionist activism would be measured against the terms of advocacy defined by the American Anti-Slavery Society at Philadelphia: Aileen S. Kraditor, *Means and Ends in American Abolitionism: Garrison and His Critics on Strategy and Tactics, 1834-1850* (New York: Pantheon Books, 1969).

32. Martin J. Medhurst, "Public Address and Significant Scholarship: Four Challenges to the Rhetorical Renaissance," *Texts in Context: Critical Dialogues on Significant Episodes in American Political Rhetoric*, ed. Michael C. Leff and Fred J. Kauffeld (Davis, Calif.: Hermagoras Press, 1989), 30 and 35-36.

33. Stephen E. Lucas, "The Renaissance of American Public Address: Text and Context in Rhetorical Criticism," *Quarterly Journal of Speech* 74 (1988): 246-52.

34. Dilip Parameshwar Gaonkar, "The Oratorical Text: The Enigma of Arrival," *Texts in Context*, ed. Leff and Kauffeld, 275.

35. For an explanation of the concept of critical or rhetorical compatibility, see Black, *Rhetorical Questions*, 14-16.

LINCOLN AMONG THE NINETEENTH-CENTURY ORATORS

Michael C. Leff

I have two purposes in writing this paper. The first and primary objective follows a conventional agenda in historical and critical studies: it is to contribute something to our understanding of Lincoln's influence on late nineteenth-century American oratory. That influence is so broad and so obvious that it would seem to command attention, but, so far as I know, no one has yet studied the matter in any detail.[1] This paper, then, attempts to help fill a gap in the historical scholarship.

Given the existing climate of academic opinion, however, this conventional objective is neither self-explanatory nor self-justifying. Traditional studies of the influence of one speaker upon others may now seem hopelessly obsolete, since they rest upon dubious assumptions about the role of agency and textuality in the rhetorical process. Mindful of this problem, I have adopted a second, broader, and more theoretical purpose, and that is to indicate how an interpretative approach grounded in speakers and their texts may yield interesting results. The success of this effort, of course, depends upon the criticism that follows, but the theoretical issues involved are complex and often treated in a rather imprecise fashion. Consequently, I want to make some general remarks about the scope of the paper and the issues it raises about agency, textuality, and the politics of interpretation.

The tendency to displace the conventional view of agent and text reflects a broader change in the conception of rhetoric itself. It is now generally agreed that rhetoric is not a property of certain kinds of texts but a process that inheres in all discursive practices and that influences social consciousness at every level of its manifestation. This stress on process encourages a corresponding de-emphasis on specific agents and the textual products that record their utterances. If rhetoric is a global, unbounded process manifested in general cultural and social practices, then attention to the particular mistakes a fragment for the phenomenon itself. It

131

follows that a critical program anchored in speakers and speeches reflects a defective and archaic rhetorical consciousness. For modernists, such as Wayne Brockreide, Samuel Becker, and Rod Hart, the individual product is not an appropriate unit of analysis since it blocks perception of the theoretical coherence needed to apprehend rhetoric *per se*.[2] For post-modernists, such as Michael McGee, Ray McKerrow, Jim Klumpp, and Thomas Hollihan, the product model sustains an ideological blindness since it blocks perception of practices that become coherent only at the level of aggregate social and cultural performance.[3]

Theoretically, I find it difficult to dispute the status of rhetoric as a global process. I do not know of any abstract principle that would distinguish some discourses as rhetorical and others as non-rhetorical. Yet, there also are some practical considerations that might encourage a restrained approach to the business of criticism. We may acknowledge, for example, that an article in *Human Communication Research* is as much a rhetorical artifact as a campaign oration. Nevertheless, this global conception should not blind us to the fact that we are dealing with very different kinds of rhetoric. The differences are obvious, and among other things, they result from the generically different conditions attached to the production of these discourses. Competent campaign orators understand, though not always at an entirely conscious level, that special resources and constraints enter into the work at hand. And so do behavioral scientists, and that is one reason their rhetoric is so far distanced from ordinary public language. Moreover, writers and speakers, even those who operate within the boundaries of orthodox science, master a genre not simply by learning abstract rules but also through the assimilation of past utterances within the genre—that is, through the interpretation and application of models or paradigms for certain kinds of discourse.[4] We choose words in order to produce an utterance suitable to a context, and the propriety of the utterance depends upon our understanding of past utterances that fall within our generic conception of the context. Thus the accumulated practices in a certain domain determine important features of the rhetoric used within it, and unless we bracket the conditions associated with the production of discourse, the view that all discourse is rhetorical expresses a theoretical truism that has limited practical value for the critic. Global conceptions of rhetoric cannot adequately account for the differing kinds of rhetoric that appear and develop in the social world.

The status of rhetorical production, however, has become a problematic issue. One of the achievements of post-modernism is to challenge the conventional assumption that authors are autonomous, seemingly isolated, agents who produce discrete texts. Instead, attention shifts to the complex network of production that superintends and shapes individual efforts and places both authors and texts within a broader ideological landscape. In a very strong version of this position, such as McKerrow's "critical rhetoric," production and performance have no status except in the work of the critic.[5] "Texts" become fragments of ideological consciousness, and their meaning remains veiled until the critic assembles the fragments and textualizes the hidden architecture that informs the whole development. On this view, the specific features of any local product are insignificant except insofar as they represent signs or symptoms of the larger discursive formations that determine an author's subjectivity. What we have traditionally accepted as texts have no integrity and should not be approached as discrete utterances.

This radical displacement of texts depends upon the assumption that agents and their rhetorical actions are captive within a totalizing structure. All local production is inert since it is drawn into the orbit of forces that it cannot alter, and hence the critic, who stands distant from the fragmentation at the surface, occupies a privileged position, since only the critic can comprehend the structure that governs the epiphenomenon of grounded utterance.

This perspective yields an extraordinarily exalted view of the critic, but it comes at the price of oversimplifying the complexity of rhetorical performance. We are asked to believe that the sense of completion, which we experience as readers and writers of texts, has no bearing on the construction of social consciousness. It is as though no circulation exists between demarcated objects and a monolithic ideological structure. Ordinary rhetors become passive receptacles, since the marks of their subjectivity and their strategic maneuvers are submerged within a larger, fixed pattern, and there is no space to re-articulate elements of that pattern into new formations. In its extreme form, then, the doctrine of fragmentation regards social and cultural constraints on production as a monolith that controls all phases of production.

Yet, even if we have cause to doubt the exaggerated claims of some variants of post-modernism, the general point about constraints on production still has real force. At the least, we need to modify the received notion that rhetors are purely strategic agents employing neutral instruments to adjust people to ideas and ideas to people. This conception ignores the placement of the agent—the socially conditioned subjectivity of anyone who enters the discursive arena. Rhetors are not only producers of discourse; they are also rhetorical products. And, as Mikhail Bakhtin has explained it, the productive process involves a complicated interaction: "The unique speech experience of each individual is shaped and developed in continuous and constant interaction with others' individual utterances. The experience can be characterized as the process of *assimilation*—more or less creative—of others words (and not the words of a language). Our speech, that is, all our utterances . . . is filled with others' words, varying degrees of otherness or of 'our-own-ness,' varying degrees of awareness and detachment. These words of others carry with them their own expression, their own evaluative tone, which we assimilate, rework, and re-accentuate."[6] Approached from this perspective, attention to the text as a complete utterance should not block perception of larger discursive developments. Instead, it should offer a way to understand the text as an assimilative social product—as something constructed through a process that submits to and reappropriates the authority of the other. The text is at once a point of local closure, an event in the ongoing development of a genre of utterance, and a productive moment in the unending process of interpreting and re-interpreting the social world.

With these general comments as background, I can now turn to the specific project at hand and define its objectives more clearly. In my earlier statement of purpose, I described my interest as an effort to understand Lincoln's influence on late nineteenth-century oratory. I used the word "oratory" rather than "rhetoric" advisedly. Though what I have to say may have some bearing on the general rhetorical ambiance of the period, my concern centers on a particular genre of discursive practice, and the question I am asking is this: How did late nineteenth-century orators use Lincoln?

The "use" of Lincoln appears in at least three related but distinguishable forms. First, orators invoke Lincoln's name—or terms, ideas, and images closely linked to his name—for some immediate strategic purpose. This is the routine and normally uninteresting use of an icon for instrumental purposes. Second, orators may imitate or re-appropriate Lincoln's textual practices in producing their own texts. At the simplest level, this involves use of Lincoln's words or phrases, but there is also a more complex process of imitating broader features of Lincoln's rhetoric through the appropriation of his stylistic or argumentative patterns. (In this respect, we might note how Lincoln used Webster's texts for just this purpose, re-working Webster's themes within his own discourse.) At a still higher level, orators might seek to capture the essence of Lincoln's rhetoric—to re-embody his rhetorical persona and the tone and spirit of his utterances. In principle, this sort of appropriation might be limited to a general but still technical exercise in composition. In practice, however, such broader imitation is associated with a third use of Lincoln—Lincoln as a moral and political paradigm. In this case, Lincoln emerges as a model for the conception and representation of the orator's own subjectivity, or through synecdoche, of some group with whom the orator identifies.

The more technical and specific of these usages—particularly those that fall into the first category—are easily isolated from the texts in which they appear, and they can be gathered together into abstract patterns that tell us something about the strategic uses of the Lincoln "ideograph."[7] But the other usages become apparent only as they are apprehended within the orator's own pattern of utterance, since they function to structure the utterance as a whole. At this level, Lincoln inhabits the text; the orator appropriates the ideograph within the metabolism of his or her own rhetorical creation, in a process that entails both a submission to Lincoln's authority and a reinterpretation and re-embodiment of that authority. Lincoln's rhetorical and ethical persona is thus recirculated through its different textual manifestations.

My interest in Lincoln's influence, then, has to do with a complex process of assimilation and adaptation, and it cannot depend upon "statistical representations" that enumerate and isolate references or bits of texts. My objective is to learn something about how Lincoln enters into the practice of oratorical rhetoric, when practice is viewed as a complete utterance or a fully realized performance within the genre. Consequently, my unit of analysis is the "representative anecdote," and I have selected three late-nineteenth-century texts that call for careful interpretation as discursive wholes.

In one sense, this orientation encourages a literary or perhaps even "formalistic" approach, but by considering a number of texts in relation to one another, I believe that we can learn something about the broader social and political issues that enter into textual practices. As we shall soon discover, the appropriation of Lincoln proves to be a complex business in which rhetorical strategies merge with ideological concerns and social myths. Consider, for example, Lincoln's status as an object of strategic use or emulation. In part, that status resulted from the texts he had produced, and late nineteenth-century orators were familiar with those texts and often referred to or invoked them. But Lincoln also had become a mythic figure, and the myth functioned as a kind of text—one that was rather diffuse and ambiguous but undoubtedly powerful, both in shaping the rhetor's attitude toward Lincoln and in structuring the use of his authority as symbolic capital. In other words, Lincoln emerged as a complex, composite figure who could be interpreted and invoked in many different ways. There were, of course, limits to the range of this activity, but they were broad, and depending on the circumstances and the interests of the orator, Lincoln could be incarnated in strikingly different guises. Thus, he became a common resource for rhetorical invention, but a pliable resource that could be constructed and adapted to fit a variety of political purposes and ideological agendas. Specific textual practices, then, should tell us something about how a key symbol of national identity could be interpreted, reinterpreted, and assimilated into the changing social and cultural milieu.

I have selected three texts for this analysis: Henry Grady's "The New South" (1886), Frederick Douglass's "Speech at the Freedman's Memorial to Lincoln" (1876), and Jane Addams's "A Modern Lear" (1894).[8] These texts are the products of influential orators, all of whom became heroic figures in their own right. Obviously, however, the three occupied very different positions in the political and social world of late nineteenth-century America. As a consequence, I believe that they offer "representative anecdotes" for differing interpretations and appropriations of Lincoln.

THE NEW SOUTH: LINCOLN AS HEROIC CAPITALIST

Delivered on December 22, 1886 before the New England Society of New York, Grady's "New South" was a classic case of rhetorical accommodation in difficult circumstances. Grady, the editor of the *Atlanta Constitution*, was the first southerner ever to address the Society, and his mission was to allay sectional tensions and encourage Northern migration to and investment in the South. Memory of the Civil War still remained a fresh and potent element in the consciousness of both sections, and real hazards attended any effort to plead for conciliation and unity. Moreover, Grady's task was complicated by the two speakers who preceded him on the podium. Both Dewitt Talmage and General Sherman rekindled partisan memories of the War, and to finish this display of rhetorical insensitivity, the orchestra in the balcony struck up "Marching Through Georgia" at the conclusion of Sherman's speech.[9]

Grady's response to the situation was tactically brilliant. Turning the apparent liability of his position as a Georgian into a positive advantage, Grady won an extraordinarily enthusiastic response from his audience, and in the ensuing weeks, the speech attracted much attention from the Northern press, almost all of it fulsome in praise of the speaker. The Southern reaction, with a few notable exceptions, was also favorable. Grady emerged as an instant national celebrity, the symbol of a new, "progressive" Southerner, who commanded respect in the North and who advanced high-minded, conciliatory principles. When he died only three years later, at the age of thirty-nine, he became the object of a heroic cult. In Atlanta, the citizens erected a monument to him, bearing an inscription that praised him as a man who "was literally loving the nation into peace." A memorial volume, edited by Joel Chandler Harris, solidified and extended Grady's reputation as a heroic agent of national conciliation and good-will.

Small wonder, then, that the "New South" became canonized as a masterpiece of eloquence. For generations, students declaimed parts of it as an exercise in elocution and citizenship; it appeared in almost all anthologies of American public address, and critics cited the speech as an example of rhetoric that rose above partisan sentiment to express a message of "justice, honesty, freedom, fairness, faith, courtesy, courage."[10]

Recent critics present a far less benign interpretation of the speech. Careful historical research, conducted by Cully Clark, Harold Davis, and others, demonstrates that Grady did not represent the South as a whole.[11] In fact, he was a spokesman for the local and special interests of the Atlanta business community and vastly (but effectively) oversimplified matters by converting its desires into a representation of the actually existing consciousness of the entire region. Moreover, for a contemporary reader, the veneer of Grady's non-partisan, inclusive rhetoric seems transparent. Although he elevates national over sectional interests, his vision of the national interest is narrowed by an Anglo-Saxon bias. Cavaliers and Puritans happily blend into a dichromatic portrait of America that excludes all other colors and textures. The treatment of the race issue is, by current standards, totally unacceptable and almost obscene; in the "New South," as in other of Grady's speeches, his rhetoric excuses an overt policy of social discrimination and disguises a covert and brutal policy of political repression. More broadly, Grady articulates a narrow version of the capitalistic ethic that has little appeal for contemporary academics.

All told, "The New South" is an ideal target for the axe of political correctness—a paradigm case of false ideology canonized as fair-minded statesmanship. Nevertheless, however we evaluate the ethical and political doctrine of the speech, it would be a mistake to dismiss it—and not just because of Grady's dexterity in responding to the immediate occasion. The speech had remarkable staying power, sustaining a favorable, if not heroic, image of the orator for several generations. That this after-dinner speech could accomplish so much for so long must surely tell us something about the rhetorical climate of the late nineteenth and early twentieth centuries and something about the way oratory could appropriate and infiltrate the ideological system.

In his careful and expert analysis of "The New South," Robert Iltis identifies Grady's key strategy as a "compensatory transformation"[12]—an effort, in Ernest Bormann's phrase, to fetch good out of evil[13] by transforming the war from a tragic conflict where one side wins and the other loses into a vehicle for redemption and rebirth for both parties. The rebirth theme echoes sentiments powerfully articulated by Lincoln in the Gettysburg Address, but Grady does not align his theme directly with Lincoln. He invokes Lincoln's symbolic authority in more subtle ways as he advances his own variant of this strategy.

The speech opens with a quotation attributed to Benjamin Hill, a fellow Southerner: "There was a South of slavery and secession—that South is dead.

There is a South of union and Freedom—that South, thank God, is living, breathing, growing every hour."[14] This image of a reborn South recurs throughout later parts of the speech, but Grady does not develop it immediately. He announces the quotation as his text for the evening, and then in keeping with the occasion, he tells some humorous stories and asks for a fair hearing.

Grady almost imperceptibly glides from this light-hearted introductory material into the body of the speech. In order to preserve "a sort of historical equilibrium," Grady notes that the Cavalier was as much present as the Puritan in the early development of the nation. But Puritan and Cavalier were merged in the storm of the "first Revolution," their blood shed in common to secure the Republic. The narrative is then pushed forward to its climactic moment: "From the union of these colonist Puritans and Cavaliers, from the straightening of their purposes and the crossing of their blood, slow perfecting through a century, came he who stands as the first typical American, the first who comprehended within himself all the strength and gentleness, all the majesty and grace of this Republic—Abraham Lincoln." Lincoln's name, withheld until the dramatic conclusion of the sentence, becomes a synecdoche for the nation, and by invoking the Union hero for this purpose, Grady surely ingratiates himself with his Northern audience. But there is more: "He was the sum of Puritan and Cavalier, for in his ardent nature were fused the virtues of both, and in the depths of his great soul the faults of both were lost. He was greater than Puritan, greater than Cavalier, in that he was American and that in his homely form were first gathered the vast and thrilling forces of his ideal government—charging it with such tremendous meaning and so elevating it above human suffering that martyrdom, though infamously aimed, came as a fitting crown to a life consecrated from the cradle to human liberty." Lincoln now becomes a Christ-figure in political form—the incarnation of perfected civic virtue, whose passion redeems liberty and opens the possibility of a reborn and reunited nation.

This invocation of Lincoln is somewhat problematic. Some Southerners could not stomach Grady's idealization of the President. Francis W. Dawson, editor of the Charleston *News and Courier*, asserted that no thoughtful Southerner would recognize "Lincoln as an ideal type. . . . He was never a typical American, unless such an American must necessarily be coarse while kindly, awkward while amiable, and weak in act while strong in word." The negative terms in this passage (awkward, coarse, weak in action) do not fit the image of the Cavalier, and Dawson suggested that Lincoln's real affinity was with "a type of new class who are rising to prominence in part of the 'New South.'"[15] Dawson, who was no friend of Grady's, had his own axe to grind, but his comments seem close to the mark. As Harold Davis has argued, it is easy to discern Lincoln's Puritan lineaments, but very difficult to cast him in the Cavalier mold.[16] A bit of perspective, then, might suggest that Grady was not yielding before Lincoln's political sanctity so much as he was using it to perfect the image of the progressive Southern capitalist.

Nevertheless, within the internal development of the speech, Grady deploys the Lincoln symbol with great economy and skill. At one stroke, he makes a gracious gesture to his audience, associates Lincoln's person with the main theme of the speech, and opens space to address this theme, first articulated by Lincoln, in his own distinctively post-bellum, Southern voice. Grady, for a variety of obvious reasons, cannot wrap himself in Lincoln's text, and that is precisely why he discovers (or manufactures) Hill's quotation as his text for the evening. What Grady can do, however, is to "textualize" Lincoln, to represent the historical figure as a symbol authorizing a progressive, Southern version of the meaning of the war and its aftermath. So, by using Lincoln without using Lincoln's words, Grady remains planted in his section even as his rhetoric stretches across the sectional divide.

After the narrative that ends with Lincoln's apotheosis, Grady proceeds to a second narrative—this one telling the story of the reborn South. He begins by depicting the Confederate soldier as he returns home after the war. The scene is one of utter desolation: "He finds his house in ruins, his farm devastated, his slaves free, his barns empty, his trade destroyed, his money worthless; his social system, feudal in its magnificence, swept away." But our Southerner is a plucky lad. Faced with this disaster, he does not whine for a moment. He rolls up his sleeves and goes to work.

The result is that restoration occurs in record time. The South has "planted" schoolhouses, "sowed" towns, "put business above politics," challenged the spinners in Massachusetts and the iron-makers in Pennsylvania, lowered interest rates, obliterated the Mason-Dixon line, achieved perfect harmony in every household, established thrift in country and city, fallen in love with work, let economy take root and spread, and produced con-artists equal to the shrewdest down-easter from Vermont. No, our Southern lad did not curse the Yankee; he was reborn as a Georgia Yankee.

This is a remarkable story—the South as Horatio Alger, the entire region yearning to become clones of Honest Abe, swallowing his values in a single gulp and striving to emulate, in economic terms, his rise from a log cabin to the White House. Starting with nothing, the South pulls itself up by its boot-straps by appropriating the virtues Lincoln had incarnated—thrift, industry, courage, self-reliance, family values, and ingenuity.

The cause of this miraculous transformation was the war, whose outcome was inevitable:

> When Lincoln signed the Emancipation Proclamation, your victory was assured; for he then committed you to the cause of human liberty, against which the arms of man cannot prevail; while those of our statesmen who trusted to make slavery the cornerstone of the Confederacy doomed us to defeat as far as they could, committing us to a cause that reason could not defend or the sword maintain in the sight of advancing civilization.

Echoing a theme embedded in the "Second Inaugural," Grady views the event as part of a divine plan: "The omniscient God held the balance of battle in his Almighty hand," and "human slavery was swept forever from American soil." The meaning of the war, however, is not to be found in the military outcome, but in its transformative power—in the recognition of progress that it forced upon Southern consciousness. "The South," Grady explains, "found her jewel in the toad's head of defeat. The shackles that held her in narrow limitations fell forever when the shackles of the negro slave were broken."

The old South was feudal and anti-capitalist; it spurned industrial development, concentrated wealth at the center, and resisted change because of its attachment to the archaic institution of slavery. The whole system collapsed with the demise of slavery, and once liberated from the peculiar institution, the social order, as though through an automatic reaction, achieved fluidity and changed to meet the demands of progress: "The New South presents a perfect democracy . . . less splendid on the surface but stronger at the core—a hundred farms for every plantation, fifty homes for every palace, and a diversified industry that meets the complex needs of this complex age."

Grady's tale of rebirth is told in dominantly economic terms, and in a spirit that captures only part of Lincoln's rhetorical vision. Although Lincoln hovers silently in the background as a symbol of the self-made man, the moral resonance of his "new birth of freedom" is lost altogether. Grady acknowledges that slavery was wrong, but for him, the matter is settled. The war brought an end to slavery, and the issue of racial equality no longer troubles him. Nor should it detain his Northern audience: "To liberty and enfranchisement is as far as law can carry the negro. The rest must be left to conscience and common sense. It should be left to those among whom his lot is cast." To a contemporary reader, these words ring hollow, but Grady knew his audience. By 1886, the capitalists of the Republican Party had abandoned the goals of Reconstruction. They were tired of the race issue, and given a reasonable pretext, they were more than willing to turn a blind eye toward it and get on with the business of economic development.

One of the defining developments of Gilded-Age America was the transformation of the Republican Party. What was once a party of reform dedicated to the principle of equality had become the party of conservative business interests dedicated to the preservation of industrial capitalism. Grady's Lincoln fits perfectly within the new scheme of things. As a Southern Democrat, Grady gains much through his identification with Lincoln, but the Lincoln he identifies is a product of a rhetorical art that highlights certain themes and commonplaces and hides others. In the end, this process of selection and composition yields a new and revised Lincoln. Removed from view are Lincoln's sense of the tragic rhythms of history, the imperfections that mark human institutions, and the struggle needed to adjust to changing circumstances.[17] Even more notably absent is the promise of equality inscribed in our founding document and against which Lincoln would measure the moral progress of the nation. Instead, we are presented with a "perfect democracy," modeled after a perfected incarnation of Anglo-Saxon virtue. In Grady's speech, the South is reborn in Lincoln's image, but it is an image transformed and gilded by the idiom of a later generation.[18]

DOUGLASS'S MEMORIAL: LINCOLN AS SELF-MADE WHITE MAN

Through a joint resolution, Congress had set aside April 14, 1876 as a national holiday. On that date, the anniversary of Lincoln's death and the freeing of the slaves in the District of Columbia, America's black citizens dedicated a monument to Lincoln's memory. A gala celebration marked the event; a march through the White House grounds was followed by an elaborate unveiling ceremony. Among those in attendance were members of Congress, the justices of the Supreme Court, and the President of the United States.[19] The task of delivering the main speech was assigned to Frederick Douglass.

In 1876, Douglass was not only America's most prominent black citizen, but also a stalwart in the Republican Party and a figure who commanded national respect. His rise to that position is, as Henry Wilson has said, "an epic which finds few to equal it in the realms of either romance or reality."[20] It is also a testament to the power of oratory as an engine of personal advancement in nineteenth-century America.

Born into slavery, Douglass somehow learned to read, and while still a boy, obtained a copy of Caleb Bingham's *Columbian Orator*. He studied the book assiduously, declaiming passages from the speeches it contained whenever he found the time and opportunity. The book deeply marked his political consciousness and offered him a vocation. After his escape from slavery, Douglass realized that vocation by enlisting as a speaker for the Garrisonian wing of the Abolitionist movement—perhaps the most truly and purely radical group in American history. He rapidly emerged as a brilliant orator and the pre-eminent

Black abolitionist, and gradually his politics shifted closer to the center of the spectrum.[21]

After the war, Douglass, like most other black Americans, became a Republican loyalist, but his prominence marked him as an especially important resource for the Party, and he functioned as an almost official liaison between the white leadership of the Party and the black community. During the election of 1872, he had used his considerable influence to help prevent black defections from Grant, and he was selected as a Republican elector from New York. In 1876, Douglass, despite earlier disappointments, still looked forward to an important office under a Republican administration, and that hope was realized the next year when Hayes appointed him Marshal for the District of Columbia.

Meanwhile, Douglass remained in demand as a speaker and earned a considerable income from his performances. No longer an agitator, Douglass often lectured on themes of general interest and while his style sometimes showed flashes of his radical and biting irony, the tone had shifted in a direction consistent with the role of a respectable citizen and senior statesman. His message fell well within the range of mainstream values. As Waldo Martin has described it, Douglass's thought entailed a distinctive but hardly radical blend of humanism, bourgeois capitalism, and Protestant morality.[22] The most popular of his lectures, "Self-Made Men," endorsed the standard set of virtues—self-reliance, independence, hard work, and courage. Douglass, of course, included black men in his list of the self-made, but his orientation was distinctively American, and for him, "Lincoln was the King of American self-made men."[23]

Douglass still remained an anomaly and an outsider. A black leader, no matter how eloquent or loyal, could not penetrate deeply into the corridors of national power or the inner circles of the Republican Party. Nevertheless, for black Americans and for some of the more liberal whites, Douglass was a heroic figure—a self-made man in the fullest sense of the term; he was to black America what Lincoln was to white America. Thus, it was altogether fitting and proper that Douglass should be invited to speak at the ceremony commemorating the Great Emancipator.

Douglass was honored and flattered to undertake the assignment, but he had misgivings about the monument itself. It depicted Lincoln standing erect, holding the Emancipation Proclamation, while a black man knelt before him, his shackles broken. Douglass thought that the freed slave ought to have been presented in "a more manly attitude."[24] And Douglass made the needed correction in his address, where he assumed the "more manly attitude." In this remarkable epideictic display, the orator rose to meet Lincoln squarely in the eye; he measured the Emancipator from within his own perspective as an emancipated black, a perspective made possible by the very fact of the memorial ceremony. To achieve this end, Douglass had to define the situation to suit his purposes. He needed to establish his primary objective not as a praise of Lincoln, but an act of memorialization accomplished by black citizens.

The speech has a clearly marked prooemium that extends for almost four pages in the printed text. Here the orator, consistent with the norms of the genre, considers the nature and significance of the epideictic situation. In keeping with the solemnity of the event and the standards of nineteenth-century oratorical prose, Douglass's language is elevated and rather florid, and the syntax sustains a formal, balanced dignity. But within this mannered and conventional format, Douglass develops an incisive and creative commentary on the key terms that might define his effort, and he proceeds to weight and align these terms in a manner that specifies the burden he assumes as a speaker.

The opening sentence is curious: "Friends and Fellow Citizens: I warmly congratulate you upon the highly interesting object which has caused you to assemble in such number and spirit as you have today." It is strange, I think, for a speaker to begin by congratulating the audience, but even stranger is the confusion about the reason for this congratulation. What does Douglass mean by "the object that has caused you to assemble?" Since he is positioned next to the monument, we might think that he is referring to the physical "object." But that hardly makes sense—one might congratulate the sculptor for his work, but certainly not the audience that comes to view it. On the other hand, "object" may refer to the "objective" or "purpose" that motivates the audience to gather. That makes more sense, but the word "object" seems a rather odd choice as a replacement for a word such as "purpose" that would make his point more clearly. Perhaps, however, the ambiguity is intentional. The physical presence of the object before the audience is palpable and might dominate its attention. Douglass may be deflecting attention from that object and what it represents in order to focus upon the less tangible purpose that informs the event.

In the next sentence, he introduces another key term: "This occasion is, in some respects, remarkable." Reference to the occasion is obviously appropriate, but why is it remarkable only "in some respects?" Douglass does not explain his qualification. Other key terms appear at the beginning of the third paragraph: "We stand to-day at the national center to perform something like a national act." Here Douglass moves toward a consideration of purpose, and the purpose is to perform an act. Again there is a strange and unexplained qualifier—it is not quite a "national" act but something like one.

To this point, and indeed through the next page of the text, we have heard nothing about Lincoln. What we have is an apparently jumbled reflection about what is or should be the significance of the event. The audience is congratulated for being present. Its presence, however, is not significant because of the object that stands before it nor because of the still unmentioned man it memorializes. Instead the focus shifts toward the occasion and the act which provides the motive for the occasion. But these crucial terms are left without definition, and they are qualified in a peculiar and unexplained fashion.

It is not until the fifth paragraph that Douglass specifies the purpose of the act: ". . . in a word we are here to express, as best we may, by appropriate forms and ceremonies, the vast, high, and preeminent services rendered by Abraham Lincoln to ourselves, to our race, to our country and the whole world." The purpose of the occasion, and hence its true significance, is to express gratitude to Lincoln. Yet, Douglass still defers comment about Lincoln, and in the next two paragraphs, which end the prooemium, he stresses the significance of the act *per se*; in other words, the act of expression is divided from and given priority over the object of the act.

Gratitude, Douglass explains, is a high and noble sentiment, and eloquent expression of it constitutes an important aspect of the life of the polity. And the present event assumes historic proportions precisely because it is the first time that black citizens have joined in "this high worship, and march in this time-honored custom. . . . It is the first time, in this form and manner, we have sought to honor an American great man. . . . I commend that fact to notice. . . . Let those who despise us, not less than those who respect us, know it and that now and here, in the spirit of liberty, loyalty and gratitude, we unite in this act of reverent homage." Finally, we can understand why the occasion is remarkable "in some respects." This is not one among the many normal epideictic ceremonies that periodically renew the nation's commitment to its heroes. Rather, it is a special event marking change and growth in the polity—it is a liminal moment, which enrolls black America into a sacred ritual. It is appropriate, therefore, to concentrate on the "here and now" aspects of the ceremony—on the performance of eloquently expressed gratitude that Douglass enacts as he speaks.

In the body of the speech, Lincoln comes into full view, but he is viewed from a distinctively black perspective, and that perspective forces Douglass to make a concession to the "truth": "Abraham Lincoln was not, in the fullest sense of the word, either our man or our model. In his interests, in his associations, in his habits of thought, and in his prejudices, he was a white man. He was preeminently the white man's President, entirely devoted to the welfare of white men." In his well exercised ironic voice, Douglass has revealed the paradox central to his own rhetorical mission. This paradox explains the complex meta-discourse of the introduction, which separates the act from the object, and we now know why the act is only "somehow" national. The black orator is asked to praise someone who is not consubstantial with him, who is not, "in fullest sense," his man or his model. He must perform the rite of citizenship by honoring someone who did not fully recognize blacks as citizens.

This paradox prevents Douglass from relying entirely upon the normal conventions of the genre. He must do some ground-breaking rhetorical work and construct a discourse appropriate to the unique requirements of an unprecedented situation. Consequently, his task involves articulating a black perspective that can allow him to express gratitude to a preeminent American who was preeminently the white man's president.

The perspective that Douglass constructs depends upon an enlarged view of Lincoln as an agent constrained by historical circumstances. In one sense, circumstances were moving in a progressive direction as the "nature of things" conspired to eliminate slavery. Lincoln stood at the head of that movement, was swept up by it, and though he "loved Caesar less than Rome" and the Union more than "our freedom," it was under his rule that blacks were raised from slavery to "liberty and manhood." Obviously, however, if judged in terms of this forward thrust of history, Lincoln deserved no gratitude; he was merely an instrument of fate and necessity—his own agency at best had no effect and at worst dragged futilely against the tide of progress.

Douglass, however, understood that history does not flow in a single, unimpeded direction. If there were forward-moving forces at Lincoln's back, there were also serious obstacles and counter-forces that he had to face. Lincoln was necessarily constrained, both as a man and as a president, by these negative forces. A just assessment of him, therefore, required a general view of his character and action within the swirl of circumstances that engulfed him.

Even during the War, Douglass asserts, blacks were able to achieve this enlarged perspective. They retained faith in Lincoln, although that faith was often "taxed and strained to the uttermost." "We were able to take a comprehensive view of Abraham Lincoln, and to make reasonable allowance for the circumstances of his position." He was not judged by "stray utterances," or "isolated facts torn from their connection," or by "partial and imperfect glimpses," but by "a broad survey, in the light of the stern logic of great events, and in view of that 'divinity which shapes our ends, rough hew them how we will.' We came to the conclusion that the hour and man of redemption had somehow met in Abraham Lincoln."

This view of Lincoln, attributed to the contemporary observer of his actions and words, is anchored in faith and still portrays the man in a rather passive position. As Douglass shifts to the present, he can assume an even broader perspective, since the passage of time allows for a better reasoned and more comprehensive judgment. "Looking back" to Lincoln's time and situation, Douglass now acknowledges that only a white man's president could have emancipated the slave. Lincoln's mission was to save the country from disunion and to free it "from the sin of slavery." He could not have achieved the second goal unless he gave priority to the first. An abolitionist position at the start of the war would have doomed the Union and left the Confederate slave system intact. The work had to be done by someone who hated slavery but who placed the Union ahead of abolition, and once emancipation became politically feasible, Lincoln seized the opportunity and moved ahead as quickly as prudence allowed. These reflections lead to a balanced judgment: "Viewed from the genuine abolition ground, Mr. Lincoln seemed tardy, cold, dull, and indifferent; but measuring him by the sentiment of the country, a sentiment, he was bound as a statesman to consult, he was swift, zealous, radical, and determined."

Thus, Douglass has articulated an enlarged view of his subject. Blacks can express gratitude to Lincoln for doing what was possible under the circumstances; he was not their man in the full sense, but he was well fitted to serve as the instrument of their liberation. Through the exercise of mature judgment, black citizen's can assess Lincoln for what he was; they can honor him without losing their identity; as befits the citizens of a Republic, they can appreciate a president "entirely devoted to the white man" without sacrificing their own integrity.

Having cleared the ground for a more conventional assessment of Lincoln, Douglass inquires into the reason for Lincoln's greatness of character. Predictably enough, that reason consists in Lincoln's status as a self-made man: "Born and reared among the lowly; a stranger to wealth and luxury; compelled from tender youth to sturdy manhood to grapple single-handed with the flintiest hardships of life, he grew strong in the manly and heroic qualities to which he was called by the votes of his countrymen." Faced with the crisis of secession, Lincoln's patrician predecessor, James Buchanan, had flinched and denied to the government "the right of self-preservation—a right that belongs to the meanest insect." Lincoln, the plebeian, responded with a strength born of common sense and hardened "in the school of adversity." He did not hesitate or falter, but remained clear, calm, and brave in adhering to his duty. His self-made character, then, was suited to the heroic task of preserving the union and freedom.

Douglass, of course, was conscious of his own status as self-made hero— indeed, it was an image that he had cultivated for himself. Anything he said about self-made men had at least some self-referential force, and the connection between Douglass's praise of Lincoln and Douglass's own person must have been obvious. But, I believe that the rhetoric of the speech involved another, rather more subtle aspect of this connection. The rhetorical action that reconstructed the "King of American self-made men" also worked to construct a powerful persona for the rhetor. Douglass defined his rhetorical problem as one that required opening new ground in the effort to locate a voice for a black expression of gratitude. As he engaged this problem, Douglass took the measure of his subject in a spirit of independent but balanced and mature judgment, and in the process, he enacted a model of responsible citizenship based upon an enlarged perspective. Moreover, the model was one of Douglass's own making; he had constructed himself through the heroic achievement of a self-made rhetoric. He had paid homage to Lincoln without either bowing before the white man's president or refusing to acknowledge gratitude to the man and his achievements.

After a brief and rather conventional passage concerning Lincoln's martyrdom, Douglass concludes with a peroration compressed into a single paragraph. This short section so effectively rounds out the speech that I need to quote it in its entirely:

> Fellow-citizens, I end as I began with congratulations. We have done a good work for our race to-day. In doing honor to the memory of our friend and liberator we have been doing highest honor to ourselves and to those who come after us. We have been attaching to ourselves a name imperishable and immortal; we have also been defending ourselves from a blighting scandal. When now it shall be said that the colored man is soulless, that he has no appreciation of benefits or benefactors; when the foul reproach of ingratitude is hurled at us, and it is attempted to scourge us beyond the range of human brotherhood, we may calmly point to the monument we have erected to the memory of Abraham Lincoln.

Significantly, Douglass turns our attention back to the occasion and the event. In effect, he now congratulates himself for a job well done. His speech has accomplished its goal, and by finding a rhetoric to express gratitude to Lincoln, Douglass has initiated the black citizen into a national rite. Dedicated through these words, the monument stands as testimony to a new and more equal attachment between Lincoln and the black American citizen.

JANE ADDAMS AND LINCOLN AS PRUDENTIAL HERO

In her autobiography, *Twenty Years at Hull House*, Jane Addams reflected about an event that had occurred during the turbulent summer of 1894, when the Pullman strike had turned antagonisms between labor and capital into overt violence and Chicago seemed on the verge of chaos. She wrote: "I walked the wearisome way from Hull-House to Lincoln Park—for no cars were running regularly at that moment of sympathetic strike—in order to look at and gain magnanimous counsel, if I might, from the marvelous St. Gaudens statue which had but recently been placed at the entrance of the park. Some of Lincoln's immortal words were cut into stone at his feet, and never did a distracted town more sorely need the healing of 'with charity toward all' than did Chicago at that moment."[25] Inspired by this silent consultation, Addams composed a speech, first delivered at the Chicago Women's Club in August, 1894, designed to apply Lincoln's sensibilities to the industrial crisis of her time.[26]

But if Lincoln inspired the speech, its structure came from another source. As its title—"A Modern Lear"—suggests, the speech was based upon an analogy between the Pullman strike and Shakespeare's tragedy. That strike, Addams argued, represented a crisis in industrial relations analogous to the crisis in family relations that unfolded in *King Lear*. "Historically considered, the relation of Lear to his children was archaic and barbaric, holding in it merely the beginnings of a family life, since developed. We may in later years learn to look back upon the industrial relationships in which we are now placed as quite as incomprehensible and selfish, quite as barbaric and undeveloped, as was the family relationship between Lear and his daughters."

In the fully developed analogy, Pullman is to his workers as Lear is to Cordelia. All of the parties in both tragedies are culpable, for all of them act out of narrow self-interest and fail to acknowledge the higher claims of the family bond or social justice. Yet, for Addams, the father-figures must assume the greater share of blame. Both Lear and Pullman do not recognize changing circumstances and refuse to accept, in the one case, the growth of a child to maturity, and in the other, the maturation of the workers' movement. Just as Lear cannot understand his daughter's need to assert independence, so Pullman turns a deaf ear to his employees when, as the demands of an industrial age require, they attempt to speak in a collective voice. The indulgent parent and the indulgent employer both respond with anger to what they can only interpret as ingratitude, and their inability to adjust to change becomes the mainspring of the tragedy.

As the speech proceeds, Addams develops an unobtrusive and paradoxical comparison between Pullman and Lincoln. In some respects, Pullman is just like Lincoln. He is a man of moral integrity who advocates and practices the virtues Lincoln had embodied—individualism, self-reliance, thrift, and hard work. These were virtues Pullman has learned in his youth—in the age of Lincoln—and moved by the spirit of philanthropy, Pullman had built a model city in order to instill the same virtues in his workers. Yet, in adhering to the letter of the tradition, Pullman has killed its spirit. Isolated by his individualism and philanthropic self-righteousness, Pullman loses contact with his workers and overlooks the changing circumstances that affect their lives. He neglects the cardinal principle of a social ethic—that values must be adjusted as the society evolves: "The virtues of one generation are not sufficient for the next. . . . Of the virtues received from our fathers we can afford to lose none. . . . But to preserve those is not enough. A task is laid out upon each generation to enlarge their application, to ennoble their conception, and above all, to apply and adapt them to the peculiar problems presented to it for solution."

Pullman, like Lear, failed to respond to social reality as he enacted the role of a self-indulgent parent, and in this respect, unlike Lincoln, he tried to rule for and not with the people: "Modern philanthropists need to remind themselves of the old definition of greatness: that it consists in the possession of the largest share of common human qualities and experiences, not in the acquirements of peculiarities and excessive virtues. Popular opinion calls him the greatest of Americans who gathered together the largest amount of American experience" and who strove to retain and represent the common people's "thoughts and feelings."

This oblique reference to Lincoln marks his first appearance in the text, and his name does not appear until the conclusion. Nevertheless, Lincoln's presence seems to pervade the text and to establish a basis for Addams's attitude toward the Pullman strike. Ironically, on her view, the moral distance between Lincoln and George Pullman consists precisely in Pullman's adherence to Lincoln's own explicit values. Inflexibly rooting his thought in the past, Pullman subverts tradition, since he treats it as a static code rather than as something that must be recovered and renewed in an interaction between past and present. The mere repetition of Lincoln's words or the unmodified re-enactment of his values subverts tradition because those words and values must come to life within the flux of changing circumstances. Implicitly, then, Addams establishes a dialogical relationship with Lincoln, and her rhetorical effort is to reach beyond a literal understanding of his words in order to comprehend the living spirit they represent. This attitude allows her to appropriate Lincoln's voice even as she addresses problems he could not have conceived, and in the process, she can revise some of his values. For Addams, Lincoln's authority is not something to be reproduced but to be imitated and emulated in new forms.

As she draws to her conclusion, Addams becomes more explicit about the connection between Lincoln's authority and social ethics. Lincoln emerges as the model for a social ethic based upon consent—an ethic that Pullman violated because his model city was run without the consent of "the men who were living in it." By contrast:

The man who insists upon consent, who moves with the people, is bound to consult the feasible right as well as the absolute right. He is often obliged to attain only Mr. Lincoln's "best possible," and often have the sickening scene of compromising his best convictions. He has to move along with those whom he rules toward a goal that neither he nor they see very clearly till they come to it. He has to discover what the people really want, and then provide "the channels in which the growing moral force of their lives shall flow." What he does attain, however, is not the result of his individual striving, as a solitary mountain climber beyond the sight of the valley multitude, but it is underpinned and upheld by the sentiments and aspirations of many others. Progress has been slower perpendicularly, but imcomparably greater because lateral.

A good many things might be said about this passage, for it implies a rather interesting theory of leadership in a democratic society and perhaps even an ethic for democratic political rhetoric. For present purposes, however, I want to focus more narrowly upon the way that passage coherently rounds out Addams's rhetorical performance—to stress the symmetry between her interpretation of Lincoln's authority as a political leader and her appropriation of that authority for her own rhetorical purposes. That authority, for Addams, arises from Lincoln's capacity to restrain his own views of the absolute right and to work within the limitations of the feasible right as he adjusts to the diversity of popular opinion. His leadership, then, is situated within historical circumstance and remains fluid. Likewise, Addams invokes Lincoln not as a fixed referent for establishing social and political values, but as a model of prudential deliberation—his is a voice that must be modulated as it is applied to differing circumstances. Her speech is at one and the same time an interpretation and an application of Lincoln's political and ethical principles, and these principles remain true to their source precisely because they are modified to meet a new situation.

Conclusion

Grady, Douglass, and Addams interpret and invoke Lincoln's authority in strikingly different ways. When taken together, their texts suggest something about the fluidity of Lincoln's influence in late nineteenth-century oratory and about the range of rhetorical and ideological purposes to which it could be accommodated. Nevertheless, one common concern does seem to emerge in all three cases—a concern that reflects the effort to deal with continuity and change in post-Civil War America. All of our rhetors are sensitive to the problem of placing new circumstances within a historical context, and all three use Lincoln as a bench-mark for charting the present in relation to the past.

Grady's "The New South" presents Lincoln as fixed point of reference dividing the nation's history into two distinct compartments. The ante-bellum phase of this history culminates with Lincoln's emergence as an ideal American who represents a blend of "cavalier" and "puritan" strands in the national character. The Civil War and Lincoln's martyrdom become the tragic redemption needed to destroy slavery in the South and remove the one obstacle to national unity. In the post-bellum phase of this history, Grady tells us of a South reborn in the spirit of capitalism and reorganized into a "perfect democracy." In this sweeping meta-narrative, history moves inexorably toward the goal of Anglo-Saxon perfection, and Lincoln becomes a static, uncomplicated symbol of its realization. Grady explicitly stresses Lincoln's role as the Great Emancipator and savior of the union, and implicitly he draws upon Lincoln's image as a self-made man. These commonplaces associated with Lincoln become Grady's vehicle for generating a rhetoric of sectional harmony and for deflecting attention from the race problem; Lincoln, in short, functions as a symbol for reconciliation between North and South in the spirit of capitalistic enterprise.

Douglass presents a more complex attitude toward Lincoln and his place in history. For Douglass, the Civil War and emancipation mark a starting point and not a culmination, and Douglass cannot accept the myth of Lincoln as the Great Emancipator. Intent upon achieving the assimilation of African Americans through self-assertion,[27] Douglass confronts a double burden when he memorializes Lincoln. He must express gratitude while he also preserves his own distinctive and independent position as an African American. To meet this burden, Douglass develops a complex, self-reflexive view of history that positions both Lincoln and Douglass himself within an evolving and changing historical context. Adopting a broad perspective, Douglass acknowledges that, in the passage of time, his assessment of the man must change. As an abolitionist before and during the war, Douglass had found Lincoln tardy and reticent, but from his current, ante-bellum position, he recognizes that Lincoln's commitments and priorities were necessary in order to make emancipation possible. This reflective stance allows Douglass to celebrate Lincoln as a symbol of white American history, but leaves space for him to articulate an African American view of that history. The speech becomes a vehicle for placing the African American citizen within the history of polity, since as the speaker positions himself in relation to his subject, he becomes an active agent in shaping and reconfiguring that history. Thus, it aptly serves the purpose of assimilation through self-assertion.

Despite the many differences between Grady and Douglass, the two shared a commitment to the individualistic values of nineteenth-century capitalism, and both celebrated Lincoln as a self-made man who embodied those values. For Jane

Addams, however, the tradition of individualism needed modification to meet the new conditions of an industrialized nation. Unlike her more radical contemporaries, however, Addams did not seek to uproot those values and break entirely from tradition. Instead, she sought a means to accommodate older values so that they could enter into a more cooperative and socially sensitive ethic. In "A Modern Lear," Addams uses Lincoln's authority as a bridge between traditional principles and a new social consciousness. Setting aside some of Lincoln's explicit views on ethical and economic issues, she stresses his pragmatism and his commitment to government by consent of the people. Thus, on her interpretation, Lincoln stands as a model of flexible, democratic leadership; his great virtue is his commitment to the "feasible right"—his willingness to bend principles to meet circumstances and attune them to public sentiment. Addams, then, renders Lincoln as the embodiment of a mobile, dynamic tradition, and in this hermeneutic key, his words are to be understood and applied in keeping with the ongoing history of the society.

If this summary indicates that each of our rhetors connects past and present through Lincoln, it also highlights the fundamental differences in their conceptions of history, politics, and ethics. Lincoln is not simply an influence on these orators; he is constructed by them, in part to serve their immediate rhetorical purposes, but also to help them account for and justify their own place in history. In an important sense, then, my study has not discovered much about Lincoln's "influence," in the ordinary sense of the term, since it has led to a consideration of how Lincoln was "used" by people engaged in their own rhetorical business. This use proves complex, since it blends historical understanding and rhetorical performance into a single process. This process, of course, is influenced by prevailing ideologies, and it operates within a common fund of lore about Lincoln. But the lore is not inert, and ideologies do not absolutely dictate how it is applied. Lincoln, in fact, exerts an influence that reflects the way he is constructed, and this construction occurs continuously and variously in the discourse of the period. By isolating specific passages about Lincoln from many texts and recombining them into ideological formations, we may learn something about the spoken and unspoken assumptions that constituted the temper of the time. But if we are to understand how that temper was developed, ordered, and reordered, we need to look at whole utterances and attempt to fathom the complexity of the interpretative and productive processes that enter into the rhetorical act.

NOTES

1. Merrill Peterson's recent book, *Lincoln in American Memory* (New York: Oxford University Press, 1994), offers a detailed and expert account of Lincoln's place in American thought. Peterson's study draws much from oratory and related genres and provides a useful frame for inquiry into Lincoln's influence on oratorical practice. Especially notable is Peterson's identification of five main themes that emerged in the memorialization of Lincoln: "Lincoln as Savior of the Union, Great Emancipator, Man of the People, the First American, and the Self-made man." These themes, Peterson argues, are "the building blocks of the Lincoln image" (27). The research for this paper, and most of its composition, was completed before publication of Peterson's book, but in what follows, the themes he identifies appear quite clearly. In contrast to Peterson, my interest centers on how Lincoln was interpreted and used in rhetorical production rather than on an understanding of Lincoln's place in American political and social history.

2. Wayne Brockreide, "Trends in the Study of Rhetoric: Toward a Blending of Criticism and Science," in *The Prospect of Rhetoric*, eds. Lloyd Bitzer and Edwin Black (Englewood Heights, N.J.: Prentice Hall, 1971), 123-39; Samuel Becker, "Rhetorical Studies for the Contemporary World," in ibid., 21-43; Roderick Hart, "Contemporary Scholarship in Public Address: A Research Editorial," *Western Journal of Speech Communication* 50 (1986): 283-95, and "Theory-Building and Rhetorical Criticism: An Informal Statement of Opinion," *Central States Speech Journal* 27 (1976): 70-77.

3. Michael McGee, "Text, Context, and the Fragmentation of Contemporary Culture," *Western Journal of Speech Communication* 54 (1990): 274-89; Raymie McKerrow, "Critical Rhetoric; Theory and Praxis," *Communication Monographs* 56 (1989): 91-111; James Klumpp and Thomas Hollihan, "Rhetorical Criticism as Moral Action," *Quarterly Journal of Speech* 74 (1989): 84-96.

4. On this point, see M. M. Bakhtin, "The Problem of Speech Genres," in *Speech Genres and Other Late Essay*, trans. Vern W. McGee (Austin: University of Texas Press, 1986), 78-91.

5. McKerrow, "Critical Rhetoric."

6. Bakhtin, 89.

7. Michael McGee, "The 'Ideograph': A Link between Rhetoric and Ideology," *Quarterly Journal of Speech* 66 (1980): 1-16. As McGee conceives the "ideograph" it is a condensation symbol which triggers powerful ideological and affective responses within a given culture. His ideographs are abstract terms such as "justice," "equality," and "rule of law," and I am here expanding McGee's notion to include a person, such as Lincoln, who commands great respect and authority and becomes connected intimately with certain ideologies.

8. For Grady's speech, I use the text printed in Ronald Reid, ed. *American Rhetorical Discourse*, 2d ed. (Prospect Heights, Ill.: Waveland Press, 1995), 551-59; For Addams's speech, I use the text in Graham R. Taylor, ed. *Satellite Cities* (New York: Appleton, 1915), 68-88; And for Douglass, I use the text printed in Douglass's autobiography, *The Life and Times of Frederick Douglass* (1892; reprint, New York: Macmillan, 1962), 481-93.

9. The circumstances surrounding this speech are reported in Raymond B. Nixon, *Henry W. Grady: Spokesman of the New South* (New York: Alfred Knopf, 1943), 243-44.

10. Charles F. Lindsley, "Henry Woodfin Grady, Orator," *Quarterly Journal of Speech* 6 (1920): 33.

11. Harold Davis, *Henry Grady's New South* (Tuscaloosa: University of Alabama, 1990), and E. Culpepper Clark, "Henry Grady's New South: A Rebuttal from Charleston," *Southern Communication Journal* 41 (1976): 346-58.

12. Robert Iltis, "Textual Dynamics of the 'New South,'" *Communication Studies* 43 (1992): 29-41.

13. Ernest Bormann, "Fetching Good out of Evil: A Rhetorical Use of Calamity," *Quarterly Journal of Speech* 63 (1977): 130-39.

14. The status of this quotation from Hill is not clear. There is no record of a speech by him at Tammany Hall in 1866. Hill did address the Young Men's Democratic Union in New York City two years later, and Raymond Nixon (*Henry W. Grady: Spokesman of the New South*, 245) reports that this speech contains sentiments close to those expressed in the quotation Grady attributes to Hill, but nowhere does the exact wording appear in the printed version of Hill's speech. In other words, Grady's text is, at least in some part, something that Grady manufactured himself.

15. The quotations from Dawson are taken from Clark, "Henry Grady's New South," 352.

16. Davis, *Henry Grady's New South*, 178.

17. Compare the image of Lincoln that emerges in Grady's speech to the one that appears in, for example, Garry Wills, *Lincoln at Gettysburg: Words that Remade America* (New York: Simon and Schuster, 1992).

18. Lincoln appears prominently in the peroration of the speech. As he concludes, Grady appropriates Lincoln's language, and from his position as a Southerner, Grady says that he speaks from "consecrated" ground—ground "hallowed" by the blood shed by both Northern and Southern soldiers. The words "hallowed" and "consecrated" obviously echo the Gettysburg Address and help in the effort to appeal for sectional unity. The images and strategies at work in the concluding paragraphs of the speech are interesting and complex, but they do not add much of consequence to my interpretation of the speech, and they already have been treated in detail by Iltis (37-39). Grady also conjures the ghost of Lincoln as he makes a last plea for Northern tolerance: "Will she [New England] make the vision of a restored and happy people, which gathered above the couch of your dying captain, filling his heart with grace, touching his lips with praise and glorifying his path to the grave; will she make this vision on which the last sight of an expiring soul breathed a benediction, a cheat and delusion?" This appeal, while perhaps appropriate at the end of the speech, is hardly subtle and requires little comment.

19. For an account of the event, see Benjamin Quarles, *Frederick Douglass* (Washington, D.C.: Associated Publishers, 1968), 276.

20. Henry Wilson, *History of the Rise and Fall of the Slave Power in America* (Boston: Houghton, Mifflin, 1872), 1:500; quoted in Waldo Martin, *The Mind of Frederick Douglass* (Chapel Hill: University of North Carolina, 1984), 272.

21. The life and career of Douglass is presented in three autobiographic books: *Narrative of the Life of Frederick Douglass, an American Slave* (1845), *My Bondage and My Freedom* (1855), and *Life and Times of Frederick Douglass, Written by Himself* (1881, with a revised edition in 1892). In addition to the biography by Benjamin Quarles, there is now William McFeely, *Frederick Douglass* (New York: Norton, 1991).

22. Martin, *The Mind of Frederick Douglass*, passim; Martin's assessment of Douglass's thought is briefly characterized in the Preface to the book, ix-x.

23. Ibid., 260.

24. Quarles, 277.

25. Jane Addams, *Twenty Years at Hull House* (New York: Signet, 1960), 38-39.

26. After delivering the speech in Chicago, Addams also presented it in Boston at the Twentieth Century Club and in other places. She submitted a version of the text for publication in several periodicals, but none would accept it. The speech was first published as an article, entitled "A Modern Lear," in *Survey*, 29 (2 November 1912): 131-37. See Alvin Davis, *Jane Addams: An American Heroine* (New York: Oxford University Press, 1973), 113-14. To my knowledge, there is no detailed critique of the work, but Ray Ginger, *Altgeld's America: Chicago from 1892-1905* (New York: Marcus Weiner, 1986), 164-67, offers an interesting, brief commentary and assessment.

27. This characterization of Douglass's objectives comes from W. E. B. DuBois, who describes Douglass's program as "ultimate assimilation through self-assertion." *Souls of the Black Folk* (New York: Bantam, 1989), 35.

Anxious Oratory—Anxious Criticism: The Substance of Deferral and the Deferral of Substance

Maurice Charland

Professor Leff is a perceptive and judicious critic. His rendering of invocations of Abraham Lincoln is instructive, telling us a great deal about the situations and stakes facing Grady, Douglass, and Addams. Furthermore, we can appreciate the innovative character of his study of the construction of an American folk hero in America's oratory. Nevertheless, there is something disconcerting in the way he locates his study within certain theoretical and ontological debates. In particular, Leff presents this analysis as a challenge to what he perceives to be the excesses of postmodern premises. At the same time, however, he acknowledges that the criticism of public oratory has often been based on a number of dubious assumptions that he wishes to avoid. As such, one might say Leff is seeking to be prudently responsive to postmodern critics. But the *ethos* of his analysis, and indeed of his orators and their Mr. Lincoln, requires detailed examination.

Leff wants to defend the practice of criticizing individual texts. He asserts that the text is a point of "local closure" and that the feeling of completion that we experience in the face of oratory has political consequences. With this I have no major quarrel. But why does he feel compelled to assert this? By his own account, he does so because certain postmodern critics have dismissed agency and reduced particular texts to fragments. In Leff's words, postmodern theorists, such as Raymie McKerrow and Michael McGee, favor "a radical displacement of texts" because "agents and their rhetorical actions are captive within a totalizing structure."[1] Consequently, the task of political intervention would fall upon the critic, who would engage in a recombinatory praxis. For Leff, such a view is flawed, an "oversimplification" that unduly exalts the critic. Leff wants us, instead, to think of the rhetor as a contingent agent, who appropriates received cultural materials.

Leff's account of postmodern theory is problematic, however. Postmodern thought does not hold that agents and their utterances are but moments within a determining totality. Postmodern thought is precisely characterized by its refusal of "totality" as a valid category. Rather, certain strains of modern thought, including "vulgar" Marxism or the critical theory of Theodor Adorno hold that the totality negates freedom and the power of human invention in history. While "radical fragmentation" is certainly a postmodern notion, it does not imply that the rhetor is "an utterly passive receptacle." Indeed, the postmodern critique might well be sympathetic to Leff's use of Mikhail Bakhtin and assertion that "rhetors are not only producers of discourse; they are also rhetorical products." Furthermore, the suggestion that Lincoln is a rhetorical construct is not inconsistent with postmodern critical practices. But does this make Leff an unwitting postmodernist, misrecognizing his opponents and allies? Not exactly, for despite his gestures towards Bakhtin's statement that "our speech . . . is filled with others' words" his analysis still betrays a romantic vision of agency.

Postmodern theory does not evacuate human freedom so much as dissolve a unitary view of the human subject. Radical fragmentation would suggest either that human agents, such as Lincoln, Grady, Douglass, and Addams, are not coherent, lacking an essence or substance; or if such coherent subjectivities once existed, they no longer do. The same would be said for rhetorical texts themselves. Leff's analysis hints at the same insight: Lincoln, even in the nineteenth century, had become an "ideograph" whose usage was imbricated in the post-Civil War political order even while its meaning was open to various constructions.[2] The real Lincoln is not accessible to rhetorical audiences and critics (or historians for that matter); what are accessible are figurings of Lincoln. Audiences and critics encounter fragments, often strategically deployed to provide, as Leff points out, a local sense of closure.

Postmodern theory goes further than Leff, not by stressing determinants but by highlighting radical indeterminacy. We do not share one Lincoln; we know several and they are the product of the figurings of Grady, Douglass, Addams, and innumerable others. More precisely, our Lincoln is an often incoherent composite of these figurings that seems to acquire a coherence and form as portions of it are called to our attention, even as fragmentation is always threatening. Like the solidity of the glow of a fluorescent lamp, the meaning of "Lincoln" is an effect of the fixing of our attention that blinds us to an ever present instability. My guess is that Leff's amicable protagonists, McGee and McKerrow, would respond to his paper by speaking to the conditions of reception. Rhetorical audiences would not interpret texts as coherent unities; they would attend to fragments, juxtaposed in the moment of reception to other fragments circulating in their culture. Or, more generously, if unities existed in the previous century, they certainly do not now. Oratory would be an archaic form, displaced by the sound bite and the headline. In a *tu quoque*, they might even assert that in seeking to recover the agent, Leff is the one exalting the critic's role. After all, the critic's knowledge and status requires an initial gesture of deferral to the authority of orator and text.

Were I to follow McGee and McKerrow's lead, I would enquire into the kind of knowledge Leff's paper produces. McGee is convincing when he claims that the analysis of single texts can produce only very limited knowledge about historical forces and events.[3] Leff's criticism, by its very scope, will not tell us why the South developed as it did after the Civil War nor how liberated slaves lived their proclaimed freedom. Thus, McGee might challenge Leff to demonstrate the correspondence between the critic's sense of completion and that of the social agent in history. McGee might want Leff to map the discursive universe into which these speeches were inserted. Finally, McGee might ask whether a speech such as Grady's, as well received as it was, was of historical consequence.

Leff might respond in a number of ways, but I suspect, especially from his introductory remarks, that he would claim that his goal is more modest than McGee would like. Leff's concern is with texts and these are furthermore set in the nineteenth century, before the fragmentation brought about by communication technologies and the enfranchisement of alternative voices and cultural formations. However, the question of fragmentation and indeterminacy remains, for beyond the dispersal of formations of reception there is a lack of fullness in the texts themselves.

What exactly is being studied here? And what kind of knowledge is being produced? Is the ultimate focus Lincoln, the rhetorical figure of invocation, or the oratory of Grady, Douglass, and Addams? These questions have no clear answer because Leff in large measure enacts, albeit not self-reflexively, McGee's recommended *praxis*. Invocations of Lincoln serve as an organizing alibi that underwrites the presentation of discrete texts whose juxtaposition requires the critical act to become meaningful. Granted, we can identify commonalities between the texts Leff considers. They are all epideictic; they all are concerned with the construction of *ethos*; and they share certain themes. Nevertheless, together they neither represent nor constitute an object with immanent integrity. As such, Leff's analysis suffers from an excess of coherence, for it does not address the incoherences both within and between the texts he considers.

Curiously, the Civil War presents both Grady and Douglass with a common predicament. There are no pre-existing speaking positions that they can comfortably occupy. In Grady's case, the old South no longer exists, the old hegemonic block has been defeated, and his oration follows General Sherman's and the band's rendering of "Marching through Georgia." As such, anxiety must inhere to the obligation to speak. Indeed, Grady's introductory remarks as cited by Leff express a rhetorical death wish:

that if, when I raise my provincial voice in this ancient and august presence, I could find courage for no more than the opening sentence, it would be well if, in that sentence, I had met in a rough sense my obligation as a guest, and had perished, so to speak, with courtesy on my lips and grace in my heart.[4]

For Grady to speak, he must repress the historical memory of the war, for his *ethos* could not withstand its presencing. And yet, the war cannot be simply erased or forgotten, for its outcome is constitutive of the rhetorical situation in which Grady finds himself. As such, Grady can only speak as a citizen by neutralizing the war's significance even while acknowledging its presence. Grady does so by inducing his audience to forget the past and in so doing forget what the South and he might be. The military installation of a reconstructed union and the myth of martyrdom make of Lincoln the uncontestable ideograph of ethical value, and Grady refills his and his region's canceled *ethos* by invoking a Lincoln tolerable to his condition. Out of the numerous narratives and textual fragments that orbit "Lincoln" as ideograph, Grady relays those that present Lincoln as a moment of historical rupture. As such, Lincoln and the reborn South are radically free from their past. Grady, the New South, and Lincoln are figured as consubstantial in that history cannot define them. Oddly, though, if Lincoln is the first American, Grady's identity and the *raison d'être* of his speech arise from what America negated, the South. The New South must paradoxically affirm and deny its difference from the North lest it cease to exist. Indeed, Grady can speak only within this tension. He is both Southerner and not Southerner, from a South whose identity is constituted through the act of denying its Southern essence.

A similar pattern can be found in Frederick Douglass's 1876 Lincoln Park address. Just as Grady was confronted with the dilemma of speaking as a citizen of the nation that had conquered him, Douglass was to speak as a citizen of a country that had once sanctioned his enslavement, and from which freedom was given rather than wrested. The monument that is being dedicated well captures the paradox of his speaking position: Lincoln stands tall, while the slave kneels before him even while being freed. The slave's traditions and historical memories are not those of the Republic; and the *ethos* of the Union's hero cannot easily be appropriated by Douglass and those for whom he speaks. The freed slave must stand, but as yet has only the title and not the substance of citizenship. Leff well appreciates this when he observes that Douglass cannot assert his consubstantiality with Lincoln. His stance must be one of deference.

Lincoln is the repository of *ethos* in this new order, and all its citizens are called to awe before him. They are all constituted in their deferential relation to him as national "father." And yet, Lincoln can at best be stepfather to Douglass's people; Lincoln was the white man's president. Thus Douglass's deference to Lincoln cannot but remain marked by difference, and this difference underlies the anxiety of his address, the trace of which can be seen in his repeated deferral of the act of praising the slain president. Although ultimately praised, Lincoln remains marked as other, and the consubstantiality of citizenship must be attained through identification with historical and ethical progress itself. Douglass and Lincoln find common citizenship only as they are both de-centered, deferring to historical circumstances and forces.

A proper appreciation of Leff's critical practice requires that attention be paid to a third text. I am not referring to Jane Addams's "A Modern Lear," which Leff has treated in less detail and which is in many respects quite unlike the two others. Rather our third text is Leff's essay itself. Leff's commentary also begins with an awkward moment. Leff expresses anxiety as to his speaking position. The role of the critic has been radically challenged, the integrity of the oratorical text has been called into doubt, and public address studies have in some accounts suffered a death. He, like Grady and Douglass, struggles with finding a place from which to speak, and his strategy is similar to theirs. Leff invokes Lincoln, whose *ethos* assures the value of his criticism. Public address critics, at least of the usual sort, acquire their *ethos* in an act of deferral. The authority of the critic is tributary of the substance of orators and oratory and to the critic's claim of privileged method. Such is Leff's stance in this case, except that it is not to a single text that he defers, but to a set of texts that themselves acquire their value in their deferral to Lincoln.

Leff's criticism thus inhabits a set of curious paradoxes. Writing in good faith, Leff acknowledges that an essentialist view of the orator is problematical. In focusing upon invocations of Lincoln, and in demonstrating that these need not be consistent, Leff de-essentializes Lincoln. The rhetorical figure of invocation, as employed by Grady, Douglass, and Addams, serves to re-figure the dead president. Nevertheless, while Leff implicitly renders problematical Lincoln's persona, he maintains and indeed depends upon the solidity of the value of Lincoln's *ethos*. That is to say, Leff's essay acquires its value in its speaking of *Lincoln* even if at a remove. Furthermore, if a discussion of Lincoln as orator is deferred through the dispersion of his identity throughout an unspecified number of texts and fragments circulating in nineteenth-century America, Grady and Douglass are rendered with remarkable solidity. Indeed, they more than compensate for Lincoln's displacement as object of study. One example is in order. Leff renders Frederick Douglass in a manner reminiscent of the most inspirational folk tales about Honest Abe:

Born into slavery, Douglass somehow learned to read, and while still a boy, obtained a copy of Caleb Bingham's *Columbian Orator*. He studied the book assiduously, declaiming passages from the speeches it contained whenever he found the time and opportunity. The book deeply marked his political consciousness and offered him a vocation.[5]

The paradoxes Douglass spoke from and the anxiety traversing his speaking position and speech do not recur here, and in this solidity to which Leff can defer, the *ethos* of the critic is maintained as is his self-effacing critical practice.

Through this circuit of deferral, we have come full circle. The status of rhetorical agents, of texts, and of critics remain in place, propping up each other even while gesturing to their own incompleteness.

NOTES

1. Both Raymie McKerrow and Michael Calvin McGee seek to chart a course for rhetorical theory and criticism devoid of humanist assumptions regarding progress and the centrality of the human subject. They consider the proper locus of rhetorical studies to be power. See in particular, Raymie E. McKerrow, "Critical Rhetoric: Theory and Praxis," *Communication Monographs* 56 (1989): 91-111; and Michael Calvin McGee, "Text, Context, and the Fragmentation of Contemporary Culture," *Western Journal of Speech Communication* 54 (1990): 274-89.
2. Ideographs are high-order abstract terms in public address that command loyalty even while their signification is contestable and historically variable. See Michael Calvin McGee, "The Ideograph: A Link between Rhetoric and Ideology," *Quarterly Journal of Speech* 66 (1980): 1-16.
3. McGee, "Text, Context," 284-88.
4. Henry Grady, "The New South," in *Three Centuries of American Rhetorical Discourse*, ed. Ronald F. Reid (Prospect Heights, Ill.: Waveland Press, 1988), 510.
5. See Michael Leff, "Lincoln among the Nineteenth-Century Orators," 133-55 in this volume.

AFTERWORD: RELOCATING THE ART OF PUBLIC ADDRESS

Robert Hariman

I magine that a warp in time brought the ancient sophists into our contemporary world. As always, they would be searching for those communicative practices that produced power. Habit would lead them to look for the great orators and orations of the day, but soon they would know better. The first time they heard some kid rev up his electric guitar, their mouths would be agape. As they cruised through the cable TV channels and then discerned how the electronic media were infiltrating all other social practices, their eyes would glitter. Their own capacity for two-sided argument might occasion a sentimental counterpoint, considering more carefully the persistence of formal public speeches, but soon they would concede the inevitability of historical change and, always nomadic anyway, leave their old art behind.

Few today would argue with the claim that oratory has experienced a precipitous decline during the past century. This idea is now common knowledge, an easily evoked intuition often used to rationalize inattention and incompetence. Even those few scholars who are fascinated with the art of oratory often prefer to study the speeches of the eighteenth and nineteenth centuries, when public speaking was widely appreciated as an art and clearly imbricated in historically decisive political actions. Yet such study, which is the subject of the present volume, is dogged by the suspicion that attention to the art of oratory is a merely antiquarian interest. The question now arises, what value is there in studying oratory when that knowledge is not likely to contribute to actual practice? More specifically, why study great speeches when no one is interested in imitating their artistry? Why study great speakers when the orator no longer is an identifiable and esteemed social character?

Of course, historical study has itself changed remarkably in the past century, and the rise of the academic profession underscores the general value of historical inquiry for a modern society while it suggests more specific historiographic applications for the study of public address. Although a history of oratory (as a relatively autonomous practice) can appear too narrowly drawn in respect to the comprehensive scope of period studies, the analysis of a canon of public speeches can identify crucial elements of understanding and action that are likely to be overlooked by historians today, who now write within a much different complex of communicative practices and intellectual norms. By valorizing public speech as a distinctive social practice having its own tradition and historical trajectory, at least three contributions to historical scholarship are possible: First, it offers a narrow yet reliable passage into the lived experience of public culture in particular historical periods. This approach will not work in all cases, of course, even when the historical record is adequate, but there have been times when public speech mattered. Their sense of themselves, like ours, was closely tied to their habits of speaking and being spoken to, their conventions of address and their modes of response, and so was dependent on the tacit knowledge and aesthetic reactions of their characteristic performances. Just as C.S. Lewis once remarked that the appreciation of rhetoric was the greatest single divide between the mentalities of the Renaissance and the modern reader, a similar canyon of incomprehension divides the mentalities of the late twentieth century and the "Golden Age" of American oratory. By entering into its public performances, one can begin to see that world from within.

The oratorical text can provide this perspective because it was part of a larger process of public composition. By seeing the texts from inside, one gets a closer look at some of the conventions of the political culture itself. This relationship between public speech and political culture is reciprocal: The speech is a means of (re)constituting the culture, and does so in part by using widespread cultural designs as inventional strategies for securing assent on the issue of the moment. Thus, a second contribution of a history of public address is that it can provide a distinctive analysis of the discursive structure of a society. The very properties of a speech that mark it as intellectually deficient in respect to more expert discourses are often the shadows of another framework of meaning that provides the culture with its basic sense of coherence, identity, and action. By understanding persuasive artistry as a skillful appropriation of typical, impersonal discursive forms, one can discern how public affairs are conducted within specific channels of interest that arbitrarily restrict imagination and intellect yet do not wholly determine specific decisions. By examining how the speech addresses a complex situation and organizes conflicting social goods through the artful interplay of conventional assurance, unspoken assertion, and distinctive restatement, one can discern how the language of the social text actually operates as a means for managing contingency and negotiating conflict.

Third, the history of public address can identify and resolve problems of historical interpretation that are themselves the result of depending on an insufficient understanding of the role of public talk in the political culture of the period. Whatever they might be, the ideas and interests of American political culture operate within specific communicative practices. Too often, the subsequent anatomy of those ideas and interests has lifted them out of their original performative context. Not only are meanings lost, but problems of interpretation are created unnecessarily for want of attention to the manner in which events turned on both general assumptions about the persuasive process and specific moments of artistic inflection. For example, the problem of identifying the essential meaning and influence of civic republicanism in American political culture is in part created by the historian's own habits.[1] Although scholarship on republicanism has been characterized by unusual attention to popular rhetorical practices such as pamphleteering and oratory, the tendency has been to use those texts to locate the doctrine rather than to understand the doctrine as it was being filled out rhetorically through textual performance. If republicanism can be understood as a performative sensibility coalescing around a repertoire of inventional strategies, its lack of coherence and its conjuncture with seemingly incompatible doctrines cease to be problematic. Or, rather, they become problems of a different sort—the problems of composition that occupied and enthused the speakers of the period—and the historical task shifts to identifying this intricate relationship between discursive performance and social order.[2]

Even as this volume and others like it contribute to these tasks, however, the problem of immediate cultural significance remains. In fact, it is compounded, for the historian of public address has a pedagogical orientation that many other historians can avoid by recourse to the norms of scholarly craft and professional identity. From classical antiquity through the nineteenth century, the study of public address was conducted for the dual purposes of training effective speakers and cultivating civic life. (The potential contradiction between these two objectives has been much discussed and need not be a concern here.) Whether schooling the next generation of the political elite or cultivating the last refinements of the mature orator, knowledge of oratory usually was acquired in order to equip individuals for effective performance in public affairs. The codification of this quest for advantage in turn provided society with the skills and norms required to cultivate and maintain high quality deliberation about public matters. In brief, the historical study of public address has inherited a particular obligation from its precursors, which is to identify the means for individual persuasive success by the citizen-orator in respect to the norms of public deliberation. This traditional program of analysis presumes an essential connection between the practice of oratory and the public sphere, and also the value of comparing, indeed, of judging the present in respect to the past.

These presumptions acquire additional significance within the context of modern democracy. A democratic political culture requires, among other things, the ability to discuss public address intelligently and also a civic memory regarding the possible warrants and models for action.[3] On each of these points the art of oratory and the historical study of that art converge. Both the oration and the scholarly treatise are reservoirs for civic memory, and particularly for remembrance of the value and means of high quality public deliberation. Civic memory can be notoriously fictional, but its stories of eloquence and action contribute to a polity's capacity for stable innovation. Academic study can be far removed from public life, but scholarly investigation, argument, and judgment can expand or constrict the art of the possible in a knowledge-intensive society. Although public speech and academic writing obviously are very different modes of communication, the better examples of each will at some point articulate a usable past.[4]

This inclination to make academic study responsive to modern cultural conditions already has stimulated considerable disagreement within the discipline of communication studies regarding the object and method appropriate to the study of public address.[5] Until the 1960s, the study of public address was virtually synonymous with the study of oratory; newspapers, essays, and other genres were included, but oratory was the master art and representative case. Since then, the definition has broadened to include every modality of public communication and, for most scholars in communication studies, oratory is but one mode among many and usually the least interesting. This change has been accompanied much of the time by others as well, including a shift from historical study to the analysis of relatively contemporary events.

This tension between the traditional study of oratory and modern communication studies has intensified of late. On the one hand, there has been a resurgence of interest in the more traditional venue; on the other hand, the study of other communicative media has acquired greater theoretical and political sophistication. To briefly summarize a well-known debate within the field, the basic standoff is between a neoclassical revival and an appropriation of poststructuralism.[6] Of course, many scholars work in an intermediate range or according to other agendas, but one way or the other, one of these two positions often ends up providing the horizon of meaning for understanding individual essays and larger programs of inquiry. Moreover, the tension between these two positions is symptomatic of the problematic of postmodernism itself, as neither innovation nor tradition provide any assurances while both prove useful in making sense of a radical plurality of discursive practices.

The neoclassical approach defines public address as situated, artistic, civic discourse: Oratory remains the premier genre of public address and the basic object of analysis is the individual speech, which is understood to address a particular situation and to be oriented towards a tangible policy or definition of civic culture. The analysis relies on the vocabulary of classical rhetoric to guide close readings of the text in order to discover a relationship between persuasive composition and political maneuver. Persuasive artistry involves use of the norms of linguistic and social appropriateness governing the situation to produce a text having formal integrity, personal distinction, and practical effect. Typically, this approach features canonical texts, focuses on the prominent governmental debates of modern British and American history, affirms the norms of liberal democratic polity, and assumes the value of identifying models of eloquence.[7]

The poststructuralist approach says good-bye to all that, claiming that oratory died while the public sphere was mutating into a media culture. This approach challenges every assumption of authorial intention, textual practice, civic context, and political privilege that is embedded in the classical model. The basic object of analysis is the social structure controlling comprehensive processes of discourse production and reception, while the analysis emphasizes the fragmentary nature of all discursive practice, the limited role of individual human agency, and the dispensability of any particular text. Public address is a ubiquitous trafficking in momentary, episodic instantiations of comprehensive processes of discursive control which are never available themselves as stable, coherent referents, and its study begins not with the speech text but with the task of assembling a collage of textual fragments in order to interpret the social order. The project also is emancipatory, directed to identifying how dominant modes of communication persistently maintain exploitation and limit freedom. Individual artistry is usually ignored except for reflexive attention to the critic's performance, which will be an adaptation of the tradition of ideology critique to the conditions of postmodern culture.[6]

Any reader of this volume will recognize at once that many of the essays are seated firmly on one side of the aisle. I see little use in arguing that any of them should have been on the opposite side. The better question is to ask how work from either perspective can contribute to the task of making public address in the nineteenth century a resource for those participating in the political culture(s) of the present. Let me begin by noting some of the liabilities that apply on each side. First, there are what could be called tit for tat criticisms, which set out each side's view of the other: For example, it is said that the neoclassical approach legitimates the status quo of the period, leaving untouched many undemocratic assumptions of social position, education, and the like; it is indifferent to authentic democratic culture while it practices a politics of exclusion, maintaining the silences in the social text and promoting models of public speech few have the opportunity to emulate; its history of public address is contrived and narrow, for it presumes the artistic merit and social value it supposedly is discovering while ignoring all forms of low culture; its method of close reading is merely descriptive rather than explanatory or critical and it depends on unexamined or outmoded theories of persuasion.

On the other side, it is said that the poststructuralist analysis is largely innocent of historical awareness and foregoes any attention to historical detail; its assumptions about contemporary social conditions are equally unfounded, the result more of a round robin of theoretical essays than of empirical study; it is too dependent on continental theory, accounting neither for the social embeddedness of that theory in its own context nor for the distinctiveness of the American experience; its claims about specific discourses also are unreliable because it produces few studies of actual public address and because its method of assemblage is self-validating; most important, its dismissal of individual agency is both incorrect and politically dangerous.

Although these criticisms might draw blood occasionally, they are not likely to be persuasive on either side since they are not based on shared assumptions. A second set of arguments might be called immanent criticisms, for they hold each project accountable to its own criteria. These should be harder to disregard and, if corrected, lead to better scholarship. In respect to the neoclassical approach, the focus on the individual text or singular event blurs perception of the comprehensive social conditions and long-term discursive effects that make its significance possible. Frederick Douglass is remembered not only because he was an accomplished speaker but also because his oratory presented a powerful challenge to slavery. One difference between a literary canon and a set of oratorical masterworks is that the latter should be a record of moments of political crisis and change, and the study of public address ought to be a means for understanding those more comprehensive processes. Furthermore, the basic sense of classical artistry is itself put at risk if either the speech itself or the situation in which it occurs is given too much emphasis—and, not surprisingly, traditional public address studies have oscillated between each of these forms of overemphasis. That is, intensive attention to either the individual text or a particular moment of reception produces a blindness regarding the larger economies of social and linguistic action that were the primary interest of the classical model. In that model, the key to effective discourse involved crafting distinctive usage of common artistic resources for a practical end—in other words, of hitting on the right combination of poesis and praxis.[9] When either artistic excellence or situational constraint are emphasized without regard for the other, the relationship between the speech and the social formation is too easily trivialized.

The poststructuralists also could improve their project on its own terms, and, once again, the characteristic shortcoming becomes apparent once the specific character of public address is highlighted. Public address, even in periods of fluorescence, differs from other forms of expression in part because it is so laden with popular culture, everyday experiences, and vernacular idioms. In fact, this is the point of purchase for the poststructuralist, for a persistent appeal to convention and uniformity are good indices that a text is but the instantiation of a process of social reproduction and, with that, all the structural inequities of the society. Stated more simply, conventional verbal forms and common sense responses seem to be the vehicles for ideological control of the audience. Furthermore, public address is a thoroughly material practice—people prepare for it, do it, recover from it, or act in response to it, usually in explicitly defined situations and in regard to specific objectives. The key to understanding processes of domination would seem to be identifying how the abstractions that organize the society as a system benefiting some at the expense of others become the lingua franca of ordinary, everyday persuasive interactions.

Yet poststructuralism also can lead to comprehensive disregard of the categories embedded in vernacular practices and everyday experiences. It should not, of course, for this inattention is contrary to related beliefs regarding the nature and value of organic political practices as well as any commitment to discursive empowerment of marginalized peoples.[10] The problem, however, is that poststructuralist linguistic theory runs directly against the grain of vernacular speech. Ordinary people prove to be poor theorists, even when they are politically creative and effective, for they believe in direct statement, verbal representation, and artistic excellence. Whether engaging in the vernacular economics of buying a car, or the vernacular politics of serving on a library board, or the vernacular rhetoric of writing a letter to the editor, they persist in thinking that words can clearly communicate intentions, that descriptions can be accurate or misleading, and that some deals and decisions and texts are more beautifully crafted than others. Poststructuralists know better, of course, for they can prove that these beliefs rely on naive ideas about language and reality while they perpetuate misleading assumptions regarding individual subjectivity and transcendental values.[11] (Of course, for the moment, the theorist has slipped into the vernacular idiom, but this *tu quoque* is avoided with the next step, which is to show that the suspect ideas are internally contradictory while the theorist is self-reflexive.) My point is not that the poststructuralist critique of modernist ideas of representation, subjectivity, and culture is wrong; in fact, I think it is largely correct and rightly influential, but this philosophical achievement is largely irrelevant at many important moments in the conduct of inquiry (as were the doctrines that it has discredited). A largely philosophical critique has encouraged disregard for a conventional mentality that is essential to the everyday practice of public address, and this disregard results not only in an inadequate account of public address but one that is at odds with democratic empowerment.

To this end, the poststructuralist has to re-admit conventional ideas of intentionality and artistry and also attend to the commonplace typology of genres, issues, personalities, and techniques that is embedded in the vernacular.[12] This revisionary criticism need not assume that everyday practices are simple, and it certainly is not beholden to traditional criticism, which has assumed that eloquence encompasses all lesser artistry. Nor does it mean attending only to familiar categories of analysis or accepting the model of the individual, autonomous subject in complete, conscious control of the text. In fact, the interesting thing about a focus on social performance is that all of these philosophical notions can be dropped without much loss to the analytical concepts. Whether shifting from agent to agency, or from scene to agency, strong emphasis on the design of the text allows near complete reconceptualization of the "extrinsic" elements of design. In addition, instead of assuming that attention to textual artistry requires belief in an autonomous subject, one can consider how artistry is a primary means for creating the effect of subjectivity, even for gaining control over the construction of subjectivity within encompassing discourses. These are hardly radical claims, of course, for the neoclassical approach already recognizes how a text can articulate subject positions for both speaker and audience.[13] If basic terms of the neoclassical vocabulary should not be avoided, however, they will need to be adapted beyond what would have been expected.

By now it should be apparent that I believe the key to finding a middle way between these two critical perspectives lies in reconsideration of the concept of persuasive artistry.[14] This argument reveals the characteristic shortcomings of each while attempting to draw together their best insights. The basic limitation within the poststructuralist approach to the study of public address is its near-complete effacement of style.[15] It is not that poststructuralists do not see the aesthetic dimension of public address but that they so relentlessly reduce it to another dimension of discourse production. Within this perspective, the values of eloquence are dispersed by the shattering of the oratorical text, artistic design is reduced to a mechanics of control, and any inflection in audience response is interpreted solely within a dialectic of hegemony and tactical resistance. The dynamics of the social order that are at the focal point of the analysis become a tissue of signifiers, then a body of arguments, finally a rigid frame of abstractions.

To this extent, and contrary to virtually all of its important provocations, it remains a modernist project, beholden to antitheses of argument and style, politics and poetics, praxis and poesis. Critique on these terms will have difficulty understanding, much less mobilizing, effective political discourse.

Unfortunately, the neoclassical approach does not do any better. Although it has corrected for an earlier scanting of style within its own tradition, the close reading of exemplary texts can be a thinly disguised New Criticism, relying on such presumptions as the autonomy of rhetorical form, the primacy of the artistic object, the subordination of theory to textual study, and a liberal bracketing of other ideological interests. Even if it is modernism with a human face, the finely nuanced attention to the internal unities of the well-wrought speech is a project that not only has limited application to the present, but also places too many constraints on the understanding of the political culture of the past. The neoclassical approach needs a stronger, more classical, sense of how public speech was an art within an art. Public address was understood to be an art form, but one that was only relatively autonomous because it functioned within a larger, concentric art of politics that in turn was a means for management of the entire social formation. Michael Leff surely is correct in his insistence that the reciprocal concepts of decorum and prudence are essential to the development of this perspective, for they articulate a social aesthetics and a social rationality that define artistic craft and aesthetic response in public address as the nexus between individual effectivity and structural constraint.[16] What has not been adequately developed is the awareness that these twin concepts supply only the barest, thoroughly formal constructs for analysis of the contemporary text, and that in a society characterized by cultural pluralism one certainly can no longer presume that a single version of either prudence or decorum can inform any public arena for long.

Thus, both approaches need to alter their conception of rhetorical artistry. The best way to do that is in regard to what each can offer the other. The poststructuralist is not so much wrong about the (lack of) integrity of the speech text as right about the importance of processes of dispersion and a contemporary hermeneutics of fragmentation. Oratory is not dead, but it has been dispersed through the mass media into a dynamic collage of free-floating fragments, disjointed images, and instantaneous commentaries that then are reconstructed by ordinary people in order to make sense of specific situations. Moreover, although public speaking no longer is a high cultural art form, it has acquired ever greater ubiquity as a vernacular practice for low-level institutional management.[17] It is alive and well every day in hotel meeting rooms, school auditoriums, and many similarly unexceptional scenes, and its importance there stems in part from its new-found function of localizing discourse that begins as the mass media's all-encompassing but displaced mediation of everyday life. That is, instead of seeing first the elite public speech and then a ripple effect through the mass public, today public speech typically begins as a practice for reconstituting mass mediated discourses in specific locales in order to establish sufficient warrants for action. Thus, I believe that important questions about the available means of persuasion in our political culture—including questions in the spirit of Benjamin and Gramsci—are likely to remain unanswered until the vernacular is taken seriously, both as a repository of traditional forms and a proving ground for new patterns of assemblage and reception. Likewise, although important governmental officials still make public speeches that have influence, the analysis of those texts now has to include at some point consideration of how they are contending with an interpretive context that is essentially incoherent. Mass media production has superseded any individual's discourse, and texts themselves are both composed and appropriated through flexible processes of *bricolage* with little regard to artistic or social permanence. Moreover, as the processes of modernization that drive these changes were underway well before the contemporary moment, there is good reason to push the analysis back into the past, considering how the public culture of the late-eighteenth to mid-nineteenth century was already showing the signs of its impending demise.

On the other hand, the neoclassical approach is not so much wrong about the social value of eloquence as it is right about the necessity of rhetorical artistry to public culture. The problem of the contemporary public sphere—and a lesson that is learned from historical study—is that high-quality public deliberation requires appreciation of the artistic possibilities and achievements in the available modes of communication. It probably matters less what mode is dominant—whether oratory or newspaper editorials, essays or live TV coverage, public debates or public interviews—than it does that the dominant mode is understood and esteemed as an art form, having known standards of quality, characteristic biases of production, and preferred effects, rather than being experienced as a relatively natural process. In the nineteenth century the available venues ranged from letter writing to public conversation to public debate to epideictic oratory to commemorative statuary to landscape architecture, among others. In our own day we are well aware that the spectrum includes much more as well. What is perhaps most distressing to me about the current status of oratory is not its displacement by other forms of public address but the poor quantity and quality of public talk about whatever performances do occur. Moreover, such inattention to the command of artistic form in public address is probably the most immediate disservice one can give to those who speak from the margins—as the examples of the many eloquent abolitionists and suffragists have made clear. Today, moreover, this appreciation for public artistry would have to include folk arts and indigenous literatures, and not as exhibits in the theme park of late-modern culture but as models for advocacy and political innovation.

Let me suggest that a common denominator for this extension of the idea of rhetorical artistry might be the concept of imitation. The idea that a text should be imitated is a hermeneutical idea: it sets in motion a process of interpreting the text which in turn defines the relationship between text and context, directs comparison with other texts, motivates construction of a canon, directly shapes the composition of subsequent texts, and can be a powerful means for reproduction of the genre and the social order. This hermeneutic is at once the weak prop under the neoclassical model and an important supplement for poststructuralist inquiry, so revision of the classical concept provides one opportunity for bringing the two approaches closer together.

This hermeneutical orientation operates at a higher level of interpretation than the related psychological processes that are at work throughout all socialization and all reading and writing, speaking and listening. Only some genres and some texts are used as templates, and the experience of personal identification with the text is explicitly self-conscious. For example, John Adams did not just happen to imitate Cicero, nor was it only one act among many in his social maturation. When the text is an example of public address, the act of imitation also has a more specialized relationship with political order. By interpreting a public speech with an eye to its imitation, one is styling oneself within an established set of political relations, presumably to one's advantage. Adams's study of Cicero was a transparent exercise in political maneuvering in the hope of securing a reputation in his own republic similar to what Cicero had achieved at Rome, and this imitative relationship was the core of his republican sensibility.[18] Finally, one characteristic of public address is that it is produced not only by means of imitation (and adaptation and innovation within that context), but also with an eye toward its own imitation. The achievement of the objective of the moment is rarely the sole end of a speech. Political actors quickly learn that most objectives are already compromised, provisional, and reversible, while some recognize that success at one level of conflict might result in failure at a higher level, and often there is the spur of fame as well. The best guarantee in respect to all of these considerations is to become an object of imitation. Thus, public exemplar and personal image merge in a complex process of self-fashioning.

Adams's example epitomizes the idea of imitation undergirding the neoclassical approach: The individual active in public life studies classical rhetorical texts to discern the model of the ideal orator in order to become such a figure in one's own time. Particular speeches provide approximations of this *orator perfectus* while the theoretical treatises depict its anatomy in more technical detail. By drawing on these examples of fully embodied eloquence and a typology of the particular means of persuasion, the author becomes equipped to reproduce similar effects. Accordingly, all aspects of rhetorical study acquire a pedagogical orientation. The rhetorical critic's task is to identify the sources of eloquence in a given text, which, presumably, are what is to be imitated by others. If current work is not explicitly dedicated towards the education of the orator, it relies on the imitative hermeneutic nonetheless. The interest now is channeled through the question of reproducing a high quality public culture and the art of oratory itself, rather than the individual accomplishment of eloquence and fame. The result remains a canon of great speeches that are models of eloquence available for imitation rather than merely representative features of a prior historical period.

Poststructuralists find this project amusing, to say the least. Yet their skepticism already has been anticipated, internalized perhaps, by the neoclassical reader, who now is finding that eloquence is a complicated process of negotiating the discursive formation, a process that can look remarkably fragmentary from within. More to the point, the question of what to imitate becomes a more interesting question, and it becomes clear that a straightforward imitation of the techniques of persuasion (as techniques) will not produce eloquence. (Isocrates had insisted this was the case, and now that claim looks less like special pleading and more like an astute observation on the social determination of discourse.) Seen from within, the achievement of eloquence becomes more than beautiful phrasing of practical ideas or giving elevated testament to common sentiments; instead, it is something closer to the use of artistic craft in civic discourse to negotiate a political conundrum. This approach culminates in the idea of a liberal political aesthetic that is identified not in terms of technique per se but in the experience of public life that results from eloquent speech.[19] The accompanying sense of craft is inevitably imitative but every successful imitation to the end of eloquence is necessarily a (pragmatic) adaptation as well.[20]

Seen from without, the process of imitation of the text by others becomes a fascinating story of dispersion and transformation. Great texts are used in a myriad of ways, as models certainly, but also as pretexts and foils and icons, and the range of identifications runs from Adams's love of Cicero to Lincoln's Birthday Sale. Instead of becoming a story of successful adaptation and democratic continuity, however, in our own day the idea of imitating any verbal work is confounded by the omnipresent popular culture which consists of ubiquitous processes of imitation, from movie sequels to youth fashions, that all are market-driven, consumption-oriented, and have no direct orientation toward political institutions. It would seem that the study of public address will have to shift the focus of any emphasis on imitation from ethos (and strong authorial control of the text) to agency (and the dispersion of both skills and learned incapacity). Instead of attention to the striking turn of phrase, the critical interest should be in the strategic value of particular persuasive designs that become widely available for use in a myriad of situations.

It should be obvious that many of the essays in this volume circle around this problem of revising the imitative hermeneutic. For example, Edwin Black laments its passing; James Farrell examines how Webster staged his comparison with the Founders; Martha Watson identifies two cases of remarkably direct appropriation; and Michael Leff illustrates three cases of freely drawn refashioning. Rather than consider the specific contributions and missed opportunities in each case, it might be more helpful to let this general interest in rethinking the process of imitation in public address lead back to the question of finding a usable past. How might we read these texts from the nineteenth century as examples of public address if they are not to provide models of eloquence? Even if acknowledged as models of eloquence, what exactly is the object and process of imitation that the critics have set before us, or should have set before us? How might we read these texts if they are to be the basis for some form of imitation directed towards maintaining a democratic culture, although not one characterized by public speaking?

The broad outlines of the political culture that emerges from these studies of nineteenth-century public address are familiar: It was a period of great debates resolved at times only by force, of progressive though fitful democratization, and of social transformation wrought by industrialization. Civic republicanism gave way to Jacksonian populism and Yankee commercialism, the constitutional consensus was confronted by abolitionists and suffragists, and by the end of the century its cultural forms were becoming increasingly inadequate for managing the multiple contradictions of an increasingly complex society. Within these circumstances, we also observe a society self-consciously caught up in public arts and public ceremonies; for example, civic remembrance was a preoccupation of sorts—commemorations and similar occasions were both taken seriously and widely enjoyed as forms of entertainment. One significant result was a public accustomed to the conventions of presentation characterizing these events. This audience was maintained in part through the mass media but the speech text was the basic unit of reproduction—today's "sound bite" is a mildly critical label because of the complete text whose absence it implies—and public address was oriented toward norms of textual integrity and comprehensiveness. Finally, political identity mattered: citizenship was prized, and speakers who were excluded from full participation in public life labored to expand the public sphere rather than repudiate it.

A different world indeed. Yet the essays in this volume also point toward characteristics of the public address of the period that have some pertinence to contemporary problems of progressive empowerment in a postmodern culture. The opening wedge is to ask how artistic craft and political motives each can reflect the other. The next step is to consider how the speakers used major ideological constructions as inventional devices in their speeches. Keep in mind that the point here, as these case studies illustrate, is not to label the speakers; quite the contrary, close reading of their speeches reveals how ideological forms can work quite differently in artistically crafted practical discourse than they do elsewhere. We then can identify several pervasive designs that were important means of persuasion in the culture and pliable material for the gifted speaker's craft.

Let me mention one example of how conventional form allowed a surprising range of improvisation. The model of the "self-made man" obviously was at work throughout the public address of the period. Whatever their cause, speakers also were dedicated to self-advancement; indeed, public speaking was prized because of its capacity for self-promotion, and oratorical skill was a commonly recognized sign of the qualities expected of anyone who wanted to get ahead. The speakers promoted those they were honoring, and themselves, as models of self-assertion, and their speeches were designed as self-help manuals adapted to the issues of the day. The persona of Webster assuming the toga of republican embodiment was very different from the calculated split personality of Booker T. Washington, but both were using self-advancement as a motivational device astutely adapted to the circumstances of their audiences. This model was explicitly male, and it is interesting to note that the suffragists offer an appropriate exception to the rule, for they drew on a model of collective self-assertion, the Declaration of Independence, and then made the adjustments necessary to ensure the proper gender identifications for their audience of women.[21]

The flexibility of this device is underscored by its use by such diverse figures as Garrison, Douglass, Grady, and Washington. Although typically self-advancement is thought of as a conservative ideology—and the nineteenth century provides many such instances of this alignment—the essays in this volume demonstrate that it also can be a powerful means of persuasion for speakers from marginal or contradictory social positions speaking on behalf of radical or unpopular proposals. I will not claim that the trope is wholly neutral ideologically, but to the extent it is a trope it also is a flexible resource and perhaps one ironically well suited to the challenges faced by the unconventional speaker. In addition, it is easy to forget how anxious a project self-advancement can be. It is not too great a stretch to see the nineteenth-century figure as a precursor of those today who want to better their condition but are well aware of their marginality, or stymied by the seeming groundlessness of all moral claims in a media culture, or discouraged by the unsettling fact that political legitimacy depends on persistent competition for public attention through often haphazard media processes.

The point I want to emphasize is that the most memorable public speakers of the nineteenth century were particularly gifted at mastering generic constraints.[22] They were well aware of how they could be stifled by the established conventions of address, often unconscionably so, and how they had few conventions of their own or appeals uniquely suited to their cause. This condition of strong discursive constraint is one of the costs of working within an esteemed public art—the public audience has strong expectations and preferences about what one might say, and there are plenty of other speakers capable of fulfilling those requirements.[23] Even so, under these conditions the opportunity for influence within the established forums and modes of public address is enormous. So it was that the speakers of the day all worked within a dialectic of conforming to known expectations while modifying or deviating artfully from those expectations. Those speakers having the more conventional messages still worked in this way in order to distinguish themselves individually while contending with the constant drag toward redundancy and boredom that characterizes any popular art. Their successes have been easily forgotten, with little loss. The radical speakers, however, faced the problem as a profound contradiction in their very mode of being. When speakers such as Douglass or Susan B. Anthony spoke publicly, they could not avoid forms of address that worked powerfully against them, and their ethos inevitably was both radical and compromised, black and white, female and male.[24] Likewise, speakers such as Grady and Washington had to speak on behalf of interests both Southern and Northern, agrarian and commercial, public and private, political and commercial (with none of these oppositions lining up neatly with the others). Although not radical (in the conventional sense of the term), they were nonetheless managing complicated definitions of public identity that were most immediately present to them as constraints on what they might say.

This observation does not account for every great speech of the period, but it does suggest why some are memorable and why understanding those speeches can be a resource for advocates in the present. For many nineteenth-century speakers, oratory offered a different persuasive range and stronger sense of audience than what thrives in the current context of identity politics and mass media production. Marginalized cultures did not require separate forms of expression, nor did dispossessed peoples have to be identified as separate interests.[25] Douglass's Fourth of July speech is the most obvious example of these differences: His harsh use of irony today might be interpreted as a proud gesture of rejection but at the time it was a creative mode of engagement with the mainstream and a means for infiltrating and appropriating the means of legitimation. Or witness how feminist orators of the nineteenth century such as Elizabeth Cady Stanton and Sojourner Truth so artfully reinterpreted the Genesis creation myths and other Biblical stories, and not merely to neutralize those powerful weapons but to turn them on their adversaries.[26] The genius of these speakers comes in part from their ability to use to their advantage exactly those powerful ideological discourses that otherwise worked against them.[27] The nineteenth-century speaker usually assumed that he or she had to speak in a common idiom that might not be suited to the cause but that nonetheless offered necessary or economical or sufficient means for changing the society.

The willingness to work within conventional forms of address for unconventional ends carries a related sense of artistic appreciation. If attempting to influence a public by modifying its conventions of public address from within, the act of crafting the persuasive text is an obvious locus of control. (Conversely, if this assumption about public action is false, then the cultivation and appreciation of persuasive artistry is merely another means for trapping and disarming the radical.) Thus, the pleasurable response to a text is twice valuable: in itself and as a means or sign of political effectivity. Likewise, performative skill and discernment are qualities that all sides will have reason to maintain: the winners (of the moment) because it worked for them and the losers because it is an economical agency that can work tomorrow.

This appreciation of public speech as an art form will be the last characteristic of nineteenth-century political culture that I will feature here. Although the essays in this volume certainly presume such a sensibility, they also validate it. The culture that emerges from these studies was one in which artistic performance of public discourse was a means for resolving political disputes. Where agreement seemed impossible, acclaim could intervene. Long-standing prejudices could be set aside in the common act of appreciation for the performance of the orator. If the performance was one aspect of his or her politics, it also was something already adapted to take the edge off of political differences. Thus, the emphasis on persuasive artistry provided a model for political cooperation, first in the speaker's dance of adaptation and then in the audience's coming together in appreciation of the speaker's artistry. This aesthetic sense was at once popular and refined, performative and practical, and shared by officials and radicals. It involved familiar, traditional models of eloquence and explicit norms of imitation, but also constant regard for adaptation and innovation.

As I have said, I believe that a similar sensibility persists in the vernacular public address occurring daily below the level of media coverage. It also is evident occasionally in the media, although typically other manners of "analysis" predominate. In fact, the public sphere could not function as merely the rational exchange of information and argument; as John Peters has argued, the artistic dimension of public communication is a blind spot in critical theory and in need of correction by recourse to rhetorical studies.[28] Some public address scholars today will continue to examine the traditional practice of oratory, while others will track the migration of discursive power into other modes of communication and culture. The challenge for all is to fully understand the *art* of public address, as it was and as it is and as it could come to be.

To conclude, we need to relocate the art of public address. This "relocating" plays on the pun in the word, referring to both a process of discovery, where one finds what had been misplaced, and a process of transference, where one moves something from one place to another. Whether to understand our culture as it is receding into the past or as it is still coming into being, persuasive artistry has to be both found and moved. Those who have largely ignored textual artistry, need to rediscover it. Those who have celebrated a too-limited version of textual craft, need to extend their attention to the whole social text. Perhaps only then can we join past and present, the traditional art of rhetoric and the fragmented forms of our political culture.

NOTES

1. Daniel T. Rodgers, "Republicanism: the Career of a Concept," *Journal of American History* 79 (1992): 11-38.

2. Robert Hariman, "In Oratory as in Life: Civic Performance in Cicero's Republican Style," in *Political Style: The Artistry of Power* (Chicago: University of Chicago Press, 1995); James Jasinski, "Rhetoric and Judgment in the Constitutional Debate of 1787-1788: An Exploration of the Relationship Between Theory and Critical Practice," *Quarterly Journal of Speech* 78 (1992): 197-218; John Murphy, "Republicanism in the Modern Age: Adlai Stevenson in the 1952 Presidential Campaign," *Quarterly Journal of Speech* 80 (1994): 313-28.

3. For sustained development of these themes, see Thomas B. Farrell, *Norms of Rhetorical Culture* (New Haven: Yale University Press, 1993).

4. The inspiration can come from Frederick Douglass's 1850 Fourth of July oration: "We have to do with the past only as we can make it useful to the present and to the future. To all inspiring motives, to noble deeds which can be gained from the past, we are welcome. But now is the time, the important time." *The Frederick Douglass Papers; Series One: Speeches, Debates, and Interviews, Vol. 2: 1847-54*, 366. See also Warren I. Susman, *Culture as History: The Transformation of American Society in the Twentieth Century* (New York: Pantheon Books, 1984).

5. Dilip Parameshwar Gaonkar, "Object and Method in Rhetorical Criticism: From Wichelns to Leff and McGee," *Western Journal of Speech Communication* 54 (1990): 290-316. The

basic acknowledgment of the paradigm shift at the time was Lloyd F. Bitzer and Edwin Black, eds., *The Prospect of Rhetoric: Report of the National Development Project* (Englewood Cliffs, N.J.: Prentice-Hall, 1971).

6. See the Special Issue on Rhetorical Criticism edited by John Angus Campbell in the *Western Journal of Speech Communication* 54, no. 3 (1990).

7. Stephen E. Lucas, "The Renaissance of American Public Address: Text and Context in Rhetorical Criticism," *Quarterly Journal of Speech* 74 (1988): 241-60. Michael Leff has been the leading advocate of the neoclassical approach: "Textual Criticism: The Legacy of G.P. Mohrmann," *Quarterly Journal of Speech* 72 (1986): 377-89; "Things Made by Words: Reflections on Textual Criticism," *Quarterly Journal of Speech* 78 (1992): 223-31; Michael Leff and Andrew Sachs, "Words the Most Like Things: Iconicity and the Rhetorical Text," *Western Journal of Speech Communication* 54 (1990): 252-73. For representative neoclassical studies, see Stephen E. Lucas, "Justifying America: The Declaration of Independence as a Rhetorical Document," in *American Rhetoric: Context and Criticism*, ed. Thomas W. Benson (Carbondale: Southern Illinois University Press, 1989), 67-130, and Stephen H. Browne, *Edmund Burke and the Discourse of Virtue* (Tuscaloosa: University of Alabama Press, 1993).

8. The major influence in this redefinition of public address has been Michael Calvin McGee, whose most recent statement is "Text, Context, and the Fragmentation of American Culture," *Western Journal of Speech Communication* 54 (1990): 274-89; see also "The 'Ideograph': A Link Between Rhetoric and Ideology," *Quarterly Journal of Speech* 66 (1980): 1-16. For another influential statement, see Raymie E. McKerrow, "Critical Rhetoric: Theory and Praxis," *Communication Monographs* 56 (1989): 91-111. Representative poststructuralist analysis includes Maurice Charland, "Constitutive Rhetoric: The Case of the *Peuple Québécois,*" *Quarterly Journal of Speech* 73 (1987): 133-50, and John Sloop, *The Cultural Prison: Discourse, Prisoners, and Punishment* (Tuscaloosa: University of Alabama Press, 1996).

9. For elaboration of this idea, see Farrell's discussion in *Norms of Rhetorical Culture* of the relationship between Aristotle's *Rhetoric* and *Poetics.*

10. For another statement of this argument see James Arnt Aune, *Rhetoric and Marxism* (Boulder, Colo.: Westview Press, 1994), chap. 4.

11. My position should not be confused with the argument by Marxists such as Perry Anderson, Terry Eagleton, and Alex Callinicos that ideology critique has been profoundly corrupted by those following the continental version of the linguistic turn. I believe this reaction is mistaken for more reasons than can be listed here. For our purposes, we need note only that the prior scholarship preferred by these critics was naive rhetorically and that the poststructuralists have made some important discoveries. See Aune, *Rhetoric and Marxism*, for extended discussion of the need for joining rhetorical study with Marxist critique.

12. For one model of how to develop poststructuralist assumptions for the analysis of vernacular speech forms, see M. M. Bakhtin, "The Problem of Speech Genres," in *Speech Genres and Other Late Essays*, trans. Vern W. McGee and edited by Caryl Emerson and Michael Holquist (Austin: University of Texas Press, 1986).

13. Aristotle's *Rhetoric* is the locus classicus. The influential essay in modern public address studies has been Edwin Black, "The Second Persona," *Quarterly Journal of Speech* 56 (1970): 109-19.

14. Perhaps this is the place to acknowledge that many scholars might already see themselves as drawing on both approaches towards this end. I certainly see myself this way—e.g., see Hariman, *Political Style*—and I have learned much in this regard from my colleagues. Yet no one should assume that the middle way is the easiest, and most of us most of the time will be depending on one set of assumptions rather than the other, and at any such moment we probably could improve our inquiry by taking more seriously the other project. Strong adherents to either side probably will counter that they already address the other's concerns, though in their own terms which are not comprehensible to those working from different assumptions. Fair enough, but this claim does not quite touch my argument that each perspective is subject to certain self-imposed limitations.

15. Surely, this is not quite right, is it? How can poststructuralists be faulted for effacing style when they have done so much to valorize the aesthetics of everyday life and even have been accused of throwing open the door to fascism by aestheticizing politics? Let me offer several observations on behalf of this provocation. First, poststructuralist study of aesthetics has been, both theoretically and critically, largely a study of commodity consumption, which does not yet encompass all discourse production. Second, whatever poststructuralists outside of communication studies have done, those within the discipline have been far more oriented toward ideological constraint than to any sense of artistic craft or aesthetic response, as they will be the first to admit. Nor is such inattention unique: Witness the statement by Michele Barrett that aesthetic questions have been "relegated to an extremely marginal position in both theoretical and critical debates" in contemporary Marxist cultural theory. Michele Barrett, "The Place of Aesthetics in Marxist Criticism," in Cary Nelson and Lawrence Grossberg, eds., *Marxism and the Interpretation of Culture* (Urbana: University of Illinois Press, 1988), 697.

16. Michael Leff, "The Habitation of Rhetoric," *Argument and Critical Practices: Proceedings of the Fifth SCA/AFA Conference on Argumentation,* ed. Joseph Wenzel (Annandale, Va.: Speech Communication Association, 1987), 1-8; "Decorum and Rhetorical Interpretation: The Latin Humanistic Tradition and Contemporary Critical Theory," *Vichiana* 3a serie, 1 (1990): 107-26; Thomas Rosteck and Michael Leff, "Piety, Propriety, and Perspective: An Interpretation and Application of Key Terms in Kenneth Burke's Permanence and Change," *Western Journal of Speech Communication* 53 (1989): 327-41.

17. Note as well that the dissolution of a high culture of oratory has been accompanied by changes in the vernacular, which much of the time now is a mid-range discourse available throughout modern society. For earlier tensions between high and low cultures of public address, see Thomas Gustafson, *Representative Words: Politics, Literature, and the American Language, 1776-1865* (Cambridge: Cambridge University Press, 1992), and Kenneth Cmiel, *Democratic Eloquence: The Fight over Popular Speech in Nineteenth-Century America* (New York: William Morrow, 1990).

18. James M. Farrell, "John Adams's Autobiography: The Ciceronian Paradigm and the Quest for Fame," *New England Quarterly* 62 (1989): 505-28; "Letters and Political Judgment: John

Adams and Cicero's Style," *Studies in Eighteenth-Century Culture* 24 (1994): 137-53. Bernard Bailyn has captured this cult of imitation in a sentence: "They found their ideal selves, and to some extent their voices, in Brutus, in Cassius, and in Cicero, whose Catilinarian orations the enraptured John Adams, age 23, declaimed aloud, alone at night in his room"; *The Ideological Origins of the American Revolution* (Cambridge: Harvard University Press, 1967), 26.

19. See, e.g., George Herbert Mead's evocation of this experience of democratic culture, "The Nature of Aesthetic Experience," *Selected Writings*, ed. Andrew J. Reck (Chicago: University of Chicago Press, 1981), 297-98.

20. Garry Wills illustrates this point superbly in *Lincoln at Gettysburg: The Words that Remade America* (New York: Touchstone/Simon & Schuster, 1992).

21. For example, see the 1848 "Declaration of Sentiments and Resolutions" in Karlyn Kohrs Campbell, *Man Cannot Speak for Her: A Critical Study of Early Feminist Rhetoric*, vol. 2 (New York: Praeger, 1989). For discussion of the masculinist bias in American oratory, see Kathleen Hall Jamieson, *Eloquence in an Electronic Age: The Transformation of Political Speechmaking* (New York: Oxford University Press, 1988), chap. 4.

22. This claim is a special case of the more general idea that public discourse always is altering traditional terms to manage changing circumstances and to bring about change. For a good example of how to put this general idea to work, see Celeste Michelle Condit and John Louis Lucaites, *Crafting Equality: America's Anglo-African Word* (Chicago: University of Chicago Press, 1993). See also Andrew W. Robertson, *The Language of Democracy: Political Rhetoric in the United States and Britain, 1790-1900* (Ithaca: Cornell University Press, 1995), which I discovered as this essay was going to press. As Robertson states succinctly, "even the most radical polemicist must rely upon familiar themes, common values, and proven rhetorical strategies if he or she is to persuade an audience" (8). My emphasis on mastering generic constraints would attempt to identify the artistry used to adapt an ideologically recalcitrant idiom for a particular cause and in respect to a specific situation. Obviously, this process of adaptation within the specific text, and in respect to the demands and opportunities of performance, would be the better basis for imitation subsequently.

23. Much more has been said, of course—e.g., in feminist and postcolonial critique—about the problems and strategies for a subordinate group speaking within a dominant language. See also Gilles Deleuze and Félix Guattari, *Kafka: Toward a Minor Literature*, trans. Dana Polan (Minneapolis: University of Minnesota Press, 1986). Today, of course, some theorists of emancipatory movements adamantly reject any reliance on conventional speech forms. Here we have to balance the chance of a breakthrough in communicative praxis against the ease with which this self-conscious stand against adaptation is co-opted into a regime of "repressive tolerance." See Herbert Marcuse, *Critique of Pure Tolerance* (Boston: Beacon Press, 1968).

24. Karlyn Kohrs Campbell, "The Rhetoric of Women's Liberation: An Oxymoron," *Quarterly Journal of Speech* 59 (1973): 74-86.

25. This claim does not cover all cases, of course, but a number of recent studies document the artful accommodationism of nineteenth-century reformers, particularly in respect to the

women's movement. See, e.g., A. Cheree Carlson, "Creative Casuistry and Feminist Consciousness: A Rhetoric of Moral Reform," *Quarterly Journal of Speech* 78 (1992): 16-32. For a contrary case of a speaker choosing ideological fidelity over persuasive effectiveness, see Martha Solomon, "Ideology as Rhetorical Constraint: The Anarchist Agitation of 'Red Emma' Goldman," *Quarterly Journal of Speech* 74 (1988): 184-200. See also the analyses of a "feminine style" in women's speech: Campbell, *Man Cannot Speak for Her,* vol. 1; Bonnie J. Dow and Mari Boor Tonn, "'Feminine Style' and Political Judgment in the Rhetoric of Ann Richards," *Quarterly Journal of Speech* 79 (1993): 286-302. It also should be clear that the relation between communication and consciousness always is complicated and burdensome for the minority speaker, even when achieving persuasive success; see, e.g., W.E.B. DuBois's discussion of "double consciousness" in chapter one of *The Souls of Black Folk* (New York: New American Library, 1969).

26. Elizabeth Cady Stanton, "Speech at the Seneca Falls Convention, 1848," in Campbell, ed., *Man Cannot Speak for Her,* 2:47; Sojourner Truth, "Speech at the Woman's Rights Convention, Akron, Ohio, 1851," 101.

27. History does repeat itself. Today the American civil rights movement of the 1950s and 1960s has been criticized for its accommodationism, while at the time many of the most important advocates were self-consciously trying to adapt to their ends the legal system that had been an instrument of their oppression. Their considerable political success was the result of mastering the dominant culture's conventions of public address. Exhibit A is the work of Thurgood Marshall, Constance Motley, and others in the N.A.A.C.P. Legal Defense and Education Fund.

28. John Durham Peters, "Distrust of Representation: Habermas on the Public Sphere," *Media, Culture, and Society* 15 (1993): 541-71. See also Aune, *Rhetoric and Marxism* and Farrell, *Norms of Rhetorical Culture.*

ABOUT THE AUTHORS

JAMES R. ANDREWS is Professor of Speech Communication, Adjunct Professor of American Studies, and Adjunct Professor of Victorian Studies at Indiana University. He is the author of numerous critical studies that have appeared in such journals as *The Quarterly Journal of Speech* and *Communication Monographs*; he is past editor of *Communication Studies*, has served on numerous editorial boards, and is the author, co-author, or editor of seven books, including *The American Ideology, The Practice of Rhetorical Criticism*, and *American Voices*. He received the Winans-Wichelns Award for distinguished scholarship in rhetoric and public address and twice won the American Forensic Association's award for outstanding research. In 1993 he received the Speech Communication Association's Douglas Ehninger Distinguished Rhetorical Scholar award.

THOMAS W. BENSON is Edwin Erle Sparks Professor of Rhetoric at the Pennsylvania State University. He is a former editor of *Communication Quarterly* and *The Quarterly Journal of Speech*, and the author, co-author, or editor of numerous books, including *Reality Fictions: The Films of Frederick Wiseman*; *Documentary Dilemmas: Frederick Wiseman's "Titicut Follies"*; *Readings in Classical Rhetoric*; *Readings in Medieval Rhetoric*; *Rhetorical Dimensions in Media*; *Speech Communication in the Twentieth Century*; *Landmark Essays in Rhetorical Criticism*; and *American Rhetoric: Context and Criticism*.

EDWIN BLACK is Professor Emeritus of Communication Arts at the University of Wisconsin-Madison. His most recent book is *Rhetorical Questions*. He is currently at work on a book-length study of the public discourses of Richard Nixon.

185

STEPHEN H. BROWNE is Associate Professor of Speech Communication at the Pennsylvania State University. He is the author of *Edmund Burke and the Discourse of Virtue.*

MAURICE CHARLAND is Associate Professor of Communication Studies at Concordia University and former director of Montreal's interuniversity Ph.D. program in communication. He is the author of a number of essays on the rhetorical construction of political community. His current research examines the interrelationships of rhetoric, constitutions, ethos, and ethics.

JAMES M. FARRELL is an associate professor in the Department of Communication at the University of New Hampshire. His work on American public address has appeared in *New England Quarterly, Classical Journal, Rhetorica, Quarterly Journal of Speech,* and *Studies in Eighteenth-Century Culture.* He was the 1991 recipient of the Karl R. Wallace Memorial Award from the Speech Communication Association and the recipient of the 1994 Excellence in Teaching Award from the College of Liberal Arts at the University of New Hampshire.

ROBERT HARIMAN is Professor of Rhetoric and Communication Studies and Endowment Professor of the Humanities at Drake University. He is the author of *Political Style: The Artistry of Power,* editor of *Popular Trials: Rhetoric, Mass Media, and the Law,* and co-editor of *Post-Realism: The Rhetorical Turn in International Relations.*

DAVID HENRY is Professor of Speech Communication at California Polytechnic State University, San Luis Obispo, where he teaches political communication, rhetorical criticism, rhetorical theory, persuasion, and argumentation. His essays in the criticism of political discourse, social movements, and public advocacy in science and technology have appeared in the *Quarterly Journal of Speech, Communication Studies,* the *Southern Journal of Communication,* and in numerous books. He is co-author, with Kurt Ritter, of *Ronald Reagan,* and he serves on the editorial boards of the *Quarterly Journal of Speech,* the *Western Journal of Communication* and the Michigan State University Press "Rhetoric and Public Affairs Series."

JAMES JASINSKI is an assistant professor in the Department of Speech Communication at the University of Illinois, Urbana. His work in rhetorical criticism and early American public address has appeared in *The Quarterly Journal of Speech* and elsewhere.

MICHAEL C. LEFF is Professor of Communication Studies at Northwestern University. He is a former editor of *Rhetorica*, and the author of numerous essays and chapters on rhetorical theory and criticism.

JOHN LOUIS LUCAITES is Associate Professor of Speech Communication at Indiana University. He is the co-author of *Crafting Equality: America's Anglo-African Word* and co-editor of *Martin Luther King, Jr., and the Sermonic Power of Public Discourse*. He teaches courses on the relationship between rhetoric and social theory, with a focus on language and social change in American public discourse. His current research is a critical rhetorical engagement of the ways in which the word "race" is configured in twentieth-century American public discourse with a focus on legal and mass-mediated usages.

MARTHA SOLOMON WATSON is Professor of Speech Communication at the University of Maryland. She is a former editor of *The Quarterly Journal of Speech* and author of books on Emma Goldman and Anna Howard Shaw.

INDEX

A

abolitionists, 55, 61, 68n. 21, 84, 94; agitation, 78-79, 84; black, 49, 52, 54, 56, 142; Douglass as, 55-57, 141-42; effect of, 106; history of, 114, 116, 119, 125; institutionalization of, 52; radical, 87n. 25; reiterated the Declaration of Independence, 91, 96-100; white, 47, 52, 55, 56, 69n. 35, 128n. 14; and women's rights movement, 102. *See also* Garrison, William Lloyd

"academic podiatry" (Gunderson), x

Adams, Henry, 12-13

Adams, John, 15, 16, 18-19, 23, 71; and Cicero, 173, 174, 182nn. 18, 22; and Declaration of Independence, 16; eloquence of, 23, 27-28, 31; reputation of, 40; speeches by, 26. *See also* "Eulogy to Adams and Jefferson"

Adams, John Quincy, 15, 35n. 53

Addams, Jane: analogy and, 148; dialogue by, 149; inspired by Lincoln, 136, 147, 148, 149, 150, 152; "Modern Lear" (1894), 136, 148-49, 152, 155n. 26, 161; oratory of, 158; paradox in, 148; on social ethics, 149-50; *Twenty Years at Hull House*, 147-50

"Address Before the Free People of Color" (Garrison), 120, 121

Adorno, Theodor, 158

aesthetic modalities, xiv, 4

aesthetics: of African American discourse, 9-10; cultural, 1-13; dispositional, xiv, 4; elocutionist's, 12; pleasures of, 4; and pretensions, 6; and propriety, 2-4; and public discourse, 1-13; in rhetoric, xiv, 1, 8; structural, xiv, 4-5, 7, 8, 12; stylistic, xiv, 2, 4, 5, 6, 8-10, 12; utilitarian, 12; textural, xiv, 4, 7, 8; values, 1. *See also* rhetoric

African American discourse, 7, 9-10; appearance motif in, 9

African American identity: Douglass on, 55-63; irony of equality and, 63-65; paradox of, 72; rhetorical problem of, 50-55; spokespersons for, 49, 55, 62

African American politics, 49, 50-52, 61, 62, 63

agency, 43, 175. *See also* agent; rhetorical tools

agent, and political change, 49

American Anti-Slavery Society, 113, 116, 122-24, 126; Garrison's instrumental